Introduction to Japanese Horror Film

This book is dedicated to my parents
David and Peggy Balmain

Introduction to
Japanese Horror Film

Colette Balmain

Edinburgh University Press

Edinburgh University Press Ltd
22 George Square, Edinburgh

Typeset in Monotype Ehrhardt
by Koinonia, Manchester, and
printed and bound in Great Britain by
CPI Antony Rowe, Chippenham, Wilts

A CIP record for this book is available from the British Library

ISBN 978 0 7486 2474 4 (hardback)
ISBN 978 0 7486 2475 1 (paperback)

Published with the support of the Edinburgh University
Scholarly Publishing Initiatives Fund.

Contents

List of Figures

Preface

> In America and Europe most horror movies tell the story of the extermination of evil spirits. Japanese horror movies end with a suggestion that the spirit still remains at large. That's because the Japanese don't regard spirits only as enemies, but as beings that co-exist with this world of ours. (Suzuki 2005)

With the exhaustion of American horror cinema, as evidenced by the recent trend towards remakes of classic 1970 films such as *The Texas Chainsaw Massacre* (Nispel: 2003), *The Amityville Horror* (Douglas: 2003) and *The Hills have Eyes* (Aja: 2006), it is not surprising that both American studios and Western audiences have been looking elsewhere for inspiration. There can be little doubt that Nakata's *Ring* (1998) has had much to do with the recent international interest not just in Japanese horror cinema, but East Asian cinema more generally.

Following the success of Nakata's *Ring*, Shimizu's *Ju-On: The Grudge* (2003) and the American remakes, Tōhō announced in 2004 the establishment of *J-Horror Theatre*, a series of six horror films from noted Japanese directors. The fact that Lion Gate Films obtained worldwide distribution rights to the films (with the exception of Japan) testifies to the increasing popularity of the Japanese horror film. The proliferation of remakes of Japanese films continues, with the most recent, *Pulse* (Sonzero: 2006), based upon Kiyoshi Kurosawa's extraordinary technological horror of the same name (2001).

However, the centrality of isolation, alienation and emptiness that defines Japanese horror cinema cannot be simply explained by a nebulous reference to a sense of loss of history and nostalgia for the past which lies at the heart of postmodern theories of identity, such as that espoused by Jameson (1991). This is too simple a comparison. Concerns around the loss of connection are much more pivotal in a society based upon a long tradition of obligations amongst individuals and communities (known as the *ie* system). Further, as Suzuki points out, the Japanese have a belief in the materiality of ghosts that is very different to Western conceptions, including the notion of co-existence of the world of the living (*kono-yo*) and the world of the dead (*ano-yo*).

Similarly, *Battle Royale* (Fukasaku: 2000), which has been taken up as a meta-discourse about disaffected youth, is on another level a commentary about the consequences of individualism (Westernisation) for the Japanese community. And if *Battle Royale* and *Suicide Circle* (Sono: 2002) are about youth violence, they need to be understood in terms of the emergence of the *Otaku* sub-culture amongst Japanese adolescents in the 1990s. It is the conflict between obligations towards the outside world (*giri*) and towards oneself (*ninjō*), specific to Japan, that leads to violence and apocalyptic destruction rather than a simple clash between the value systems of adults and adolescents. The fetishisation of the schoolgirl in Japanese horror cinema, in films such as *Stacy* (Tomomatsu: 2001) and *Eko Eko Azarak: Wizard of Darkness* (Sato: 1995), also has its roots in the sub-cultural formations. Both films explore the obsession with *kawaii* (a term used to refer to cute schoolgirls) and *Aidoru* (young pop idol schoolgirls, who were at the height of their popularity in the 1990s). However, whilst Misa, in *Eko Eko Azarak*, remains the virginal *shōjō*, the zombie schoolgirls, or Stacies, in *Stacy*, articulate the politics of the *kogal* (a sub-cultural formation of young Japanese teenagers, noted for their linguistic and aesthetic challenge to prevailing norms), and in so doing offer a very different female subjectivity to that found in traditional Japanese films and anime. In the same vein, although the female avenger of films such as Ishii's *Freeze Me* (2000) and Miike's *Audition* (1999) bear some similarities to female avengers in other rape-revenge films, they need to be contextualised in relation to the violated bodies of female victims of Japanese sadomasochistic pornography and, from the 1960s onwards, pink cinema (called *pinku eiga*, a type of soft-core pornography notable for its low budget, short running time – usually one hour or less – and radical politics).

The emergence of the erotic ghost story, a sub-genre specific to Japan, is also made possible by the newly burgeoning Japanese pink film industry. And it is significant that many third-generation Japanese directors, including Nakata, gained their training within the pink film industry. Therefore an understanding of the intersection between the pink film industry and Japanese horror is important to any history of Japanese horror film.

Although most contemporary Japanese horror is modelled along the lines of the social problem film or *shakiamono*, Japan has a long history of period (*jidaigeki*) films which have provided the background for tales of ghostly happenings, forbidden desires and capitalist greed. The emergence of Edo Gothic in the 1950s and 1960s has much in common with the gothic horror films being produced by Hammer in the United Kingdom and Roger Corman's Edgar Allen Poe adaptations in the United States. However, Edo Gothic, underpinned by Buddhist beliefs, does not provide the spectator with an Absolute Other, whose destruction reaffirms the protagonist's (and viewer's) sense of self. This is the case in films such as Nakagawa's *Ghost Story of Yotsuya* (1959) and Mori's *Ghosts of Kaqami-Ga-Fuchi* (1959), in which the boundaries between good and evil are blurred and the protagonist's actions, however terrible, pave the way for an emptying of self and salvation through suffering. Nakagawa's *Hell* (1960), a Grand Guignol exercise in visceral gore and transgression, almost bankrupted the director, but at the same time has provided the template for many contemporary Japanese horror films.

While the remakes of Japanese horror films often fall far short of the originals, with perhaps the exception of Shimizu's *The Grudge* (2004), their success in terms of box-office receipts means that there can be little doubt that Japanese ghosts and monsters will be around to terrify us for some time to come.

Acknowledgements

I would like to thank Sarah Edwards at Edinburgh University Press for her patience and expertise. Special thanks go to all my students over the past few years; without their discussion and enthusiasm for Japanese horror, this book could not have been written. I would also like to thank my colleagues, in particular Dr Lois Drawmer and Dr Alison Tedman. The book would not have been possible without the support of my family, especially my sister, Louise Balmain.

A Note on Language

It is traditional in Japan to put family name first and forename last. I have used the Westernised form, forename before family name, instead for directors and actors/actresses. This is because the book is written for general audiences, as well as specific audiences. Japanese words are italicised throughout and I have used a macron or long sign over vowels in Japanese words, such as Shōjo, which stresses the sustained vowel sound. I have put the name of the actors/actresses next to their character names, where information was available.

Introduction

The key defining feature of Japanese culture, according to Donald Richie in his writings on Japanese cinema, is the ability of Japan to assimilate and transform other cultures. So just as Japan has integrated components from China, India and other pan-Asian countries into its culture and socio-political structure, this can also explain Japan's relationship with the West. However, even a brief discussion of this relationship makes it clear that this is an over-simplification and that in fact culture, ideas and ideology flow in both directions.

In 1853, after a long period of isolation, Japan opened up its borders to trade with the West. At the World Exhibitions, held every few years in major Western cities, 'Japanese arts and crafts were introduced to Europeans and Americans'. This inaugurated a 'Japan boom', an enthusiasm for all things Japan that came to be known as *Japonaiserie* (Avella 2004: 6). In 1872, Phillippe Burty, a French art critic and collector, first used the term *Japonisme* to describe 'the elements of Japanese art that influenced, and were integrated into, Western art' (Avella 2004: 6). Of particular interest were woodblock prints, known as *ukiyo-e* (pictures of the floating world), which offered images of traditional Japan, including geishas and teahouses, alongside pictures of spirits, ghosts and monsters, whose inspiration was taken from Japan's rich mythology.

Avella points out that the distinctive features of *ukiyo-e* included 'solid areas of color; strong contour lines; decorative shapes; and little, if any, chiaroscuro (shading or modeling)'. The result of this was 'a conception of space and mass that emphasised two-dimensional qualities', which 'disregarded the mathematical perspective that was faithfully adhered to in Western aesthetic systems' (2004: 6). The use of perspective in these prints would often dispense with the idea of the spectatorial gaze, by cropping the image, using the prominence of empty space and adopting 'unusual angles and viewpoints', in which 'figures are seen from behind, in shadow, or partially obscured' (Avella 2004: 10).

These qualities were not confined to *ukiyo-e*, but were a central component of Japanese art and architecture generally. *Japoniste* elements began to appear in Western painting and graphic design, in the work of such luminaries as Degas, Van Gogh and Toulouse-Lautrec. The name used to refer to these cultural crossings is *Japonisme*. Thus the impact of Japanese culture on the West is nothing new, but what is new is the emphasis on the popular – video games, manga, anime, toys and film, associated with what has been termed Japan's soft or 'pink' power. In his highly influential article, 'Japan's Gross National Cool', Douglas McGray writes:

> Japan is reinventing superpower – again. Instead of collapsing beneath its widely reported political and economic misfortunes, Japan's global cultural influence has quietly grown. From pop music to consumer electronics, architecture to fashion, and animation to cuisine, Japan looks more like a cultural superpower today than it did in the 1980s, when it was an economic one. (2002)

Not only have children across the world (in more than 65 countries) grown up with Pokémon and Hello Kitty, but also 60 per cent of all animated cartoons generate from Japan. The popularity of Pokémon was such that it made the cover of *Time* magazine on 22 November 1999. In addition, the influence of anime and manga can be seen in many best-selling video games for the Playstation 2 and Nintendo 64 consoles such as *Biohazard* (known in the West as *Resident Evil*), *Final Fantasy* and *Silent Hill*. The impact of this on the Japanese economy has been profound, with Japanese cultural exports tripling between 1993 and 2003, bringing in $12.5 billion. Yano argues that Japan's 'pink globalization', led by the monstrous figure of Godzilla who has been transformed into the cute (*kawii*) – and less threatening – figure of Hello Kitty, 'suggest[s] a broadening of Japanese popular culture global flows' (2006: 154).

All this paved the way for the success of Japanese horror cinema in the West, which broke out of its cult status with the critical and commercial success of Hideo Nakata's *Ring* in 1998. Taking approximately $13 million at the Japanese box-office, *Ring* is the most successful horror film in terms of box-office receipts in Japan. The American remake opened in the United States on 20 October 2002 and rose to number one at the box-office. *Ring* took $15,015,393 in its opening weekend. Eventually, the film took $129,094,024 in the United States alone, and $249 million globally. In Japan, *Ring* grossed over $2 million in its first week, taking over $14 million in Japan alone and making more money than the Japanese version. The success of the remake of *Ring* inspired similar, sometimes not altogether successful, remakes of films such as Nakata's later *Dark Water* (Salles: 2005), Shimizu's *Ju-On: The Grudge* (Shimizu: 2004) and, most recently, Kurosawa's *Pulse* (Sonzero: 2006).

ANALYSES OF JAPANESE CINEMA

In *Kurosawa: Film Studies and Japanese Cinema*, Yoshimoto critiques ......
and Eurocentric approaches to the study of Japanese cinema. He identifies
two dominant trends: firstly, the focus on universal themes – the humanist
approach – which negates cultural specificity; and secondly, the concentration
on the differences between Japanese and Western cinemas – the Orientalist
approach – which ends up confirming Western stereotypes around Japan's
exoticism and irreducible difference. Specifically in terms of both Japanese
and Western analysis of the films of Kurosawa, Yoshimoto notes 'a certain type
of anxiety, an apprehension about the validity of the conceptual frameworks
… because his films problematise Japan's self image and the West's image of
Japan' (2005: 2). In terms of cross-cultural studies, Yoshimoto contends that
the inherent problem with this type of analysis is that it can work to 'reinforc[e]
the identity of the West as something transparent, natural and self-evident'
(2005: 27). Similarly, Dennison and Lim, writing about world cinema, argue
that to see world cinema as the opposite or antithesis of US or Hollywood
cinema 'is to disregard the diversity and complexity within both cinema in the
US as well as cinema from the rest of the World' (2006: 7). In 'Orientalism or
Occidentalism? Dynamics of Appropriation in Akira Kurasawa', Hutchinson
explains:

> Criticism of Japanese cinema has often been dominated by an Orientalist
> construction of 'Japaneseness' as Other to a homogeneous West and has
> tended to focus on how 'Japanese' or 'Western' a given film or director
> is. (2006: 173)

Hutchinson continues, 'The Japanese cinema is set up as confined, limited
and in need of techniques and ideas from the West, achieving success when
it assimilates or incorporates Western cinema. This model is then applied to
individual directors, including Kurosawa' (2006: 174). She argues that the
processes of self-appropriation of Orientalist stereotypes (Occidentalism),
as in the case of Kurosawa, can provide a mechanism of counter-discursive
opposition. She writes, 'The film as discursive act implies power is invested in
the "adaptation" in its political, counter-discursive, aspect' (2006: 181).

In his analysis of the relationship between modernity and early Japanese
cinema, through the works of Junichirō Tanizaki (1886–1965), LaMarre
writes: 'What is ominous about film is its potential to be produced everywhere
and nowhere, and to be distributed globally' (2005: 113). LaMarre argues that
the phantasms generated by cinema mean that 'racial origin is at once marked
and unmarked, located and dislocated, everything and nowhere' (2005: 113).
In his analysis of Tanizaki's 'The Tumor with a Human Face', LaMarre points

out how, for Tanizaki, 'the repulsiveness of the Japanese face [on the cinematic screen] is linked to the possibility of seeing one as a dark, colonial other' (2005: 112). These fears around the erasure of racial and cultural difference, via the situating of the West as the ideal/idealised image through which the Other identifies itself in the global marketplace, are also articulated in Iwabuchi's work on self-orientalism and cultural odour (1994; 2002) (see Chapter 1).

GENRE

Writing about the history of critical approaches to horror cinema, Jancovich argues that it has been dominated by two main questions:

> First, there is the question of what one might mean by terms such as 'horror', and this usually becomes a question of how one defines the horror genre and so identifies its essential features. This first question also presupposes a second and more fundamental question: what is a film genre, or more properly what should be meant by the term 'genre' when it is used in film studies. (2002: 1)

Genre theory seeks to identify patterns of similarity and difference across films through which genre as a discrete area of study is constructed and audiences are targeted. Although genre predates cinema, the industrial mechanics of the studio system in Hollywood meant that the separation of films into 'types' enabled the maximisation of economic potential and profitability. In 'Reusable Packaging: Generic Products and the Recycling Process', Altman argues that there has been a tendency to see genres as both stable and permanent, particularly in approaches which stress the mythic quality of genre. By doing so, Altman writes that two generations of genre critics 'have done violence to the historical dimensions of genre' (1998: 2). He argues, 'Instead of imaging this process in terms of static classification, we might want to see it as a regular alternative between an expansive principle – the creation of a new cycle – and a principle of contraction – the consolidation of a genre' (1998: 18).

This is also true of the horror film. In 'The American Nightmare: Horror in the 70s', Wood identifies a basic formula, shared by all horror films, in which 'normality is threatened by the monster' (2002: 31). It is in fact, according to Wood, the relationship between normality and the monster that 'constitutes the essential subject of the horror film' (2002: 31). In *The Philosophy of Horror, or Paradoxes of the Heart*, Carroll foregrounds the importance of the process of repulsion in the specific form of art-horror, pointing out that this repulsion must be pleasurable, as evidenced by the genre's popularity (2002: 33). The epistemological desire to know, although fundamental to other genres, is central to horror because the monster at the heart of the narrative is 'in principle *unknowable*' and 'outside the bounds of knowledge' (2002: 35). For Carroll, therefore, the 'paradox' of horror lies in the twin processes of repulsion and attraction. Similarly, Creed, in *The Monstrous-Feminine: Film, Feminism and Psychoanalysis*, using Kristeva's theory of the abject, argues that the monstrous in horror articulates a morbid desire 'to see *as much as possible of the unimaginable*' and horrifies because the threat of the monster is connected to 'fear of losing oneself and one's boundaries' (1993: 29).

In his 'Introduction' to the BFI *Companion to Horror*, Newman traces the origin of horror to the gothic novels of the eighteenth and nineteenth centuries. Like Altman, Newman argues that, while films such as the Universal Cycle of Horror Films in the 1930s are easily identifiable as such, the further away from such 'default horrors we travel, the more blurred distinctions become, and horror becomes less like a discrete genre than an effect which can be deployed within any number of narrative settings or narrative patterns' (1996: 11). Newman continues, 'the horror film proper did not exist until the genre started concreting in its foundations by imitating itself.' In these terms it is *The Mummy* (1932), a variation on the earlier *Dracula* (1931), that is the first horror film (1996: 13). However Newman does point to the hybrid nature of horror film, and its overlapping with the genres such as science fiction and the crime thriller as articulated in the manner in which scenes are 'explicitly designed to provoke horror' (Newman 1996: 15).

In the simply titled *Horror Films*, Frank points to horror's similarity to nightmares as constitutive of horror as genre (1977: 16). For Wells in *The Horror Genre: From Beelzebub to Blair Witch*, the prevalence of images of death in horror film, and the representation of the undead 'literally embod[ies] states of "otherness" which are intrinsically related to humanity but are ultimately a parallel and threatening expression of it' (2000: 10). Other critics, such as Grant in 'Sensuous Elaboration: Reason and the Visible in the Science Fiction Film', seek to understand horror in terms of its opposition to other genres, specifically science fiction. He writes, 'the appeal of science fiction is primarily cognitive, while horror, as the genre's name suggests, is essentially emotional' (Grant 2004: 17). In response to hybrid science fiction/horror films in the late 1970s and early 1980s such as Cronenberg's *Videodrome* and Ridley Scott's *Alien*, in 'Horrality: The Textuality of Contemporary Horror Films', Brophy introduced the term 'body horror' as that which constituted the dominant theme in the horror cinema:

> The contemporary horror film tends to play not so much on the broad fear of Death, but more precisely on the fear of one's own body, of how one controls and relates to it ... conveying to the viewer a graphic sense of physicality, accentuating the very presence of the body on the screen. (1986: 8)

THEORISING HORROR

In *Horror Film and Psychoanalysis: Freud's Worst Nightmare*, Schneider emphasises the manner in which psychoanalysis has proved to be one of the most popular ways of interpreting horror. As he argues, since the late 1970s 'there has been a tremendous diversity of psychoanalytic approaches' (2004: 2). Insightfully, Schneider points to a number of theorists, including Creed, who see the horror film as a repository of male castration anxieties and (patriarchal) fears around female sexuality. Other theorists, such as Neale, in *Genre*, focus on the male monster, although female sexuality is to blame for the psycho-sexual pathology of the male killer. Women's sexuality, Neale argues, 'renders them desirable – but also threatening – to men', thereby constituting the main problem of horror, and that which is seen as 'really monstrous' (1980: 61).

Utilising the theory of the male gaze, as laid down by Mulvey in 'Visual Pleasure and Narrative Cinema' (1975) and the later 'Afterthoughts on "Visual Pleasure and Narrative Cinema"' (1981), feminist interpretations of the genre such as those espoused by Clover (1992), Creed (1993) and Williams (1984) focus on the gendered assumptions behind representations of the monstrous in horror film, using theories of absence and lack derived from Freud and Lacan. Schneider writes:

> According to this paradigm, the threat of castration (absence and lack) posed by images of the female form in Hollywood cinema is contained through a sexualised objectification of that form, whether fetishistic-scopophilic (woman displayed as erotic spectacle, rendered unthreatening by the controlling male look) or sadistic-voyeuristic (woman investigated, demystified, and eventually controlled through punishment) in nature. (Schneider 2004: 5)

This type of approach to horror film can be reductive, especially if it is utilised unproblematically in the study of non-Western forms of horror, as Totaro points out in her article 'The Final Girl: A Few Thoughts on Feminism and Horror', in which she writes, 'American horror, like its popular culture in general, is generally prudish and too deeply entrenched in a Puritan past to really engage in sexuality, which is so important to the horror film' (2002).

As the theoretical approaches to horror film criticism, as we have seen, operate almost exclusively using the form of American horror cinema as the paradigmatic example, it becomes difficult to adapt these wholesale to Japanese cinema without erasing historical, cultural and racial difference. In the 'Preface' to McRoy's *Japanese Horror Cinema*, Sharratt points out that, in the projection of nihilism, Japanese horror represents 'a view that is a rejection of social transformation long embodied in the western horror film' (2005: xiii).

In addition, McRoy foregrounds the complexity of the socio-political context which provides the background to modern Japanese horror cinema, referring to:

> a myriad of complex political, social and ecological issues, including – but by no means limited to – apprehensions over the impact of western cultural and military imperialism, and the struggle to establish a coherent and distinctly Japanese national identity. (2005: 1)

In *Nightmare Japan: Contemporary Japanese Horror Cinema*, McRoy contextualises Japanese horror cinema as a sub-genre of 'New Asian Horror' (2008: 3). He argues that 'As a substantial component of Japanese popular culture, horror films allow artists an avenue through which they may apply visual and narrative metaphors in order to engage aesthetically with a rapidly transforming social and cultural landscape' (2008: 4). However, the emphasis on directorial visions and extreme cinema means that, while McRoy's book covers some of the same ground as this book, it does so in a substantially different manner.

Not only traditional theatrical forms such as Nō and Kabuki, but also belief in the supernatural, as embedded in both Buddhism and Shintō alongside a rich tradition in cultural mythology, have influenced the development of Japanese horror film. Perhaps most crucial are Japan's experiences during the Second World War and the subsequent Allied Occupation, the trauma of which underlies many, if not all, Japanese horror films from the 1950s onwards, as demonstrated through the prevalence of the discourse of *hibakusha* (female victims of the bombings of Hiroshima and Nagasaki) as one of the defining features of modern Japanese horror cinema. In *Shocking Representation*, Lowenstein argues that to 'speak of historical trauma, is to recognise events as wounds'. He continues, 'Auschwitz. Hiroshima. Vietnam. These are names associated with specific places and occurrences, but they are also wounds in the fabric of culture and history that bleed through conventional confines of time and space' (Lowenstein 2005: 1). It is necessary therefore to locate cinematic texts historically and culturally rather than using a grand narrative that can erase differences. This – historical trauma – as Lowenstein points out can help to think through theoretical impasses in film theory (2005: 2).

Finally, Kawai's discussion of Japanese fairy tales in *The Japanese Psyche: Major Motifs in the Fairy Tales of Japan* is particularly insightful and can help explain the specific cultural context and intertexts of horror cinema. Kawai argues that, 'While fairy tales have a universal nature, they concurrently manifest culture-bound characteristics' (1996: 3). The same is true of horror cinema.

ORIGINS/THEMES/CONVENTIONS

This book focuses on the origins, themes and conventions of Japanese horror cinema from 1950 to date. It is divided into two broad sections, the first of which considers the origin of contemporary Japanese horror film during and in the aftermath of the Second World War. The forced modernisation of Japan, while largely an economic success, had a profound social effect on Japan's sense of nationhood and identity as different from the West. Japan's incomplete modernity is often embodied within the figure of the pre-modern monster, a revenant of traditional Japanese culture and mythology, in the horror film, which threatens apocalypse and disaster. In addition, the imposition of democratic values on what was still a largely feudal state, with the emperor at the centre, caused social and cultural anxieties around the demise of tradition, as embedded in the *ie* system of obligations and duties that determined relationships. Untrammelled individualism is often the cause of horror, as in *Tales of Ugetsu* (Mizoguchi: 1953) and *The Ghost Story of Yotsuya* (Nakagawa: 1959). In addition, unrestrained appetites, linked with commodification and materialism, also lead to death, as in *The Empire of Passion* (Ōshima: 1978). The figure of the 'salaryman', along with that of the absent father, embody anxieties negotiated in films such as *The Discarnates* (Obayashi: 1988) and *Vengeance is Mine* (Imamura: 1979). Internet and mobile technologies wall in individuals, isolating them and killing them, as can be seen in films like *Suicide Circle* (Sono: 2002). The increase in domestic violence as a result of the recession provides the major theme in contemporary films, including *Ju-On: The Grudge*. Absent mothers, bad fathers, and abused children seem to be all too present in Japanese horror films such as *Ring* and *Carved: A Slit-Mouthed Woman* (Shiraishi: 2007).

In addition, as much of Japanese horror, especially in the 1970s and 1980s, was concerned with sexual violence, issues around gender representation and the theme of rape as a major trope in Japanese culture are explored in some detail. In order to do so, the book focuses on the manner in which cultural mythology and folktales, including traditional archetypes such as 'the tragic lovers', 'the wronged woman' and 'the vengeful ghost', have provided a mechanism through which to negotiate transformations in the social and political structure of Japan from the early 1950s to date.

Part I
Origins

CHAPTER 1

Laying the Foundations

First the enthusiastic acceptance of a new idea, then a period of reaction against it, and finally the complete assimilation and transformation of the idea to Japanese patterns. (Anderson and Richie 1982: 34)

In their analysis of Japanese culture, Anderson and Richie delimit three stages by which ideas become incorporated into the Japanese worldview: acceptance, assimilation and transformation. However, as we have seen, this is a two-way process, as shown by the influence of Japanese decorative art and aesthetics, or *Japonisme*, on the West in the late nineteenth and early twentieth centuries. At the same time, there can be little doubt that Western ideas and beliefs, as well as cultural forms, have had an impact on Japan, especially during the Allied Occupation that followed Japan's defeat in the Second World War. It would seem that the pendulum has swung back again, with the popularity of the super-flat aesthetics of artists such as Murakami, who designed the cover for Kanye West's recent number one single *Stronger* (2007), video games such as *Silent Hill* and *Resident Evil* (originally titled *Biohazard* for its Japanese release in 1996), anime and manga – not forgetting, of course, Japanese horror cinema.

Without doubt, the growth of the studio system in Japan in the early twentieth century owed as much to the model of Hollywood cinema as it did to the emphasis on genre, especially during and after the Allied Occupation. State Shintō, which placed the emperor at the centre of a complex system of obligations and duties, based upon Confucian concepts of loyalty, was abolished. In its place Western democratic values and structures were imposed by the Allied powers, transforming Japan's political infrastructure beyond recognition. These profound socio-political changes impacted on material social relations, and were expressed in the cultural landscape as a tension between the pre-modern and the modern, communalism and individualism, Japanese tradition and Western democracy. This conflict not only is a dominant theme of Japanese horror cinema in the 1950s, but also is perhaps the very condition of its emergence. At the same time, Japanese horror cinema is influenced as much by Japanese traditional theatrical forms, including Nō and Kabuki, as it is by the West. This chapter explores the relationship between Japanese cinema, traditional aesthetic and theatrical forms, and the West in the first part of the twentieth century until the early 1950s and provides the foundation for subsequent chapters.

THE STUDIO SYSTEM

> The silent Japanese film industry ... was closely connected with the theatre industry, and drew on the theatrical repertoire for its narratives and performance styles. Popular stage hits, as well as popular novels, were adapted to screen, and exhibited in theatres alongside the live performances of a star dramatic narrator and musicians. Japanese adaptations of European and American stories were also made, but shifted to Japanese locations and peopled by Japanese characters. (Freiberg 2000)

Following the success of magic lantern shows in the late 1890s (mainly imported from France), the first cinematograph was introduced into Japan in 1897, and in 1899 a screening of the first Japanese film was shown at the Kabuki-za (a Kabuki theatre in Ginza, Tokyo). Kabuki, one of the foremost traditional Japanese theatrical forms, would provide rich material for the burgeoning art of the visual image and would become the template for many Japanese horror films since. Surprisingly, although Kabuki was originally the theatre of the ordinary people and working classes – unlike Nō, which was aimed at the ruling classes – the first film screened at Kabuki-za was shown solely to royalty and the upper classes.

The development of the studio system in the 1920s and 1930s, analogous in many ways to that associated with early Hollywood, would enable films to be seen by a much wider demographic group as well as maximising profitability. As Chaudhuri writes, 'The base for Japan's prolific production until the 1970s was its studio system, run along similar lines (oligopoly and vertical integration) to the Hollywood studio system' (2005: 102). However, while most Hollywood directors had little or no power in terms of choice of material, with the selection of their crew, including the cinematographer, being made from the contract employees of the studio, in Japan the director system meant that directors were able to gather around them teams of people whom they trusted and would be associated with for most, if not all of their careers. Ozu is a case in point, with Yuharu Atsuta (cinematographer), Yoshisaburo Senoo (sound engineer),

Tatsuo Hamada (art direction) and Yoshiyasu Hamamura (editor), remaining an integral part of Ozu's team for nearly ten years. As Knowles writes, 'The studio system, moreover, emphasized the ultimate authority of the director, as opposed to Hollywood's more producer-oriented system' (2002).

The oldest film company, Nikkatsu, was founded in 1912, and divided production between its Kyoto and Tokyo studios. The Kyoto studio concentrated on traditional period dramas, *jidaigeki*, while the Tokyo studio focused on contemporary dramas, or *gendaigeki*, set after 1868. These days Nikkatsu is remembered more for its *roman porno* (romantic pornography) of the 1960s and 1970s. Nikkatsu would eventually close its doors for good in 1988.

In 1920, Shōchiku was founded. Originally a theatre playhouse, the Kabuki-za, established by Takejiro Otani, it would become one of the most profitable studios, associated with directors such as Yasujiro Ozu and Akira Kurosawa, and more recently Miike, of *Audition* and *Ichi the Killer*. In opposition to traditional historical dramas, Shōchiku saw the evolution of *shingeki*, a radical movement in the theatrical arts and cinema influenced by Europe and the West. Shōchiku released a prospectus, which clearly indicated the aim of utilising 'the latest and most flourishing of the Occidental cinema' (cited in Anderson and Richie 1982: 41). Shōchiku was also the first to use actresses, rather than *onnagata* (male actors dressed as women). In the 1930s, after the coming of sound, Shōchiku would come to be most associated with *shomingeki*, issue-led dramas about the lower middle classes, while Nikkatsu developed socially informed dramas in modern settings (McDonald 2006: 5).

By the late 1920s, Shōchiku and Nikkatsu had a stranglehold on the exhibition of films in Japan, owning over three-quarters of theatres. This allowed the 'Big Two' to compete effectively with Hollywood, often screening domestic products alongside Hollywood films. At the same time, linguistic and cultural barriers meant that Hollywood films were less easily consumed by Japan than in the West (Freiberg 2000). But in 1923 the Great Kantō earthquake devastated Tokyo and much of the surrounding area, almost calling a total halt to domestic film production and boosting sales of imported film. The strength of the Japanese studio system is clearly demonstrated by the fact that, within a year, domestic films accounted once more for most of the films screened (Wyver 1989: 151).

In 1936, the business tycoon and owner of Hankuo Railway, Ichizo Kobayashi, founded Tōhō. Kobayashi bought two other film companies, and built a large production studio in Kinuta. Abandoning the star system, which was the driving factor in Japanese cinema at the time, Kobayashi established a producer-based approach to cinematic production. Examples of popular genres at Tōhō were vaudeville-style comedy and musical genres (McDonald 2006: 5). Before the Second World War, Tōhō was the largest producer of propaganda pictures. After the Second World War Tōhō would give birth to the most perennial of all movie monsters in Godzilla, who first emerged from the watery depths in Honda's groundbreaking *Godzilla* in 1954, marking the beginning of the popular *kaijueiga* (monster) genre.

Ten years later, the Japanese government created Daiei Studio by consolidating the production studios of Shinko, Daito and Nikkatsu, with Nikkatsu remaining as an independent distribution company. In 1947, Daiei financed a separate cinematic production company called Shintōhō. Due to the success of *Three Hundred and Sixty Nights* (Ichikawa: 1948) – a melodrama about a love triangle between two girls and a boy – Shintōhō was able to distribute its films itself and eventually gained independence from Tōhō. Shintōhō would be known for popular genre films including action films and thrillers. Due to competition from foreign films and from television, Daiei went bankrupt in 1971, only to emerge as Kadokawa Pictures in 2002, renamed Kadokawa Herald Pictures when it merged with Herald Pictures in March 2006.

Tōei, founded in 1956, remains one of Japan's most important studios, as evidenced in the statistics for 2005, which show that Tōei produced nine out of the ten best-selling films in Japan. Noted worldwide for its animation division, Tōei is the home of Hayao Miyazaki, director of such international hits as *Spirited Away* (2001) and *Howl's Moving Castle* (2004).

Davis argues that independent films have overtaken studio-produced films, writing that '234 out of 287 total films released in 2003 were technically independents' (2006: 194). But the distinction between independent and studio films is not as easily identifiable as in the US, as Domenig points out:

> The term 'independent', i.e. independent of the big studios, has become almost meaningless nowadays, at least on the production level. The studios Shochiku, Toei and Toho make very few in-house productions and participate in barely a dozen films as co-producers annually. (2004)

A brief discussion of the Japanese New Wave helps to illuminate the relationship between studios and independent productions. Earlier attempts at independent film in the 1920s and in the late 1940s were doomed to failure, as they were unable to compete effectively with studio-produced films. In fact, independent film was totally squeezed out of the market in 1959 at the apex of the studio system, when there was not one independent production (Domenig 2004). However, Shōchiku was the main financier of the Art Theatre Guild (ATG) (*Nihon ato shiata undo no kai*). Even the Japanese New Wave (*Nuberu bagu*), unlike its counterpart the French New Wave or *Nouvelle Vague*, originated within rather than outside the studio system. While ATG's primary purpose was the exhibition of foreign films, it also allowed directors considerably more freedom than under the studio system. Ōshima's animated manga, *Band of Ninja* (1967), which innovatively used manga panels instead of film stills, was one of the first films to be distributed and exhibited through ATG. And in the 1960s, independent pink cinema (*pinku eiga*) outperformed studio productions struggling to compete with television and foreign cinema. Pink cinema would prove to be the saviour of the main studios, including Nikkatsu, as independent *eroductions* were transformed into sexploitation cinema.

Just as the studio system influenced the production of films, it was traditional Japanese art forms, and in particular theatre, that would influence the shape and form of these films.

FROM STAGE TO SCREEN

> Performers and directors moved back and forth between the two entertainment media, popular plays were adapted to screen, theatrical genres and performance styles were employed in the cinema, and the two largest film companies of the late 1930s, Shochiku and Toho, were part of giant entertainment complexes with major theatre interests, companies that derived their profits from live theatre as well as movies. (Freiberg 2000)

Early Japanese cinema had a tendency towards the theatrical, utilising traditional Japanese dramatic forms including Kabuki, Nō and Bunraku (puppet theatre), elements of which persist through to contemporary Japanese cinema, including the horror genre. All three dramatic arts were derived from travelling storytellers who used a *biwa* (a type of short-necked lute) to accompany the relating of their stories. The *biwa* would later be replaced by the *shamisen* (a three-stringed instrument like a guitar), and would form a central part of the performance in Kabuki theatre. Both Kabuki and Bunraku can be traced to the Tokugawa Period (1600–1867). From 1734 onwards, Bunraku's life-size puppets have required three men (although recently women have been allowed to train and work in Bunraku) to operate them: one puppeteer who controls the movements of the legs, the other the left arm and any props needed, and finally the master puppeteer who controls the puppet's facial expressions and right arm movement. The master puppeteer is the only one visible, as the other two wear black and have hoods covering their faces.

Japan's most famous playwright, Chikamatsu (1653–1724), has often been compared to Shakespeare. Chikamatsu's plays were either historical dramas relating the tragedy of following society's rigid rules (*jidaigeki*), or plays about contemporary situations (*gendaimono*) in which choosing personal happiness over filial and feudal loyalty often led to suicide. Tragic lovers, doomed to be together only in death, were a dominant trope in Chikamatsu's work, and tales of these influenced Japanese horror cinema, particularly in the 1950s and 1960s.

Chikamatsu was a prolific playwright who wrote 130 plays, mainly for Kabuki but in the latter 20 years of his life for Bunraku. Two of Chikamatsu's most famous plays are *The Love Suicides at Sonezaki* (1703) and *The Love Suicides at Amijima* (1721), both Bunraku plays. Shinodam's *Double Suicide* (1969) is based upon the latter Chikamatsu play, and merges elements of Bunraku with live action. Similarly, Kitano's *Dolls* (2002) begins with a scene from a traditional Bunraku puppet play, which mirrors the themes of love and sacrifice, integral to the work of Chikamatsu, updated to a modern society in which three intertwining narratives play out. The film ends with the double suicide (often a central trope of doomed love in Chikamatsu's plays) of the main characters, a pair of 'leased beggars' joined together with a thick red rope, whose love places them outside the regulatory boundaries of Japanese society.

Like Bunraku, Kabuki is a formative influence on both early and contemporary Japanese cinema. One of the most famous Kabuki plays, which has been adapted for the screen no less than thirty times, is *The Ghost Story of Yotsuya*, first performed in 1826. The first film adaptation was by Makino in 1912, but the most famous is the 1959 Nakagawa version. Interestingly enough, a temple priestess invented Kabuki, and yet it quickly became a patriarchal (male-centred) art form, with all the female parts being played by men (*onnagata*) after the reigning Shogun put a stop to women being entertainers.

Kabuki and Bunraku share obvious similarities: the use of richly decorated costumes, the *shamisen* providing mournful and emotive music to accompany the unfolding events, and highly decorative make-up used to signify both character type and internal emotion. However, the component elements of Kabuki would have more of an impact on the newly minted art form of the moving image. In particular, the use of a revolving stage (*kabuki no butai*) allowed the seamless and uninterrupted flow of the story with no need for halting the narrative in order to change the scenery. In *The Ghost Cat of Otama Pond* (Ishikawa: 1960) the camera is used to mimic the revolving stage, joining together present and past in one flowing circular motion from right to left. The stage itself in Kabuki was particularly suited to ghost stories, with a number of trapdoors (*seri*) beneath the stage allowing ghostly apparitions to emerge at will. Further, the Kabuki stage has a passageway (*hanamichi*) coming out into the auditorium at right angles, dissolving the spatial distance between the actors and the spectators. The *hanamichi* allowed actors spectacular exits, and they would stop at a certain point down the passageway (known as *shichisan*), using exaggerated poses and expressions to draw the attention of the spectators to themselves. Depending on the play, the *hanamichi* could signify a body of water, a corridor, a road: in short, any type of passage between one place and the next.

In many ways Kabuki provided the raw elements of cinema with these exaggerated poses, comparable to the freeze frame and stop-motion cinematography. Another integral element of Kabuki is the use of sound. As already mentioned, Kabuki utilises the *shamisen* to provide musical accompaniment (*shamisenongaku*), played by musicians on a raised platform at the back of the stage. The use of make-up and costume, again as in Bunraku, completes what are known as the four elements of Kabuki. There are more than fifty types of make-up used to signify character and emotion in Kabuki. Colours are central to the meaning-making system, with red signifying youth and justice, whilst blue, black and brown are used for monsters and wicked people. The final element of Kabuki is the stunning costumes – rich, highly decorated kimonos, noted for their beauty and complexity. However, in contemporary Japan, Kabuki is seen by some critics as an outmoded form, as a consequence of its highly formal language.

Whilst both Kabuki and Bunraku are popular theatrical forms, Nō is associated with the upper classes and has its origins in the fourteenth century. Nō is highly stylised, combines music, poetry, drama and dance, and is particularly noted for its use of masks. Like Greek plays, Nō utilises the mechanics of a chorus (*jiutai*) to narrate the background to the story and at times to express the emotions and feelings of the characters on stage. Music in Nō is called *nogaku* and consists of traditional Japanese musical instruments such as the *tsuzumi* drum and *hayashi* flute. Unlike Kabuki, Nō used to be performed on an outside stage with a roof supported by four pillars; however, during the Meiji Era (1868–1912), indoor stages were created which attempted to recreate the ambience of the outdoors.

There are five main types of Nō play, each distinguished by type of character: gods; warriors; beautiful women; mad women or contemporary and other types of figures; and finally ghosts and demons. Traditionally, a Nō performance would consist of a highly ritualised set piece called *Okina-Sanbaso*, followed by a play of each type in order, and would take place over the whole day. Central to Nō is transformation from human to ghost or other supernatural entity with the duplicity of being articulated through the use of highly stylised masks. The only character not to wear a mask in Nō is the secondary character known as the *waki* because, unlike the central character, the *shite*, the *waki* is the only character to be human. In many cases, the *waki* would take the form of a wandering priest whose journeys would bring him into contact with these strange supernatural beings. Often in early Japanese horror, the figure of the *waki*, or wandering priest would function in a highly symbolic manner, appearing to warn the main character(s) of the appearance of a ghost and/or curses. A variation on the *waki* can be found in *Tales of Ugetsu*, *The Ghost Cat of Otama Pond* and Kurosawa's *Sweet Home* (1989).

As in Kabuki, men played female roles in Nō until very recently. Focusing on emotion rather than plot, Nō would mainly recreate scenes from well-known traditional literary works, such as *The Tale of the Heike* (*Heike monogatari*). *The Tale of the Heike* is an example of what is called in Japan *gunki monogatari* (military tales in which the core themes were loyalty, sacrifice and honour). Some Nō plays took the form of historical dramas, with a dead character returning to the scene of a terrible defeat, re-enacting the scene through dance and/or song. In the award-winning *Kwaidan* (Kobayashi: 1964), an anthology of four stories based upon traditional ghost stories, we can see the influence of Nō. In 'Mimi-nashi-Hoichi' ('Hoichi the Earless'), the third segment of the film, a blind man, famed for playing the *biwa*, is entreated by a retainer to visit his lord to play the story of the Battle of Dan-no-ura (the last battle between the Heike and the Genji, in which the Heike perished). What Hoichi does not realise is that the lord and his entourage are in fact ghosts of Heike. On an open platform, such as would be used in the Edo Period to stage Nō plays, Hoichi plays the *biwa* night after night, retelling in song the dreadful tale of the defeat as the ghosts of the Heike watch and the drama of their loss unfolds, through both song and image. The dead are not necessarily figures of horror, as we will see in the following chapters, but tragic suffering entities unable to come to terms with their defeat or the untimely manner of their deaths.

Nō is marked by restrained understatement and abstraction as compared to Kabuki. Dance and poetry, in conjunction with masks, are used to express emotion rather than narrative or dialogue. Plot is not as important in Nō as it is in Bunraku or Kabuki. Just as with Bunraku and Kabuki, the influence of Nō could be found in both early Japanese cinema and the horror genre, in particular. *Kuroneko* (1968) and *Onibaba* (1964), both directed by Shindō, contain visual references to Nō. In *Kuroneko*, as Shige (Kiwako Taichi) attacks her male victims, the film cuts away to her mother-in-law, Yone (Nobuko Otowa), performing a Nō dance in the background. In *Onibaba*, a woman (Nobuko Otowa) and her daughter-in-law (Jitsuko Yoshimura) find themselves forced to kill and steal from warriors returning from the war in order to feed themselves in the absence of any patriarchal figure to take care of the household. The daughter-in-law finds herself attracted to a deserter, Hachi (Kei Sato), and starts a passionate affair with him, much to the older woman's horror. One day, the jealous older woman steals a demonic mask from a passing Samurai in order to frighten her daughter-in-law and put a stop to her passionate affair with Hachi. Her plan works to begin with, but slowly the mask takes over the woman; try as she might, she is unable to remove it. In the tradition of Nō, the mask is an external expression of the internal self, as outer appearance is in fact inner subjectivity. *Onibaba* falls into the fourth category of Nō play, which deals with mad women and other miscellaneous characters. As in Nō, the dialogue is sparse in *Onibaba*; instead the film relies on performance as spectacle to motivate the story of jealousy, lust, passion and revenge. Hand stresses the centrality of traditional theatrical forms to Japanese horror cinema:

> An argument can be advanced that the Japanese horror film draws on the storylines, structures, performance practices and iconography of traditional theatre as much on the traditions and mechanisms of western horror. (2005: 22)

The influences of theatre on cinema were many. First and foremost was the figure of the *benshi*, adopted from Bunraku. Rather than onscreen intertitles, Japanese films utilised a narrator or *benshi*, who from an off-stage position would relate the story of the film, acting out all the different character roles. This allowed the assertion of the spectacular form of the cinematic image. Freiberg comments:

> By relieving the film text of the need to narrate a story, he enabled Japanese film-makers to concentrate on extra-narrative embellishments of the visual text, on surface play, and thus transgress the norms of Hollywood-style narrative efficiency (continuity editing, crisply cut to tell a story, shot-reverse-shot dialogue exchanges, eyeline matching, use of 90 degree shooting space). (2000)

By February 1927, there were 7,500 *benshi* (Freiberg 2000). *Benshi* became stars, with fan followings, and could command a great deal of money for their performance. In many cases people went to the cinema, not to see the film, but to listen to the *benshi's* interpretation of the film. The *benshi* became so powerful that Japan was later than other countries in introducing sound to film. Silent film also used male actors in female parts (*onnagata*), as did Kabuki and Nō, although this practice had been abandoned by 1923. McDonald argues that the three characteristics of early Japanese cinema were the use of *onnagata*, the *benshi* as narrator and finally the centre-front long take which followed strict continuity guidelines (2006: 2).

In addition, one of the most overt connections between theatre and early cinema was, following the practice of Kabuki theatre, the division of cinema into two main genres: the *jidaigeki* and the *gendaimono*. These two genres were different not only in terms of time period, but also in terms of location. The *jidaigeki* were set in Kyoto, Japan's former capital, with its temples, castles and decorative gardens, whilst the *gendaimono* were set in the urban megalopolis of Tokyo with its high rises, neon lights, office blocks and restaurants. In addition to this, it was common for films to use theatrical actors: Kabuki-trained actors for the period films and Shimpa (New-Wave Meiji-Era theatre, largely melodramatic)-trained actors for contemporary films. (Freiberg 2000). Stars of Kabuki and Shimpa became the first stars of the silver screen.

Hollywood cinema and the coming of sound would irrevocably change the style and form of Japanese cinema; the *benshi* became redundant and the use of single fixed shots was supplanted by the mobile camera, tracking shots, quick editing and cross-cutting, while the close-up was added to the Japanese filmic vocabulary. The first Japanese film to show the influence of American cinema directly was the 'realist' melodrama, *Souls on the Road* (Murata), in 1921. *Souls on the Road* introduced the close-up to Japanese cinema, bringing with it a sense of intimacy and humanism that was new to audiences, used to the static shots and presentational perspective of the fixed camera along the imaginary fourth wall. Freiberg writes:

> In the late 1920s, fast cutting, dramatic angles and moving camera were increasingly employed … in *jidai-geki*, and swordplay scenes became much more exciting, in part through studying the action and shooting style of the Hollywood western. But the stories were taken from the Japanese theatre – late kabuki plays about the escapades of disreputable *ronin* and *yakuza* and popular sentimental plays about wandering outlaws (the sub-genre known as *matatabi-mono*); and the swaggering gait, wild grimaces and macho posturing of the heroes in scenes of confrontation followed by the *aragoto* style of *Kabuki* performers. (2000)

TRANSFORMATIONS

> Narrative as such is not foreign to Japanese tradition; it is, on the contrary, omnipresent, but its modes are radically different from ours … in kabuki and the doll theatre the primary narrative dimension is isolated, set apart from the rest of the theatrical substance, designated as one function amongst others. In the West on the other hand, since the eighteenth century, our major narrative arts – the novel, the theatre and more recently the cinema – have tended towards a kind of narrative saturation; every element is aimed at conveying, at expressing, a narrative essence. (Burch 1979: 78)

Burch argues for the specificity of Japanese cinema in terms of its approach to narrative. Indeed, the use of the *benshi* in early Japanese cinema meant that, as in Bunraku, narrative was separate to spectacle, rather than an integral component of it. Famous *benshi* were well known for embellishing narratives and thus transforming their meanings. In these terms, early Japanese cinema, before sound, was presentational rather than representational. It was, however, the outbreak of the Second World War which would ultimately have the biggest impact on the direction that Japanese cinema would take in the 1940s and 1950s.

In 1939, in response to the German invasion of Poland, Britain and France declared war on Germany, marking the beginning of the Second World War. The war was subsequently fought on two fronts: in Europe and in Asia. On 4 December 1941, Japan attacked Pearl Harbor. The following day the United States declared on war on Japan. It would take two atomic bombs, the first on Hiroshima on 6 August 1945, and the second on Nagasaki just three days later, to bring an end to the war in the Pacific. The Allied Forces insisted on unconditional surrender from the Japanese, the worst possible result for a nation that favoured honourable death over defeat. Between 1945 and 1952, the former colonial power of Japan became itself a colonised power, occupied by the Allied Forces. The trauma of defeat left scars on Japan's national psyche which have never fully gone away, and many horror films from the 1950s onwards would use the scarred face of the archetypical Japanese wronged woman, 'Oiwa', to signal metonymically the continuing impact of the Second World War on Japan.

The occupation of Japan would have a significant impact on the direction of Japanese cinema. Traditional Japanese films dealing with issues of honour, feudal loyalty and community were largely banned in favour of a more 'democratic' product modelled on the lines of Hollywood cinema. Often this would be expressed as a conflict between the pre-modern and the modern, the Japanese *ie* system and the democratic values of the West. The domestic drama was perhaps the most open to Hollywood influence, as it was the least traditional of Japanese film genres (Freiberg 2000). In addition to this, audiences would have been widely exposed to American films as they premiered on double bills with Japanese films. As in Hollywood, film was carefully policed by a set of regulations, which were introduced in Japan in 1917. These regulations were put in place to ensure that no film would in any way at all undermine the emperor; contain obscene references; focus on inappropriate sexual relationships between people; and show criminal violence. In 1925, responsibility for ensuring the propriety of Japanese film and its adherence to the regulations was placed under the control of the Ministry of the Interior.

Censorship in Japan, as elsewhere, had an impact on Japanese cinema, with Article 175 of the Penal Code becoming law in 1907. Article 175 regulated the sale, distribution and possession of obscene images, with a fine or up to two years in prison for breaking the law. The law was vague as to what constituted obscenity, with definitions changing over time. For example, in 1920 obscenity was considered to be anything that went against national policy. Yet by the 1960s, obscenity was fixated on female genital hair – which, as Allison points out, is a paradox in a society predicated on masculine potency and female violation, and given the ubiquity of sadomasochistic imagery: 'Imagining a woman tied up, held down, or forcibly penetrated is acceptable, in other words, whereas revealing the reality of her pubic hair is not' (Allison 1998: 195).

The films of the Japanese New Wave would challenge traditional interpretations of obscenity, as did pink cinema: for example, in the furore over the explicit scenes of sex and violence in Ōshima's *Empire of the Senses* (1976), based upon the true story of Sada Abe (which took place in 1936), whose sadomasochistic relationship with her married lover, Kichizo Ishida, concluded in his death and castration during sex. Sada was eventually arrested after being found to be carrying Ishida's penis in her kimono sash. Ōshima was charged with obscenity. In particular, the close-up shots of male and female genitalia were considered to be particularly repugnant to the Japanese sensibility. Even in the pink film, with its soft-core pornographic visuals, genitalia could not be viewed and female pubic hair was always airbrushed out of any sex sequences. In 1982, the charges against Ōshima were dismissed and the ruling allowed the more explicit representation of sex and sexuality in Japanese cinema.

However, censorship represented the incorporation and transformation of Western values, rather than an inherent sense of decorum vis-à-vis the sexualised body. Shintō's carnivalesque approach to sexuality can be clearly seen in the myth of the Sun Goddess Amaterasu's concealment. In the myth Amaterasu is persuaded out of the cave where she is hiding from her brother, Susanoo, by the laughter of the Gods when they catch sight of Goddess Amenouzume's genitalia (Kawai 1996: 50–1). With the arrival of Admiral Perry in 1853, Japan's borders opened up to the West, and the concern was that such images would give an impression of Japan as morally lax and primitive. It was this that directly led to the regulation of sexuality and images associated with sex. Allison writes:

> To counteract this negative image of its culture not based on Japanese categories of morality or social mores but Eurocentric ones stemming from Judeo-Christian ideology, the Japanese government imposed regulations on such customary practices as mixed bathing ... In order to gain face as a modern nation, in other words, Japan inscribed shame where it had not been located before: onto body parts and bodily functions regarded as natural by Japanese traditions. (1998: 197)

As already mentioned, female pubic hair became in modern Japan a particular source of anxiety, constructed as obscene in that the sight of a stray pubic hair was considered enough to provoke sexual excitement (Allison 1998: 200). Allison argues that this (patriarchal) anxiety over female pubic hair can be explained in terms of gender relationships in Japan, which seek to infantilise women and codify male dominance over the female as object.

In Japan in the 1920s, as elsewhere, there were concerns over the tension between cinema as entertainment and cinema as education and purveyor of public morality. In Japan, there were two main categories that caused anxiety:

ko-an (issues relating to public security) and *fuzoko* (issues relating to public morality) (Freiberg 2000). The left-wing tendencies of some films in the 1920s were of particular concern to censors. The *Prokino* (Proletarian Film League of Japan) movement, founded in 1929 and influenced in particular by Soviet Film, aimed to produce films (documentaries mainly, but also fiction films) that examined the 'realistic' lives of working-class people and documented historical events of importance. The *Prokino* was outlawed in 1933, but these leftist tendencies would re-emerge in the New Wave cinema of the 1960s, and many of the horror films of the decade, such as *Pitfall* (Teshigahara: 1962) and *Kwaidan*, would utilise codes and conventions of horror in order to criticise modernity and capitalism obliquely.

In the 1930s fear of a foreign invasion and corruption by Western consumerist society shifted the direction of film production towards national propaganda emphasising traditional Japanese values of self-sacrifice. This, however, would shift in the aftermath of the Second World War and the subsequent Allied Occupation. Alongside political and economic reform, the Allied Occupation regulated the output of Japanese cinema, making it unlawful to produce films that in any way valorised the old feudal system and glorified military history. The Civil Censorship Division, formed by the Supreme Commander of the Allied Powers (SCAP), listed types of film that could be made in order to ensure 'that Japan will never in the future disturb the peace of the world'. These regulations restricted:

> 'anything infused with militarism, revenge, nationalism, or antiforeignism; distortion of history; approval of racial or religious discrimination; favouring or approving feudal loyalty or treating human life lightly; direct or indirect approval of suicide; approval or oppression or degradation of wives; admiration of cruelty or unjust violence; antidemocratic opinion; exploitation of children; and any opposition to the Potsdam Declaration or any SCAP order'. (cited in Tucker 1973: 33–4)

Instead, Western values of democratic freedom and individual expression were imposed on Japanese cinema. As Standish explains, 'The CIE [Civil Information and Education Service] sought to encourage the development of ideals associated with American "democracy" while preventing the media from disseminating anything considered unsuitable or dangerous to the Occupation Government' (2005: 155).

In particular, Kabuki narratives, with their emphasis on feudal loyalty and themes of revenge and self-sacrifice, came in for criticism. According to Standish, one of the main perceived obstacles to the so-called democratisation of Japan was identified by officials as 'an inherent conflict between Japanese Neo-Confucian-derived concepts of loyalty and revenge on the one hand, and the Western-derived concepts of the rule of law based upon universal concepts of good and bad' (2005: 157). Consequently, *jidaigeki* films, with their sword-fighting sequences (*kengeki*), were prohibited. Traditional Japanese drama, Kabuki and Bunraku, with their feudal settings and codes of loyalty towards one's superiors, were also banned. However, plays and films managed to circumvent these restrictions and continued to relate traditional stories. One way of doing this was to change the historical period by situating the action in the Meiji Period. Another way was to copy foreign sources. Remakes of Frank Capra's films were particularly popular, as Anderson and Richie explain: 'Kiyohiko Ushihara's *A Popular Man in Town* (*Machi no ninkimono*) took direct inspiration from *Meet John Doe*, and Naruse's *The Descendents of Taro Urashima* (*Urashima taro no koei*) was indebted to *Mr. Smith goes to Washington*' (1982: 175).

At the same time, the Occupation saw the liberalisation of traditional Japanese values towards sexuality, which, as we have seen, were paradoxically constructed in relation to the West. Both Anderson and Richie (1982: 176) and Standish (2005: 162–5) point out that the 'cinematic kiss' was one result of new, more liberal values during the Occupation. Previously, even in Japanese films with romantic overtones, couples were never seen kissing. On May 1946, two films opened simultaneously: Yasaki's *Twenty-Year-Old-Youth* and Chiba's *A Certain Night's Kiss*, both of which featured (heterosexual) kissing, giving birth to the *seppun eiga* (kissing film). Standish suggests that films of the 1940s and 1950s denied questions of sexual and gender difference through the exclusion of woman in narratives. The promotion of romance by the Occupation Forces, as symbolised by the cinematic kiss, was to a certain extent an attempt by the American censors to make the private public, thereby making the Japanese less 'inscrutable' – a stereotype that still has currency today – and therefore less able to remain 'secretive' in the eyes of the West. In these terms, in keeping with 'democratic' ideologies of capitalism and the mechanics of the system of exchange, the 'scripts of masculinity and femininity that are at the heart of Western social and capitalist exchange' had to be relearned (Standish 2005: 164). The myth of romance, as embodied by the cinematic kiss, became a mechanism through which dominant (heterosexual) constructions of sexuality are 'defined, negotiated, learnt and perpetuated and as such, romance was actively re-inscribed within the traditions of Japanese post-war popular culture' (Standish 2005: 165). This myth of romance, used as a way of re-establishing traditional values, can be seen in foundational horror films such as *Godzilla* and *Tales of Ugetsu*. It is hardly surpising that, when the Japanese New Wave came to challenge traditional values in the 1960s, the discourse of romantic love, which underpinned much of Japanese cinema, was replaced with the materiality of the sexualised and/or violated body.

American fears of the possibility of communist tendencies taking hold in

Japan as a result of the new democratic processes led to the reinstatement of the Emperor; thus the main symbol of the imperial system was left unchanged and unchallenged, albeit with little real political power. For the occupiers, the emperor seemed to be the lesser of two evils. Richie points out how this enabled a return to traditional Japanese values:

> Directors and Screenmakers were thus, as the Occupation deepened, no longer so interested in subjects which advertised the rosy future and their country's changed ways. The Japanese no longer needed to regard themselves as model citizens of the future. It was now possible to return to being 'Japanese' in the traditional sense. (2001: 115)

It is no surprise, therefore, that in the 1950s, the emergence of both the ghost story and the monster movie in Japan would focus on the conflict between the pre-modern and the modern. Cazdyn defines the conflict in terms of a need to find a middle ground between the demands of the collective and those of the individual:

> It can now be framed between the individual and the collective, between the need to differentiate individual wants and desires (to appeal to the ideals of democracy as well as cultivate a domestic consumer market) while restricting these needs and desires to the requirements of the collective (in order to idealize sacrifice and legitimate exploitation). (2003: 27)

There can be little doubt that Hollywood cinema influenced Japanese film, especially in terms of the move towards more realistic slice-of-life dramas and away from the fixed patterns and immobile camera of period dramas derived from Kabuki. However, directors such as Ozu would return to traditional aesthetics as a point of resistance against the Westernisation of narrative forms.

JAPANESE CINEMA AS NATIONAL CINEMA

Although Japanese cinema was clearly influenced by the West, it managed to retain the traditional elements of a presentational aesthetic, both in the theatre and in film. And while the dominance of Hollywood cinema on a global scale is often taken as read, in fact, in 'the mid-1950s, Japan was the most prolific film producer in the world, reaching the marks of five hundred feature films a year' (Nagib 2006: 31). Neither can Japanese cinema be understood in terms of a distinction between art and popular cinemas. An approach to the understanding of Japanese cinema in terms of its difference from America, within a

Self/Other binary, is inadequate to understanding the complexity of Japanese cinema. Examples of this type of approach are epitomised by the work of Burch (1979) and Desser (1992). Yoshimoto points out that: 'studies of non-Western cinemas based upon the axiomatics of Self/Other opposition cannot but reproduce the hegemonic ideology of Western neo-colonialism' (2006: 33). This means that the positioning of Japanese cinema as radical and oppositional, in comparison to the inherent and perceived conservative ideology of mainstream American cinema, functions simply to consolidate Japan as a place of inalterable difference and exoticism.

In 'The Concept of National Cinema' Higson points out that this concept is often used 'prescriptively rather than descriptively, citing what *ought* to be the national cinema, rather than describing the actual cinematic experiences of popular audiences' (2002: 133). The construction of a national cinema therefore presupposes a 'coherence and unity' and as a consequence proclaims 'a unique identity and a stable set of meanings.' Higson continues:

> The process of identification is thus invariably a hegemonising, mythologizing process, involving both the production and assignment of a particular set of meanings, and the attempt to contain or prevent the proliferation of other meanings. (2002: 133)

What it is important to understand in the case of Japanese national cinema is that the very concept of a homogenised national identity was always fraught with difficulty because of the close relationship between Japan and the West. In reaction to the threat to Japan's construction of nationhood through the menace of Westernisation, studies of Japaneseness, known as *Nihonjinron*, proliferated. And while generally *Nihonjinron* is associated with post-war Japan, its origins can be found much earlier, as a response to the modernisation undertaken as a consequence of the Meiji Restoration. Burgess writes: 'With the period of nation-building following the Meiji Restoration (1868), discussions of Japanese identity acquired both a new Other – the West – and a new urgency (Pyle 1969)' (2004).

During the Meiji Restoration, Japanese cultural identity was constructed in opposition to the 'Other' (not-us). The word for foreigner was *ijin* (a different person) and was used mainly to refer to white foreigners because of their marked difference, from the 'self'. Burgess continues:

> Nihonjinron is formulated on the basis of evaluative comparison (Befu 1993: 113). It aims to demonstrate not only that Japan (and Japanese language, culture, people) is different (uniquely unique) from the rest of the world but also that it is superior or better. Difference – a stark and evaluative comparison – is central to the maintenance of identity. In

Japan, this manifests itself in a sharp distinction between what it means
to be a Japanese and what it means to be a foreigner. (2004)

Further, and paradoxically, Western discourse about the inherent difference
of the Japanese, which utilised adjectives such as 'inscrutable', 'exotic',
'anti-individualistic', provided a mechanism through which Japan would
redefine itself. Iwabuchi labels as self-orientalism the process by which Japan
defined itself in terms of existing definitions on the part of the West (1994).
In *Orientalism*, Said defined Orientalism as 'an exercise of cultural strength'
in which the West determined 'that the Orient and everything in it was, if
not patently inferior to, then in need of corrective study by the West' (2003:
40–1). An example of this approach can be found in Ruth Benedict's book,
The Chrysanthemum and the Sword: Patterns of Japanese Culture (1946), based
upon interviews with prisoners of war in Allied camps; in fact, Benedict never
visited Japan, instead basing her conclusions solely on interviews with Japanese
immigrants and extant written materials. These conclusions constructed Japan
as a 'shame' culture in opposition to the 'guilt' culture of Western societies,
and through the processes of Orientalism and self-Orientalism (or complicit
Orientalism), became a mechanism through which to distinguish Japan from
the West, and indeed the West from Japan. As such, the search for what was
distinctive about Japanese society operated within pre-existing Orientalist
assumptions about Japan and the Japanese rather than differing from them.
The idea of the community as fundamental to the *ie* system of kinship, was
situated in opposition to the traits of an imaginary America associated with
rampant individualism, selfishness and commodity fetishisation. Iwabuchi
writes:

> Japan is represented and represents itself as culturally exclusive, homoge-
> neous, and uniquely particularistic through the operation of a strategic
> binary opposition between two imaginary cultural entities, 'Japan' and
> 'the West'. (2002: 7)

Underlying this binary distinction between Japan and the West is a
convenient forgetting of Japan's own colonial past. Victory in the First Sino-
Japanese War (1 August 1894 to 17 April 1895) led to the successful annex-
ation of Korea, as well as control over Taiwan ceded by China. Japan's colonial
ambitions were thwarted during the Second Sino-Japanese War (7 July 1937 to
9 September 1945), at which time defeat forced Japan to give up her colonial
territories. While Iwabuchi (1994) recognises the importance of Said's work on
Orientalism, he critiques Said's treatment of Japan as a 'non-Western, quasi-
Third World nation which has been the victim of Western (American) cultural
domination' in Said's *Culture and Imperialism*. Iwabuchi remarks that the 'total

absence of a consideration of Japanese imperialism/colonialism in his analysis of imperialism and culture is striking to me' (2002: 3).

From the pre-war slogan '*wakon yōsai*' (Japanese spirit, Western technologies), which allowed Japan to reinforce its cultural and colonial superiority in the pan-Asian world, to the contemporary '*Datsuō nyuō*' (Escape the West, Enter Asia), Japan's search for national identity has shifted from global to local identification with East Asia. Indeed, Japan's nostalgic glance backwards at Hong Kong articulates a desire for 'a different mode of non-Western mimetic modernity' (Iwabuchi 2004: 152). And as Chaudhuri points out, East Asian territories have a unified experience of late modernity when compared to the West. In addition, Chaudhuri writes that pan-Asian countries:

> share many centuries old cultural traditions: Confucian ethics, based on filial obligations and loyalty between rulers and their subjects, and between family members and friends; Buddhism; supernatural beliefs; classical theatre ... and Chinese classical painting, characterized by the subordination of figures to landscape and the absence of the illusion of depths. (2005: 93)

As such, and as LaMarre points out, the Japanese empire (like Japanese modernity) cannot be construed as a simple repetition of the British or American empires. Nor can its difference be dismissed as a failure, a failed imitation of Western models, or as a sort of non-imperial empire (2005: 358–9).

Iwasaka and Toelken argue that the prevalence of stereotypes in the West either constructs 'the Japanese as narrowly ethnocentric and nationally aggressive, and sees their behaviour as a hold from the samurai era', or else consider them too 'Westernised' (1994:1). Instead, these myths are a result of cultural nostalgia on the part of the West, for some exotic imagined Japan of cherry blossoms, geisha and tea ceremonies (1994: 2–3). The success of both *The Last Samurai* (Zwick: 2003) and *Memoirs of a Geisha* (Marshall: 2005) seems to attest to the perpetuation of these myths. Indeed, *Memoirs of a Geisha* caused uproar in both China and Japan, particularly around the casting of Zhang Ziyi, a Chinese actress, in the lead role as Sayuri. In fact, the other two leading female roles are also played by Chinese actresses (or Chinese-Singaporean in the case of Michelle Yeoh). Japanese actresses had to be content with secondary roles. China promptly banned the film, as no one had bothered to think about the atrocities committed by Japan on China in the 1930s. In Japan, the fact that a Chinese actress was cast to play a geisha, instead of a Japanese actress, was no less palatable.

Iwabuchi (2002) utilises the term 'cultural odor' in order to affirm the national identity of cultural exports positively, even when relying heavily on stereotypes. This odour becomes a fragrance, 'a socially and culturally accepted smell', through the process of identification with pre-existing symbolic images. Cultural odour, according to Iwabuchi, can be erased through the deletion of racial, ethnic and bodily characteristics associated with the nation of origin. For Iwabuchi anime and computer games are paradigmatic of this erasure of bodily odour: 'Consumers of and audiences for Japanese animation and games, it can be argued, may be aware of the Japanese origin of these commodities, but those texts barely feature "Japanese bodily odor" identified as such' (2002: 29). In opposition to this is Shapiro's argument that 'The ostensive Western setting and features of the characters allow filmmakers to create and audiences to receive intense subtextual undercurrents of very sensitive, contemporary sociocultural problems in Japan' (2002: 268).

GLOBAL FLOWS

The relationship between Japan and the West is a complex one, and therefore to understand Japanese cinema in opposition to Western forms is perhaps to be complicit in the promotion of myths around Japan as a place of inalterable difference. Neither is distinguishing between Japanese cinema as art cinema and Western or First World cinema satisfactory, as Japanese genres, such as horror, often merge the formalist modernism of directors such as Ozu with the melodramatic nature of mainstream narrative. In addition, Japanese cinema shares common features with other nations in the pan-Asian world and therefore cultural proximity is as important a factor in the construction of Japanese cinema as its relationship to the (imagined) West.

The importance of film as an industry and the development of a studio system, the transformation of cinematic vocabulary as a result of the relationship with Hollywood cinema, and the importance of indigenous theatrical arts and religious belief systems all lead to an understanding of Japanese cinema as national cinema in terms of cultural specificity without denying the impact that the relationship between Japan and the West had on the construction of Japanese cinema from its early days until after the Allied Occupation.

CHAPTER 2

Horror after Hiroshima

There can be little surprise that the aftermath of the Second World War, and the Allied Occupation (1945–52), would give rise to vengeful ghosts from the pre-modern past, or indeed give birth to monsters, including Godzilla. The facts and figures are stark: 1.8 million dead and 680,000 missing or wounded; cities demolished; and Japan's position as a Pacific power totally destroyed. Saturation bombing raids on Tokyo and the dropping of the atomic bomb, first on Hiroshima on 6 August 1945 and then on Nagasaki three days later, left much of Tokyo in ruins, Nagasaki devastated and Hiroshima a burning wasteland. Victims not immediately killed by the bombs would die slowly and painfully, and generations to come would be effected by the fallout as the full horror of radiation poisoning became evident.

In addition, the indignity of the Allied Occupation, during which Japan was forced to adopt Western democratic values and abolish state Shintō, functioned to call into question the very foundations of Japan's intricate obligations system, which dictated the relationship of the individual to the community, and thereafter to the State. And whilst the emperor was reinstated towards the end of the Occupation, his role was reduced to a largely symbolic one, with no real power. This was a major upheaval in the very foundation of Japanese societal values and obligation, as the emperor was seen as a descendant of Amaterasu (the Sun Goddess, Shintō's chief deity) and had become synonymous with Japanese nationhood since 1868 (Littleton 2002: 47).

POST-OCCUPATION CINEMA

This tension between pre-modern Japanese paternalism and modern Western democratic values would constitute the main thematic trajectory of post-Occupation Japanese cinema. It was not a question of abandoning traditional

Japanese values for seemingly more democratic ones, but of co-opting one in order to re-establish the other. Standish points out how, in post-war Japanese cinema, American 'individualism' was utilised as a mechanism through which to reassert traditional Japanese ideology around the primacy of the nation-state: 'individualism, as expressed through the Hollywood-derived "goal-orientated hero" was co-opted to the narrative needs of a hyper-masculinist ideology underpinning total mobilization' (2005: 179).

Films with a contemporary setting (*gendaigeki*) continued to be popular in the immediate period after the Occupation, and a variation on the genre, the politically committed *shakiamono*, or social problem/tendency film, associated with directors such as Sekikawa Hideo and Kamei Fumio, emerged (Richie 2001: 146). There was also a return to the period film, or *jidaigeki*. Whilst many social dramas adopted a 'realistic' (Western) form of filmmaking, the *jidaigeki*, influenced by traditional theatrical forms, continued to be presentational and formalist with its emphasis on spectacle and visual style.

Not surprisingly, given the physical devastation and psychological trauma that the Japanese had suffered during and after the Second World War, the 1950s saw a rise in popularity of the horror film. In 'Nightmare and the Horror Film: The Symbolic Biology of Fantastic Beings', Carroll contends that horror and science fiction films proliferate at times of economic and political anxiety, in that they allow the expression of the 'sense of powerlessness and anxiety that correlates with times of depression, recession, Cold War strife, galloping inflation, and national confusion' (1981: 17).

The two most important films that would influence the growth of the horror genre, and pave the way for its contemporary success in a global market, are *Tales of Ugetsu* in 1953 and *Godzilla* in 1954. At a time of societal disruption, shifting relationships between men and women, the demise of rigid distinctions between classes and the rapid modernisation of Japan, the horror film provided one of the most suitable mechanisms through which to articulate anxieties and concerns over the changing nature of Japanese society at a time of unprecedented upheaval. In *Godzilla*, the monstrous mutant reptile with its atomic breath functions as a reminder of the devastation caused by nuclear weapons and critiques modern technological warfare, whilst simultaneously mourning the loss of tradition. Similarly, *Tales of Ugetsu* expresses fears around modernisation, implicit within the growth of a consumer society dictated by material desires, as embodied by the seductive female ghost. Even more significant is the embedding of the discourse of *hibakusha* in both films to articulate the persistence of historical trauma and the collective denial of culpability. This often took the form of 'a tragic young heroine suffering from atomic-related illness' (Lowenstein 2005: 86). In this way, 'the figure of woman enables a historical narrative of forgetting, where victimization replaces responsibility for aggression' (2005: 85). The active forgetting of both Japan's colonial past and the attack on Pearl Harbor which initiated war in the Pacific is rendered invisible through this myth of victimology which dominated post-war Japanese cinema.

Whilst it is not my intention to discuss the monster genre, or *daikaijueiga*, generally in Japanese cinema, *Godzilla* clearly elucidates societal, economic and political concerns in Japan at the time of production that are mirrored in the ghost story, which emerges almost simultaneously. While better known in its truncated version in the West as *Godzilla: King of Monsters* (Honda and Morse: 1956), the original Japanese version has only recently been released on DVD. In terms of the ghost story, *Tales of Ugetsu* not only lays down the foundations for the 'erotic ghost story' or *kaidan pinku eiga* (discussed in Chapter 4), but also contains key themes and characters that will be identifiable to contemporary audiences whose awareness of Japanese horror has been formed by the success of Nakata's *Ring* and Shimizu's *Ju-On: The Grudge* with their sequels and American remakes. These include the vengeful female ghost with long black hair; the haunted house; themes of abandonment and alienation; doomed love – all of which are framed by the ghostly aesthetics of the mise-en-scène and musical score. Both films emerge from the Kabuki and Nō traditions (as discussed in the last chapter), the special effects and spectacle influencing *Godzilla*, and the stories of ghosts, demons and other supernatural beings forming the basis of *Tales of Ugetsu*.

FROM THE ASHES

During the Second World War, the director of *Godzilla*, Honda, had been stationed in China. On his return to Japan, Honda not only was present during the saturation bombing of Tokyo, but also saw first-hand the devastation caused by the dropping of the bomb, code name 'Little Boy', on Hiroshima – 68 per cent of the city destroyed and an estimated 70,000 people instantly killed, this figure rising to around 200,000 as a result of radiation sickness. It is no surprise therefore that *Godzilla*, which some critics argue is loosely based upon *The Beast from 20,000 Fathoms* (Lourié: 1953), is both a thinly disguised metaphor for historical trauma and a warning against its repetition. At the same time, Godzilla is also represented as an unstoppable force of nature, 'like an erupting volcano, or a devastating Tsunami, which is more or less how many Japanese remember World War II anyway' (Buruma 2006).

It is significant therefore that the opening image of the film is a long shot of dark waters and crashing waves accompanied by a crescendo of violins, trumpet horns and the clashing of cymbals. In the following scenes, an explosion, from which emanates a brilliant white light, sets a fishing trawler, the *Eiko-Maru*, alight. Long shots of the boat on fire are cross-cut with medium and close-up shots of the victims on the trawler. In this sequence, a series of associations are made between nuclear bomb (the explosion), nature (the savage seas) and human suffering (the fishermen).

At the same time, the image of fishing boats caught up in a nuclear explosion would have been all too familiar to Japanese audiences, not only in light of the use of the atomic bomb, but also coming soon after another incident in which, once again, the Japanese were unwilling victims of nuclear warfare. On 1 March 1954, a tuna trawler, the *Lucky Dragon*, became caught up in testing of the H-bomb, being carried out by the United States. Many of the fishermen became ill with radioactive poisoning and some of them would later die. It is not surprising that this was a major news story in Japan at the time or that it caused a public outcry against nuclear testing. Allsop contends that these scenes of destruction at sea also allude to the battles lost by the Japanese at sea during the Second World War and the reluctance of the Japanese government to 'report losses to the public, wishing to maintain an illusion of victory at all costs' (2004a: 65). This can be seen in the manner in which the cross-cutting between the doomed fishing trawlers and the fishermen on board not only provides a human face for the scenes of devastation, but also constructs a discourse of victimology which helps to deflect any guilt associated with the historical events that underlie the images.

Although an investigation is started, neither the fishing company nor the military is able to provide a reason for the mysterious destruction of the *Eiko-Maru* or that of two other ships that are sent to the scene of the explosion, which suffer the same fate. The explosion wakes Godzilla, a prehistoric and pre-modern monster, from his repose on the ocean bed. During a terrible storm on the Island of Ōdo, near where the explosion happened, Godzilla attacks, crushing wooden houses underfoot. A fact-finding team is sent to Ōdo, led by Professor Yamane (Takeshi Shimura), a respected palaeontologist. Yamane discovers giant footprints, the presence of radiation (strontium-90) and trilobite (an ancient fossil) in the sand by the shoreline. Like many scientists in science fiction films, Yamane wants to study the monstrous Godzilla as a past object emblematic of a new type of scientific knowledge. In Yamane's terms, Godzilla is not a monster but a victim. Anderson writes:

> His concern to save the monster's life appears to arise out of an identification with a fellow war victim who is metaphorically Japanese, and also as a source of as yet untapped scientific knowledge that unthinking destruction will eliminate before it is decoded. (2006: 30)

Central to the narrative is the romance between the daughter of Professor Yamane, Emiko (Momoko Kochi), and Ogata (Akira Takarada), a dashing young naval salvage officer who works for the Southern Sea Company. Tsutsui points out that:

> One of the most surprising aspects of the 1954 *Gojira* ... is how little time the monster actually spends on screen. Indeed, as much attention is given in the film to a melodramatic, sentimental subplot as the rampages of Godzilla. (cited in Gunde 2005)

The romance between Emiko and Ogata is crucial, in terms of providing a counterpoint to the primal Godzilla. Scenes of Emiko and Ogata together are cross-cut with those of Godzilla throughout. It is key, therefore, that we are introduced to the couple immediately after the scenes of the sinking of the trawlers. It is clear from expression, body language and the brief words that they exchange with each other that Emiko and Ogata are romantically involved. However, as Ogata receives a phone call from the shipping company, shadows fall over the couple, hinting at the presence of some malevolent force which threatens their happiness. In Japanese culture, according to Shintō, the indigenous religion of Japan, the inside (*uchi*) is associated with safety, the family and Japan as a whole; Littleton writes, 'The interior of a home is, after all, a "sacred space" compared to the outside world' (2002: 61). The outside (*soto*) is a place of danger, consisting of marginal groups or 'outsiders'. Nadeau argues that the inside is the 'nation, in opposition to what lies beyond the seas' (1996: 110). While *uchi* and *soto* are shifting signifiers constantly in flux in Japanese linguistics (in which one person's *soto* is another's *uchi*) rather than fixed binary oppositions, it could be argued that the United States is envisaged as the ultimate outside here. But this is an outside which is also on the inside. Godzilla, as we shall see, is aggressor and victim, self and other, his identity as subject caught up in the discourse of the situated self, which is central to Japanese linguistics. In this scene, danger from the outside has been brought into the 'safety' of the inside, as expressed visually through the use of chiaroscuro lighting as strips of darkness descend over Emiko and Ogata. In Shintō, the inside is constituted as a sacred space, and the outside, a profane space. Nadeau explains, 'Shinto, with its emphasis on defilement and purification, associates profane space with pollution and evil, and sacred space with purity and brightness' (1996: 110).

In a later scene, Emiko is momentarily blinded by a flash of bright light when she witnesses the full extent of the danger of the 'oxygen destroyer' (see below). The visual imagery associated with Godzilla is that of the profane – darkness, disease, and death. Tanaka writes, 'Godzilla's preference for darkness and intense dislike of light evokes the behaviour of B-29 bombers, which flew at night and sought to evade searchlight beams' (2005). In opposition, the visual imagery associated with Emiko and Ogata is that of the sacred and the inside, as expressed through the concepts of purity and brightness. Purity, however, is not an original state of innocence, as associated with Christianity in which Adam and Eve are tempted by earthly pleasures and fall from grace. Instead, Shintō 'inscribes humanity as fundamentally good, with evil as an ephemeral state of being rather than an innate quality' (Balmain 2007b).

It is important, both visually and in terms of narrative motivation, that Godzilla's rampages are cross-cut with scenes of Emiko and Ogata together. This situates heterosexual romance as a mechanism through which to defeat the destructive Godzilla. Standish argues that the functioning of romance in post-war cinema provides a point of departure from the social repression (and often the absence) of woman, which was at the centre of national policy or propaganda films:

> Romance provided both a vehicle through which the requisite dominant constructions of sexuality were inscribed in cultural and economic terms of masculinity and femininity, whilst simultaneously becoming synonymous with an antiwar imperative that challenged the underlying text inherent in images of masculinity predicated on sexual repression that dominated 'national policy' films. (2005: 210)

Emiko's engagement to the mysterious Dr Daisuke Serizawa (Akihiko Hirato), who lives with her and her father, is situated in direct opposition to her romance with Ogata. As such, Serizawa is aligned with Godzilla, as he also threatens the happiness of the couple who can be considered as emblematic of the nation as a whole. Serizawa is a recluse, who spends most of his time in the darkened gothic laboratory where he carries out his experiments, and as such he is visually connected to Godzilla. Whilst Godzilla is metaphorically a weapon of mass destruction, Serizawa possesses the power to obliterate all living things with his invention called the 'oxygen destroyer'. Significantly, the presence of facial scars on the left-hand side of Serizawa's face feminises him by situating him as the archetypal 'A-bomb' victim whose self-sacrifice functions to displace 'Japanese national responsibility for the trauma itself' (Lowenstein 2005: 86). As such, both Godzilla and Serizawa are doubles in that they are both positioned as victims of nuclear war.

The romance between Ogata and Emiko also functions to map out changes in the social structure in Japan after the Allied Occupation. Writing about the radical changes in Japanese socio-economic structures as a consequence of the democratisation of Japan during the Allied Occupation, Noreiga points to the fact that most of the reforms implemented went far beyond what could be found at the time in America:

> Reform gave women full legal equality and ended the authority of the clan over the family and the father over adult children. Compulsory

education was extended to nine years, further reducing paternal influence. So-called reform exceeded what American society would have accepted for itself at that time, indicating that the purpose was more to undermine the patriarchal basis of Japanese society than to reform it. (2006: 43)

These reforms were not, in fact, motivated by a genuine concern for the oppression of women and children under Japanese patriarchy. Instead, the changes were instigated by America's desire to ensure that Japan would never again be a military threat to the West. American capitalism invaded Japanese feudalism, bringing with it the ideal of the bourgeois nuclear family and a concept of the boundaried self that was foreign to the collectivism that had underpinned Japanese society for centuries.

The relationships between individuals, the community and the state, following the Confucian principles of loyalty and benevolence, as articulated within state Shintō (which the Americans tried to abolish through reforms), was based upon what is known as the *ie* system. Although the democratic values of the West, as applied to Japan during the Occupation, attempted to break down the rigid vertical structure of Japanese society, remnants of the *ie* system can still be found at work in contemporary Japan, dictating relationships with parents, employers and perceived superiors. As this is such a fundamental structure of Japanese society, elements of which still exist today, and often provides a pivotal theme in Japanese horror cinema, it is worth sketching out the *ie* system in some detail.

The foundations of the *ie* system were laid down during the Edo Period (1603–1867), during the reign of Tokugawa Ieyasu (the Shogunate or Shogun). At this time, a strict class system was enforced that can still be seen within corporations, and especially as embodied within the figure of the 'salaryman'. This system consisted of five classes with the Samurai on top, followed by peasants, then artisans and finally merchants. A fifth class was formed of 'outcasts', people involved in what were seen to be impure professions. Responsibility for the family was clearly defined as belonging to the head of the household, who was then responsible to the larger community, and ultimately to the emperor. The eldest son of the family was the automatic successor, while younger sons were expected to make their own way in the world and arranged marriages were made for daughters of the household. In the absence of an heir, it was common for families to adopt a suitable successor who would then carry on the family name. The system, however, was predicated on the repression and oppression of women, for whom the rules of appropriate behaviour were dictated by her obedience to her parents, husband and children, in that order.

The *ie* system, based upon the worship of ancestors (Davies and Ikeno 2002: 120), rests upon the often competing concepts of *giri* and *ninjō*. *Giri* refers to a strong sense of obligation, and is the 'social cloth' that binds Japan together, whilst *ninjō* denotes 'generosity or sympathy towards the disadvantaged, and sympathy towards each other' (Dubro and Kaplan 1986: 28). *Ninjō* promotes the avoidance of conflict, and should take precedence over *giri*, or duties towards one's superiors, family, relatives and ancestors, people from whom a favour or gift has been received, duty to clear one's reputation (i.e. a vendetta), and finally observance of social proprieties, in that order (Hunziker and Kamimura 1994). It is clear to see how and why *giri* might well come into conflict with *ninjō*.

Understanding the functioning of the *ie* system, along with the rapid changes in Japanese societal structures, can therefore elucidate our understanding of the centrality of romance in *Godzilla*. Serizawa, to whom Emiko is engaged, is the natural (and adopted) successor of Yamane as dictated by the *ie* system. Emiko and Ogata's romance therefore seems to threaten the very structures of Japanese society, in that *ninjō* (personal feeling) comes into conflict with *giri* (social obligations). As such Emiko's duty to her father, under the *ie* system and the wider notion of *On*, should take precedence over her own feelings. *On* is the system of obligations that bind the living to the dead in terms of the debt (*giri*) that is owed to them. Filial piety, after all, was the central tenet of Confucianism and 'lay at the foundations of all forms of authority, especially that of a master, who was regarded as the "father of the mind"' (Buisson 2003: 39). This model became so firmly entrenched within daily life and the education system in Japan that it became appropriate to sacrifice one's own life when either one's master or one's parents were dishonoured. Littleton foregrounds the need in Japan to maintain face (known as *tatame* in Japanese), in which the loss of face necessitates acts of atonement on the part of the community in order to make up for the violation of the social code (2002: 59). When Japan surrendered at the end of the Second World War, the War Minister Anami, Head of the Imperial Army, committed ritual suicide as an act of penance on behalf of the 'shamed' nation. Serizawa's suicide has a similar function in *Godzilla*, providing a mechanism through which to save and restore 'face' in the aftermath of defeat.

However, with the threat of Western democracy to the underlying structures of Japanese society, the emergence of Godzilla can be interpreted as expressing anxieties over the erosion of pre-modern Japanese structures, or indeed over the very notion of 'Japan' as a nation, constructed through difference from the West. Napier argues that, in Japanese mythology, pre-modern monsters are external aliens or 'outsiders who threaten the collectivity, but who can be avoided or appeased' (1996: 95). Again, this can be understood by reference to Shintō beliefs. According to Shintō, Japan is home to over 8 million deities. (Ross 1996: 27). Known as *kami* (often translated as deity), they are found everywhere: in mountains, rivers, trees, rocks and everyday household items. *Kami* are inherently neither evil nor good, and indeed, according to Shintō, the nature of the *kami* depends on the circumstance that gave rise to it:

> The Shinto tradition does not believe that there is an absolute dichotomy of good and evil. Rather, all phenomena, both animate and inanimate, are thought to possess both 'rough' and 'gentle', or negative and positive, characteristics and it is possible for a given entity to manifest either of these characteristics depending on the circumstances. (Littleton 2002: 26)

Godzilla's negative energy is therefore not constructed in terms of an absolute evil, as many critical readings of *Godzilla* have suggested. Instead, Godzilla can be interpreted as a physical manifestation of the disruption of *wa*, or the harmony between man and nature. Littleton writes, 'Rules governing human behaviour are considered necessary for the maintenance of *wa*, without which both society and the natural world would disintegrate into chaos' (2002: 59). For Shapiro the distortion in the relationships between people and nature is the main theme of post-war Japanese cinema: 'It is this distortion that must be analyzed if we are to understand fully Japan's atomic bomb cinema' (2002: 271). This explains the reason why Japanese atomic bomb cinema focuses less on the protagonists than in comparable Western films dealing with the atomic bomb. Instead, the emphasis is on a 'vague but nonetheless important concept … of the restoration of balance and harmony' (Shapiro 2002: 271). Shapiro suggests that this emphasis is most clearly seen in Japan's monster films, such as *Godzilla*. It could be argued that, in American cinema, monsters are often interpreted as symptoms of an (individual) psychosexual crisis with their fairy-tale structure (hero defeats monster and rescues the damsel in distress, undergoing a transformation – from boy to man – in the process). In *Godzilla* none of the protagonists goes through this transformation of self and, as such, it is difficult to interpret the monstrous Godzilla as a projection of inner sexual conflict, unlike King Kong in the film of the same name (1933). For Shapiro, rather than interpreting *Godzilla* as an overt condemnation of America's use of nuclear weapons, it is more productive to consider the film in terms of how war (and masculinity) disrupts the fragile balance between man and nature. He writes: 'Thus, the world is dangerously unbalanced. Something must counterbalance the male element in this film' (2002: 275). It is therefore up to Emiko, caught between her father, her fiancé and her lover, to restore harmony, as the male element here, as elsewhere, is aligned with violence and disharmony. Shapiro argues that the fighting between the men over Godzilla and Emiko creates a vacuum or *ma* (the term in Japanese aesthetics for an empty or blank space which needs to be filled), which can only be remedied by Emiko as representative of the female principle. The visual result of this can be seen when Emiko breaks up the fight between Ogata and Serizawa over the use of the oxygen destroyer – she steps in and unites the two men in a common purpose. However, her actions indirectly cause the death of Serizawa, thereby opening up an empty space that is so powerful 'that it draws Gojira back into our lives again and again' (Shapiro 2002: 278).

The repeated images of pollution and bodily corruption are central to the imagistic system of destruction, disease and death associated with Godzilla, and are thus associated with the disruption of harmony. In *Godzilla*, pollution is signalled by the annihilation of all life from the water near to where the explosion happened. This is made clear in a series of short scenes in which we see fishermen returning back to Ōdo with empty nets and, later, poisoned fish being put back into the water. It is also significant that, as a consequence, many wells on Ōdo are polluted and it is unsafe to drink from them.

At the same time, pollution was becoming a cause of concern in Japan, not only as a lingering aftermath of the Second World War, but also in terms of industrial pollution, caused by a mass exodus of people leaving the country for the cities. One such example is Minamata Bay, used as a dumping ground for industrial waste in the 1920s by the Chisso Corporation. The resulting pollution contaminated the fishing waters and impacted on the livelihoods of a substantial proportion of the villagers living in Minamata, a small factory town 570 miles from Tokyo. Estimates suggested that in a period of 36 years, between 1932 and 1968, 27 tons of mercury compounds found their way into Minamata Bay. By the mid-1950s some villagers were displaying symptoms associated with a degenerative condition, which became known as Minamata disease. The dark surging waters from which Godzilla emerges condense references to industrial pollution and the 'black rain' of Hiroshima, and are therefore linked to the profane. In *Purity and Danger*, Douglas argues that in primitive societies uncleanliness functions as a 'spiritual state of unworthiness' (1966: 11). As such, the sacred is separated from the profane by 'rules expressing its essentially contagious character' (Douglas 1966: 21). This opposition between purity and impurity, an essential component of Shintō, is a basic theme in *Godzilla*.

This can be clearly seen in the confrontation between Ogata and Emiko, and Serizawa, when the lovers try to convince Serizawa to use the oxygen destroyer to kill Godzilla. In this sequence, the three are sitting around a table, on which stands a square fishbowl with fish swimming in it. The fishbowl functions as a symbol of life and harmony. This is opposed to the death of the fish in the large tank seen earlier when Serizawa demonstrates his invention to Emiko. This visual symbology of death/life, darkness/light and disease/purity structures the filmic imagery, only giving way to purity when Serizawa and Godzilla die.

The tension between past and present, tradition and modernity is emphasised visually and thematically in *Godzilla*, through the direct opposition between the island (Ōdo) and the city (Tokyo). The rural spaces of Ōdo stand in contrast to the neon Tokyo. The difference between the pre-modern and the modern is foregrounded through the doubling (a literary device which allows the representation of competing ideas/ideologies by splitting the subject into two separate characters) between Professor Yamane and Gisaku (Kokuten Kodo), an old villager who lives on Ōdo. Yamane and Gisaku utilise different interpretative frameworks to explain Godzilla, although both agree that it is the nuclear testing that is to blame for Godzilla's appearance. For Gisaku, Godzilla is an enraged god, brought to the surface by the lack of belief in traditional values demonstrated by the younger generation's abandonment of appropriate rituals of appeasement that were necessary to retain harmony, including the sacrifice of a shrine virgin and *gigaku* performances (a type of music and dance theatre which predates both Kabuki and Nō, often used to exorcise evil spirits). Anderson writes:

> the lecture of the island elder could also stand in for a Japanese folklorist lecturing on the consequences of the loss that comes with neglecting traditional ways, and failing to respect and sustain indigenous, non European-American identity. (2006: 27)

The name Gojira is a composite of the words for 'gorilla' and 'whale', which further suggests a link between Godzilla and the supernatural. There are a number of ghosts and monsters associated with water, including the *Kappa*

Fig. 2.1 Godzilla's rampage, *Godzilla* (Ishirō Honda, 1954, Tōhō / The Kobal Collection)

or Water Imp. Others include the playful *Shojo*, a sea ghost with red hair who enjoys nothing better than a good party; the giant mermaid or *Isohime*, who tortures and then devours her victims; and *Umi Bozu*, a gigantic bald ghost with staring eyes. Then there are *Funayūrei*, or ghosts of those that die at sea. Godzilla's appearance evokes *ukiyo-e* images of water dragons who were associated with thunderstorms, and whose breath was thought to cause lightning and/or rain. It is significant that Godzilla first appears during a terrible storm, which devastates the island of Ōdo.

Godzilla's thirteen-minute rampage through Tokyo and its aftermath evokes the imagery of the Second World War – including the aftermath of Hiroshima and Nagasaki and the saturation bombings of Tokyo – as buildings are crushed underfoot by Godzilla, who is framed against the skyline by a wall of flames. The Diet building, the Nichigeki Theatre and the Matsuszakaya department store, signifiers of modernity and progress, are razed to the ground in Godzilla's wake. In the middle of these scenes of disaster, the fate of a young mother and her two children adds a tragic dimension to the scenes of destruction. Huddled in a corner by the Matsuszakaya department store, she passively awaits her fate, telling her children that they will soon be in heaven with their father. The centrality of the relationship between mother and child is prevalent in post-war Japanese cinema, especially in a type of domestic melodrama known as 'mother films' or *hahamono*. Buruma goes as far as to suggest that all 'Japanese love stories are all variations of the *haha mono*' (1984: 32). A key scene in *Godzilla*, which takes place after Godzilla's rampage across Tokyo, ends with Emiko cradling a young child in her arms. This is an iconic image of mother and child that, as we will see, becomes a key feature, if not the key feature, of Japanese horror cinema from the 1950s onwards.

The horrific nature of Godzilla's rampage around Tokyo would have had resonance with Japanese audiences at the time. Hamamoto comments on the reception of the film in Japan:

> One critic said the scariest part of 'Godzilla' is the screams of the people running away. Their terror, he feels, came across as authentic, because they were able to draw on the real horror of witnessing entire cities firebombed into burning rubble. (2006)

The apocalyptic mise-en-scène of Tokyo as a burning wasteland the next day, with the remains of the city laying submerged under swirling smoke and the bodies of the sick and injured being taken to a hospital, again visually mirrors Tokyo after the saturation bombing raids during the Second World War, as well as the lingering aftermath of the atomic bombs at Hiroshima and Nagasaki. In the light of the merciless destruction caused by Godzilla, some Western critics have dismissed the creature as both profoundly alien and absolutely evil:

The monster's allegorical power also is more terrible (and obvious) in the original. Incinerating and crushing whole cities, Godzilla – evil, overwhelming, and profoundly alien – clearly is intended to embody nuclear warfare, waged against helpless Japanese civilians. (Steele 2005)

However, to interpret the figure of Godzilla as a simple symbolic representation of the threat of America to Japan, as Steele does, is too simplistic. Noreiga argues that 'Clearly Western conceptions of the "Other or monster as repressed sexual energy" (Wood), class struggle (Jameson), or "archaic, conflicting impulses" (Carroll) do not fully explain the Japanese monster' (2006: 46). This is a linguistic difference, in that the Japanese language does not distinguish between the personal pronouns 'I' and 'you', or 'self' and 'other'; instead, the relationship between self and other in Japanese culture is one in which 'the self immerse[s] itself in the other' (Noreiga 2006: 46). This concept of the relational self suggests a mobility of identity as encapsulated within the shifting boundaries of inside, *uchi*, and outside, *soto*. This then enables us to make sense of Noreiga's statement that 'Godzilla comes to symbolize Japan (Self) as well as the United States (Other)' (2006: 46). As Napier explains, 'the traditional Japanese 'self' is more diffuse and other-directed than the more individualistic Western self' (1996: 94). In these terms, as we have seen, the anxieties expressed about Godzilla are as much about Japan, as *uchi*, as about the threat from the United States, as *soto*.

In order to restore the harmony between man and nature, life-strengthening rites, or *naobi*, are necessary. In these terms, Serizaw's sacrifice not only co-opts democratic individualism, as in the service of traditional Japanese nationalism in an attempt to bridge the gap between the two, but also provides a mechanism through which harmony between man and the environment is restored. Standish argues that the sacrificial hero is an important mechanism through which traditional identity is restored in the face of encroaching Westernisation. Drawing on Terry Eagleton's concept of the sacrificial victim as a figure standing for the expiation of communal guilt, Standish argues that the development of the 'sacrificial hero' of 'the humanist war-retro film can in general terms be understood as forming part of the process of communal internalization of the values of the nascent American-dominated world order' (2005: 203). Serizawa's sacrifice restores purity and brightness. Here individualism, as articulated through the 'goal-orientated' hero, Serizawa, is co-opted in the service of the greater good of the nation-state. His suicide is the triumph of light over darkness, purity over pollution, and thus restores temporary harmony to the world.

The death of Serizawa metaphorically signals both the breakdown of the traditional Japanese value system and the reaffirmation of those same values. At the same time, Emiko and Ogata's romance is made possible only through Serizawa's sacrifice. In addition, the romance, just like the monstrous rampages of Godzilla, undermines the paternalistic function of Yamane and his position of power within the household. As such, Yamane is a predecessor of the absent father, who, like the iconic mother, will become another identifiable trope of Japanese horror. In a key scene in which Yamane and Ogata argue about whether to study or kill Godzilla, Ogata is placed in a higher and more dominant position within the frame than Yamane, thus mirroring the disruption of the vertical boundaries that determined relationships between people in the *ie* system. But with the final words of the film, which are given to Yamane, who warns of the possibility of the emergence of another Godzilla, it could be argued that lost power is restored to the symbolic father figure. As Shapiro insightfully comments, in his criticism of Noreiga's identification of Christian symbolism at work in *Godzilla*, 'Can you have latent Christianity without Jews or Christians, or even the concept of self?' He concludes: '[A]ll the early *Gojira* films portray the men, and the male Gojira, as the cause of the problem (with the men receiving far less sympathy than the monster)' (2002: 278).

GHOSTLY RETURNS

> In Old Japan, the world of the living was everywhere ruled by the world of the dead – the individual, at every moment of his existence, was under ghostly supervision. In his house, he was watched by the spirits of his fathers; without, he was ruled by the god of his district. (Hearn 1904: 134)

Mizoguchi's *Tales of Ugetsu* is often cited as the prototypical Japanese ghost or avenging spirit (*onryou*) film. Along with Ozu and Kurosawa, Mizoguchi is considered one of the most important directors of Japanese cinema. Unlike Kurosawa, Mizoguchi was concerned with depicting the struggles of ordinary people rather than the exploits of Samurai and emperors. Based upon short stories in Ueda's (1734–1809) *Tales of Moonlight and Rain* (1776), *Tales of Ugetsu* is a morality play about the system of obligations that binds men to women in Japanese society, and the dreadful consequences of failure to abide by this. According to Tucker, Mizoguchi:

> films a world whose social system is one immediately recognizable to his Japanese audience. Rarely do his characters attempt to act against that system. Most of them suffer under these social codes but their suffering is shown as something that happens, 'that is the way things are', rarely with any implication of 'the way things should be'. (1973: 58)

At the same time, by criticising that social world in which his characters become caught up, through the representation of feckless men and downtrodden women, Tucker contends that Mizoguchi's films 'have done much to liberate Japanese women from the position that they held until recently of being second-class citizens' (1973: 59). Whilst Mizoguchi's films are noted for their strong female characters, they also champion traditional Japanese values, as we shall see is the case in *Tales of Ugetsu*.

In *Tales of Ugetsu*, two peasants, Genjuro (Masayuki Mori) and Tobei (Sakae Ozawa), see the war as an opportunity to progress up the social scale. Whilst Genjuro desires to be a master potter, Tobei – providing the film's comical moments – wants to be a Samurai. Their interwoven narratives provide a savage indictment of post-war masculinity and the loss of traditional Japanese values in the light of encroaching Americanisation, associated with commodification and materialism. Both men associate happiness with material wealth and status, and are discontented with their simple life. As such, 'modern' selfish individualism associated with the city is situated in opposition to the pre-modern 'selflessness' of rural Japan. As in *Godzilla*, the pathological nature of modernity is situated as threatening to a sense of national identity based around collectivity, filial obedience and frugality.

After their village is ransacked, Genjuro and Tobei are determined to escape the confines of the village and their peasant status, and attempt to leave by boat. The fog-enshrouded waters, menacingly absent of all life, hint at the presence of the supernatural. Eventually, however, the group come across another, seemingly empty, boat. As the boat draws near, they find a dying man in it, who warns them of danger ahead. Concerned for the safety of his wife, Miyagi (Kinuyo Tanaka), and his son, Genjuro persuades them to return to the village. However, Tobei's wife, Ohama (Mitsuko Mito), insists on accompanying them, not trusting her husband on his own: fears that all too soon prove justified.

Through the vagaries of fortune, both brothers find what they seek. Tobei becomes a Samurai by duplicitous means and Genjuro's pottery is admired and sells for a high price. The theme of abandonment runs throughout the film, with both men abandoning their wives and their duties as husbands for the empty trappings of material success. The dereliction of their duties as husbands and, in Genjuro's case, also as a father has horrific consequences; Tobei discovers that, in his absence, his wife has been raped and forced into prostitution, while Genjuro finds his homestead deserted and his wife dead when he eventually returns home. The film works within Shintō beliefs in which calamitous happenings are seen as punishment for not complying with the complex obligations systems that structure societal relations. In *Tales of Ugetsu*, the suffering of the women is brought about by a failure to act in accordance with these obligations, as selfishness (associated in Japan with the West) is privileged over selflessness.

Fig. 2.2 The first meeting between Genjuro and Lady Wakasa, *Tales of Ugetsu* (Kenji Mizoguchi, 1955, Daiei / The Kobal Collection)

Once in the city, Genjuro finds his pottery appreciated by the beautiful and ghostly Lady Wakasa (Machiko Kyō). Dressed in white, with a kimono veiling much of her features, Lady Wakasa has a status which is signalled both by the opulence of her kimono and by the fact that her servant accompanies her. The shots of their first meeting make the class differences between the two clear; Genjuro is framed from the point-of-view of Lady Wakasa who looks down on him as he sits on the ground surrounded by his wares. When she invites him back to her house to deliver his pottery and to collect his money, Genjuro finds himself unable to say no. In a sequence echoed in later Japanese ghost films he follows her home, walking behind her servant, to a grand mansion. Once there, seduced by Lady Wakasa's beauty and the opulence of her lifestyle, Genjuro forgets about his wife and son. He succumbs to Lady Wakasa's spell and marries her. His life with Lady Wakasa is in direct opposition to the scenes of simple peasant life with Miyagi and his son with which the film begins. Unrestrained physical appetites associated with materialism, including carnal desire and gluttony, are situated as the causational factor leading to the neglect of family duties and obligations.

Parallelism is utilised effectively to foreground the dangers of these unrestrained appetites and highlight the suffering of Genjuro's wife and son, who Genjuro has abandoned for a life of luxury and idleness. Just as Genjuro declares his undying love for Lady Wakasa and tells her that he must be in heaven, the film cuts to Miyagi's desperate struggle to return to their home. The idyllic and pastoral mise-en-scène of cultivated grass and gentle waters, as Genjuro and Lady Wakasa picnic, is in contrast to the dark house where Miyagi and her son are hiding, as bandits ransack it. The sumptuous picnic that is laid out on a blanket in the former scene further functions to highlight Miyagi's plight. It is thus particularly poignant that Miyagi not only is forced to beg for food for her son, but is attacked by a group of men for that scrap of food. In the ensuing altercation she is fatally wounded, and the last shot shows her struggling to make her way home, using a large branch to aid her. The rich, as epitomised by Lady Wakasa, are shown as idling their time away, whilst the poor are forced into animal-like behaviour in order to survive.

Too late, Genjuro comes across a priest, who tells him that he bears the mark of death. He learns that Lady Wakasa is a ghost, who, having died prematurely, has become tied to the world in order to experience love. The priest paints Buddhist mantras on his body to keep him from falling under her spell. The use of Buddhist mantras to keep dead spirits away is a common trope of the Japanese ghost story, although it does not always work, as in Sone's *Hellish Love* (1972) and 'Mimi-nashi-Hoichi' ('Hoichi the Earless') in *Kwaidan*. Realising that his life with Lady Wakasa is an illusion, Genjuro is freed from the spell she has cast on him. Determined to return home to his wife and son, he rejects Lady Wakasa's pleas to join her in the afterlife. In the ensuing fight, Genjuro faints. When he wakes up, the palace is a deserted and burnt-out shell, and Lady Wakasa and her nurse have disappeared. To make matters worse, the money that he has managed to save is then taken off him, and he returns home as poor as he was when he left.

When Genjuro returns, he finds his house empty and in a state of disrepair. However, the second time he walks into the house, he is surprised and overwhelmed to find Miyagi and his son are waiting for him. Overcome by guilt, Genjuro begs for Miyagi's forgiveness, which she gives. He sits with Miyagi and his son, a picture of domestic bliss. Later that night, Genjuro falls asleep with his son in his arms. Awaking the next morning, he finds his wife gone and his home destroyed. In an ironic twist, he discovers that, whilst he has been living a life of luxury, his wife also died and, like Lady Wakasa, she too is a ghost. The film ends with both men picking up their duties as head of the household, with a voice-over by Miyagi mourning the fact that it is only now that she is dead that Genjuro can be a proper husband.

In an interview with Schilling, Japanese director Juzo Itami discusses how the demise of the *ie* had catastrophic consequences for Japanese society after the Second World War. According to Itami, this produced a generation of people who 'live[d] only according to their desires' (cited in Schilling 1999: 80). Itami locates this as a result of the breakdown in traditional Japanese paternalism, a direct consequence of the defeat in the Second World War:

> the role of the father [is] to teach their children they need gamen, or perseverance and fortitude, that they cannot live simply according to their own desires, that there are morals and laws that human beings must follow. But in Japanese society that role has become extremely weak, particularly in the post war period. Because Japanese men fought the war and lost it, their value as role models has really declined. (cited in Schilling 1999: 79)

Tales of Ugetsu seems to suggest that a return to traditional values is necessary for a post-military masculinity. When the film begins, Genjuro is situated as a poor role model in that he abandons his wife and child without hesitation. Harmony is only restored and guilt expiated through the death of Miyagi.

Linked to consumerism and illusion is the figure of Lady Wakasa. She is the physical embodiment of seduction and sensuality, and therefore aligned with capitalism and modernity. As such, she is the opposite of the self-sacrificing Miyagi, aligned with tradition, who puts her family before herself and whose death is dictated by her husband's selfish desires. Barrett argues that Lady Wakasa is a malevolent spirit, who is 'restless because she died inopportunely before she could become a bride and experience fulfilment as a woman' (1989: 105). According to Barrett, as Lady Wakasa has no living descendants, she can be classified as a '*muenbotoke*' – a spirit kept tied to this world as there is no one to deliver the appropriate death rites which would enable her to pass on. Richie views Lady Wakasa more sympathetically, as the double of Miyagi: 'Rather, both women died wanting love. The spirit in the haunted mansion is to be equated, not contrasted, with the loyal and loving wife. They are equal' (2001: 130).

Lady Wakasa is the prototype of the beautiful but dangerous Japanese ghost who haunts Japanese horror cinema. Napier suggests that the seductive female ghost represents the 'intense attraction of the Other, of the outside, an Other that the collectivity seeks to shield its members from' (1996: 1000). In Japanese mythology vengeful ghosts are called *yūrei*, and more often than not are female. Cinematic representations of *yūrei* are very similar to those in traditional *ukiyo-e* prints. Dressed in white (white kimonos are used for burial in Shintō), with long unbound black hair, *yūrei* are often depicted with no legs, and hands that dangle uselessly from the wrist. Their appearance is often accompanied by floating flames, called *hitodama*.

DEADLY OBLIGATIONS

Tales of Ugetsu also introduces what will become a distinguishing feature of Japanese horror: the concept of *On*. Again, as this is such a fundamental component of Japanese horror, it seems worthwhile exploring it some detail. Iwasaka and Toelken define *On* as:

> the kind of obligation that one assumes (in Japanese idiom, one *wears* it) when one has been the recipient of love, nurturance, kindness, favor, help, or advice – especially from a superior in the social system. *On* entails not only an awareness of having received a favor, but carries with it the absolute necessity to respond and repay. (1994: 19)

These obligations do not end with death but continue afterwards, both in terms of people who have died without fulfilling their obligations or paying their debt, and those left behind who have an obligation to the departed. For the Japanese, the world of the living and the world of the dead are therefore intimately bound together, as demonstrated by the Buddhist *Obon* festival in which the dead are honoured. Toelken writes about the importance of the continuing responsibilities towards ancestors in Japanese culture: 'In Japan and elsewhere today, celebration of Obon certainly focuses on the idea of responsibility to departed parents, the "debt that can never be repaid"' (1994).

Often, it is the non-fulfilment of these familial and societal duties that leads to the emergence of the vengeful ghost, as 'when these responsibilities are unfulfilled or violated, the resulting imbalance opens the door to malevolent entities' (Hochberg 2000). Further, the etymology of the worlds of the living and the dead suggests a close connection between the two. When someone dies, his or her spirit moves from *kono-yo* (the world of the living, or this world 'here') to *ano-yo* (the world of the dead, the world over yonder, 'there'). As such, the two worlds exist simultaneously, occupying the same space and time, with permeable boundaries between the two. This permeability of the boundary between *kono-yo* and *ano-yo* provides the plot line for many Japanese horror films, including *Tales of Ugetsu*. Toelken argues that obligations are intensified rather than negated by death:

> If the proper memorials and celebrations are observed by the living family, the spirit slowly evolves into a local deity, called a sorei or kami, and responds to the petitions of the living by exercising concern for their fortunes: enhancing the catch of fishermen, assuring the fertility of crops, easing childbirth, and influencing the financial stability of the whole family. In other words, the obligations and debts that are thought to exist between generations of a Japanese family are not interrupted by death but are intensified by it. (1994)

PRE-MODERN MONSTERS

Both *Godzilla* and *Tales of Ugetsu* meditate on the relation between the pre-modern and the modern in a rapidly changing society. Godzilla and Lady Wakasa are transitional figures, caught between tradition and modernity, mourning the loss of an authentic identity as embedded in the community, in the light of the imposition of Western democratic values on Japanese socio-economic structures through a problematisation of the family unit.

Anderson, writing about the 'Overcoming Modernity' (*Kindai no chōkoku*) conference in 1942, draws our attention to the fact that 'Japan's only hope was to overthrow the foreign corruption of the Japanese body politic by returning to Japan's traditions and roots as best as it could' (2006: 23). Further, the disruption of *wa*, as constructed through the fragile relationship between man and nature, is reformed in *Godzilla* and *Tales of Ugetsu* through the female principal: Emiko in the former and Miyagi in the latter. Shapiro comments, in relation to Emiko, 'Only when she has resolved what direction she will take and reveals her love for Ogata is harmony and balance restored' (2002: 277). In her study of Japanese fairy tales, Kawai argues that the 'woman of will' 'best expresses the Japanese ego' (1996: 170). If Emiko is a woman of will, Miyagi is a typical example of the suffering woman who endures selflessly and becomes more beautiful through this endurance, as such embodying the iconography of the *hibakusha*. The iconic imagery of the mother and child, and the valorisation of the maternal bond, is an important visual and thematic trope in Japanese horror cinema, as is the absent or 'bad' father. Further, the idea of individual sacrifice as atonement for guilt of another, as articulated by the self-sacrificing Serizawa and Miyagi, is another feature that can be seen in Japanese horror cinema.

If *Godzilla* adds the atomic bomb and the possibility of apocalyptic destruction to horror cinema, *Tales of Ugetsu* foregrounds a number of themes that will become central to the Japanese ghost story: doomed love, adulterous affairs, beautiful female ghosts seeking love (and/or revenge), and haunted houses. Both Godzilla and Lady Wagasa are external aliens, who threaten social order from outside and problematise the concept of identity in a rapidly trans-forming society. Napier says 'the Fantastic Other may be seen as an important means by which post-Restoration Japanese began to construct a Westernized sense of the self' (1996: 97).

CHAPTER 3

Edo Gothic: Deceitful Samurai and Wronged Women

With its period setting, deceitful Samurai and wronged women, *Tales of Ugetsu* laid the foundations for the Edo Gothic ghost story, which accounted for most Japanese horror films during the 1950s and 1960s. Once again, an obsession with status and material wealth provides the narrative motivation for murder, blackmail and adultery. Instead of the film focusing on the lower working or peasant classes, the male protagonists in Edo Gothic are down on their luck and displaced Samurai, or *rōnin*, who break with the code of the *bushidō*, Samurai code of conduct, in order to enhance their status. Once again, it is the women that suffer the most. Unlike the passive Miyagi in Mizoguchi's *Tales of Ugetsu*, who remains the spiritual focus of the family even in death, the wronged women in Edo Gothic do not forgive their husband's sins so lightly, instead returning after death to wreak a terrible vengeance. As Hughes writes in 'Familiarity of the Strange: Japan's Gothic Tradition', 'Although women in Japanese Gothic fiction are often victims of male abuse, their spirits are capable of powerful revenge' (2000).

Japanese cinema in the late 1950s and early 1960s can be best understood in terms of a distinction between mind (*seinshin*) and body (*nikutai*), as expressed through the opposition of romantic love and carnal desire. Whilst the socially informed films of the Japanese New Wave were concerned with the 'materialism of the body', the period drama continued to constitute the subject through an 'abstract ideological essence associated with the spirit' (Standish 2005: 223). Tucker distinguishes between directors of the ethical right, or 'traditionalists', and those on the ethical left, whom he terms 'protestors' (1973: 42). On the left were the directors of the Japanese New Wave, including Hani, Ōshima, Masumura and Teshigahara, whilst on the right were directors such as Ozu, Mizoguchi, Naruse and Gosha (Tucker 1973: 43). Fatalism is a key convention of the traditionalists, and is associated with what is known in Japan as *mono-no-aware*, a type of resigned acceptance of one's fate. Richie defines *mono-no-*

aware as 'an observance of the way things are and a willingness to go along with them. … an acceptance of adversity, and an appreciation of the inevitable' (2001: 63). For Shapiro, Richie's definition is inadequate. Instead he argues that *mono-no-aware* is both an appreciation of the ephemeral nature of existence, or the 'impermanence of things', and 'a profound sense of sympathy that is more difficult to define' (2002: 2004).

The difference between films on the left concerned with *nikutai* and films on the right concerned with *seinshin* can be thought of in terms of acceptance of the status quo on the one hand, and social protest on the other, although, as Tucker points out, this division is actually more complicated than it seems:

> Yet films can be made in which characters exemplify completely *mono-no-aware* and yet be implicit criticism of the status quo, and at the other extreme a number of films have been made which had an overt intention of being critical towards the accepted social mores yet ended by supporting them. (1973: 43)

The period dramas of Edo Gothic were the opposite of the *shakiamono* film, the social problem film, which represented one of the other dominant genres in Japanese cinema in the late 1950s and early 1960s. Edo Gothic films were traditional and tended to reinforce conservative values, with their helpless victims trapped in nightmarish gothic landscapes, articulated through the expressionistic surfaces of a subjective rather than objective reality. In Standish's terms, Edo Gothic can be seen as expressive of a type of 'post-defeat victimization' or *higaisha ishiki* (victim consciousness). We saw one manner in which this post-defeat victimisation worked in the discussion of *Godzilla* in the last chapter. Like Daiei studio's 'black' films, Edo Gothic focuses on 'the examination of morality in an age of rampant materialism' (Standish 2005: 2004). In Edo Gothic this is embodied within the physical scars of the vengeful ghosts, through which individual and historical trauma become displaced from the 'self' on to the 'other'. However, the boundaries between self and other become increasingly problematised, as the external alien turns inward.

It needs to be noted that Japan was not the only country to use a period setting and the gothic form to articulate anxieties around modernity, identity and rationality. There was a definable trend in the 1950s towards gothic horror. In the United Kingdom, Hammer was producing its own period gothic horrors with films such as *The Abominable Snowman* (Guest: 1957), *Curse of Frankenstein* (Fisher: 1957) and *Dracula, Prince of Darkness* (Fisher: 1966). And in America, Roger Corman directed some of the all-time classic adaptations of the work of Edgar Allen Poe, including: *The Fall of the House of Usher* (1960), *The Pit and the Pendulum* (1961) and *Tales of Terror* (1962).

Not only did Western gothic find its roots in medieval society with a dominant imagistic system derived from Catholicism, but in some cases gothic texts also utilised the 'Orient' as a place of exoticism and eroticism. In Beckford's *Vathek* (1786), supposedly based loosely on some of the stories in *The Arabian Nights*, the main character, Caliph Vathek, is a tyrant whose decadence is such that he sacrifices fifty of the most beautiful children in his desire for arcane knowledge and power. Botting writes: 'Translations of Arabian stories led to a vogue for Oriental tales and a love of the exotic. The East constituted another space in which the expanding imagination could freely roam' (1996: 59).

In Japan, as in the West, gothic fiction served to function not only as a mechanics of transgression (of propriety, morals and values of patriarchy), but also, somewhat paradoxically, as a means of reasserting social and ethical boundaries (Botting 1996: 7). In the West, gothic literature and film allowed a reconstitution of identity through its confrontation with sheer otherness (Botting 1996: 9). At the same time, in its Buddhist sensibility and privileging of spirituality, Edo Gothic is markedly different. Hughes writes:

> Buddhist suffering aris[es] out of desire and craving in a spirited world. Desire may cause self-division, dramatized by the dangerous doppel-ganger, but the Japanese solution is rarely found in the reaffirmation of self. It is, instead, the emptying of the self that constitutes cosmic achievement ... In translation, life is not a battleground for God and the Devil – the two grow naturally together in the field of life. (2000)

For Kawai this concept of nothingness is 'beyond negative and positive values' (1996: 20). The centrality of suffering to Edo Gothic, connected to the quest for the empty self, is commonly expressed in the symbiotic relationship between mother and child. Further, while the concept of ancestry is important to Western gothic forms, it does not have the same currency as it does in Japan. The *ie* system and the symbolic functioning of debt as fundamental to *On* mean that the concept of ancestral duties has a much greater currency in Japanese gothic literature and Edo Gothic film. And instead of the rich symbolism of Catholicism that provides the backdrop to many a gothic tale, Japanese Edo Gothic draws on an eclectic mixture of religions, from Confucianism to Buddhism and Shintō. On the occasions when Japanese horror does draw on religious iconography derived from Christianity and Catholicism, it is usually for aesthetic rather than symbolic reasons. In spite of these differences, in Japan, as elsewhere, the story of the vengeful ghost 'capture[s] the adultery, conspiracy, betrayal and revenge common to the modern Gothic' (Hughes: 2000). However, belief in the ontological materiality of ghosts often separates Western gothic from Japanese:

> The Japanese artist has for centuries presented the real as unreal and

the unreal as real … In fact a strongly-held belief in the reality of the dead, both in religious and psychological terms, does much to explain the presence of ghosts in Japanese films. (Tucker 1973: 110)

THE BACKGROUND

Although some are set later, during the Meiji Period (1868–1912), Edo Gothic films are generally set during the Edo Period (1603–1867), during which the Samurai became obsolete. The period setting is important, as it parallels contemporary concerns at the time over the breakdown of social structures in the face of economic expansion and the perceived Westernisation of Japanese society. During 1953 and the early 1970s, Japan experienced what is known as 'Miracle Growth' or the 'Economic Bubble' through the enforced modernisation of Japan, and with it the rapid development of consumer culture and massive migration of people to the city. In fact, by 1968, Japan's GNP (gross national profit) was second only to that of the USA. At the same time, as Standish points out, these radical transformations in Japan's economy led to the increasingly alienated individual, with men constantly at work and women left fending for the children with little or no help:

> In short, high economic growth offered in the same instant greater levels of material security but at the cost of self-abnegation as security and welfare were built upon acquiescence; and concurrently urban society spawned increasing feelings of alienation. (2005: 309)

One reaction to this shift in Japanese society from production to reproduction was the emergence of neo-nationalism and discourses of Japaneseness (*Nihonjinron*). In 1970, the writer Yukio Mishima (1925–70) committed ritual suicide, or *seppuku*, whilst crying out, 'Long live the emperor'. In 1961, Mishima published *Patriotism* as a response to the growing materialism underlying Japanese society, as articulated through what he saw as the moral and spiritual degeneracy of Japan. In *Patriotism*, Mishima promoted 'the code of the bushidō' and with it traditional morals and values. Mishima wanted to put an end to Japan's so-called democratic system and reinstate the emperor in his rightful place as the political and spiritual leader of Japan. In the immediate aftermath of Mishima's death, Philip Shabecoff wrote:

> What he really was seeking was a return to the samurai tradition, which he saw as an ethical and esthetic system truer to the spirit of Japan than a modern army. He deplored most of the signs of Westernization in Japan. Western influence, he felt, was corrupting Japan and robbing her of her essential spirit. (1970)

DECEITFUL SAMURAI

In Edo Gothic, the loss of *wa*, or the spiritual connection between man and nature, is symbolised through the privileging of selfish desires and desire for status over selflessness (*seisen*). In Edo Gothic deceitful Samurai, who abandon the code of *bushidō* and neglect their filial and societal duties for material gain, demonstrate a lack of *ninjō* (compassion) towards others. Unlike Mishima, who wished to return to traditional values as embodied by the (mythical) Samurai, the *rōnin* in Edo Gothic has little compassion for others; instead he places self-interest before the needs of the community. The *rōnin* leaves a trail of bodies in his wake, as he dispenses with the code of the *bushidō* in an attempt to progress up the social scale, as in *Ghost Story of Yotsuya* (1959) and *Ghost of Kagama-Ga-Fuchi* (Mori: 1959). Further, women are often the victims of the dispossessed Samurai's social ascent: either abandoned, whether intentionally or unintentionally, as in the 'Black Hair' segment of *Kwaidan* and *The Ghost Cat of Otama Pond*, or murdered, as in *The Ghost Story of Yotsuya*. The figure of the wronged woman, returning from the dead as a vengeful ghost, is the figurative and symbolic outcome of the loss of traditional and pre-modern values. Ross writes of Edo ghost stories, 'especially exciting was the idea of a wrathful female ghost returning to exact vengeance for former mistreatment' (1996: 129).

The most famous director of Edo Gothic in the late 1950s and early 1960s was Nobuo Nakagawa (1905–83), who directed *The Ceiling at Utsunomiya* (1956), *The Mansion of the Ghost Cat* (1958) and *The Ghosts of Kasane Swamp* (1957), to name but a few. His most famous films are his seminal adaptation of the Kabuki play, *Ghost Story of Yotsuya* (1959), and his vivid depiction of Buddhist hell and torture, *Hell* (1960).

Adapted for the screen over thirty times, with its deceitful Samurai, Iemon, and its wronged woman, Iwa, *Ghost Story of Yotsuya* is the archetypical Edo Gothic narrative. The Kabuki play by Tsuruya Nanboku IV, first performed in 1821, was based upon an old Japanese folktale of Oiwa in which a man brings about the death of his wife, only to have her spirit wreak vengeance on him from beyond the grave. Nanboku gave the story a contemporary twist by integrating two real-life events within the narrative: the murder of their masters by two servants, and the story of a Samurai who, discovering his mistress was having an affair, brutally killed both her and her lover (who was a servant) and nailed their bodies to a board before throwing them into the Kanda River. In the play, 'The object of her [Oiwa's] wrath does not feel any guilt for his actions, but still is presented as a despicable character responsible for the heroine's plight' (Barrett 1989: 99). Of the figure of Iwa, as vengeful *yūrei*, Barrett writes: 'Perhaps she could have been created only during Nanboku's degenerate times when the social fabric based on loyalty towards superiors was coming apart'

(1989: 99). The re-emergence of Oiwa from her watery grave in the late 1950s provides a point of parallelism between past and present, times at which the social fabric of Japan was torn apart:

> The bond of parent and child lasts through this world,
> But that of husband and wife lasts forever.
> How can you kill one who is yours body and soul,
> who is bound to you for generations to come?
> I cannot leave this baby, innocent of any sin!
> O, the fury of a woman maddened
> *is truly like unto the greatest terror there is.* (My emphasis)
> (Nakagawa: 1957)

Nakagawa's film begins with a long shot of a Kabuki stage, on which a figure dressed in black sings about the obligations and ties that bind women to men, and parents to their children. This use of the song acts as a typical gothic frame. As in the folktale, and subsequent play, Iemon (Shigeru Amachi) is a *rōnin* in love with the beautiful daughter of a rich merchant. The film is divided into three distinct sections, each signalled by a fade to black, mimicking the structure of classical tragedy. The first, the beginning or 'incentive moment', begins with the murder of Iwa's father, Samon (Shinjirō Asano), and ends with that of Yomoshichi (Ryozaburo Nakamura), the fiancé of Iwa's sister. The middle section or 'climax' focuses on the events leading up to Iwa's (Kazuko Wakasugi) death and ends with the tormented Iemon mistakenly killing his new wife, Ume (Junko Ikeuchi), and her grandfather, Ito, as he is pursued by the ghosts of the dead. The final section is the denouement or 'resolution', in which the ghosts take their revenge.

In the high stylised and theatrical opening scene, Iemon is seen pleading for Iwa's hand in marriage but is ridiculed by Samon and his retainer. The impenetrable class differences between Iemon and Samon are projected on to the mise-en-scène. The frame is artificially divided into two vertical sections, by a tree that separates Iemon and his servant from Samon and his retainer. On the left, Iemon and his servant are seen kneeling, while on the right-hand side, Samon and his retainer are standing up. The tree functions as a visual marker of the importance of vertical hierarchies and boundaries in pre-modern Japanese society. Iemon oversteps the boundaries, both literally and metaphorically: firstly, by stepping into the space occupied by Samon and his retainer, and then by taking out his sword and slaying both of them. Barrett comments, 'In Nakagawa's version Iemon becomes a somewhat more sympathetic character, since he kills Iwa's father in a fit of indignation on account of his lower-samurai-class origins' (1989: 100). Here it is pride which leads to Iemon's violent act, which links to the formal characteristics of classical tragedy in which the tragically flawed hero (or anti-hero) is situated as the pawn amongst circumstances beyond his control.

As in tragedy, one act of violence leads to another in a never-ending spiral that can only be resolved through the tragic hero's death. Parallelism and mise-en-scène are utilised visually to foreground Iemon's suffering as a result of his downfall from honour. Iemon's servant, Naosuke (Shuntaro Emi), like Shakespeare's Iago, uses blackmail to persuade Iemon to help him get rid of Yomoshichi, as he desires Sode (Noriko Kitazawa), Iwa's sister, who is in love with Yomoshichi. Greed also motivates Naosuke to encourage Iemon to get rid of Iwa, who stands in the way of a profitable match with the Ito family. The parallelism between the two couples, Iemon and Iwa, and Naosuke and Sode, is used to emphasize the magnitude of Iemon's downfall, visually and thematically constructing him as the double of Naosuke, rather than his superior. Indeed, when Naosuke reminds him of this fact in the scene at Snake Temple, Iemon takes out his sword and cuts him down.

The tragic dimension of Iemon is signified by the constant framing of him against blood-red backgrounds: against the red flag in the scene when he rescues Iwa; reflections of a blood-red night sky flickering on Iemon's face as he agrees to murder Ume; and red banners blowing in the wind when he receives the poison from Naosuke. In the aforementioned scenes, the red background functions not just as signifier of desire and symbol of impending doom, but also as an externalisation of Iemon's inner conflict and guilt. Sedgwick uses the metaphor of the veil in gothic fiction as that which connotes sexuality through the interplay of concealment and revelation (like the kimono in Japanese culture), as a 'metonym of the thing covered and as a metaphor for sexual prohibitions by which sexual desire is enhanced and specified' (1986: 143). In addition, the framing of Iemon through vertical iron bars, as in the scene where he offers Iwa to the masseur Takuetsu (Otomo Jun), in repayment of a debt, and then its repetition when he convinces Takuetsu to sleep with Iwa, constitutes a mise-en-scène of imprisonment and confinement. This also links to the tragic figure of Henchard in Hardy's *The Mayor of Casterbridge* (1886), who, in selling his wife and child, demonstrates a lack of concern for the needs of others and therefore brings about his own downfall. Iemon's pride is similar to Henchard's, interpreted as hubris. According to the rules of classical tragedy, hubris is the existence of a fatal flaw, usually an excess of pride or ignorance, which leads the tragic hero to believe that he can violate the moral and ethical laws of the community without retribution. According to Bachnik, 'The Japanese equivalent to the apple in the Garden [of Eden] ... is personal pride, or hubris, which leads to the use of social power on the basis of purely personal designs for control.' Bachnik explains:

The expression of personal power is destructive of society, since self is indexed in relation to society. The more the self operates in purely opportunistic terms, the more the potential for destruction of others and even for the social organization involved. Finally, this imbalance is ultimately destructive to self as well, *since the organization of self hinges on its relationship with society*. (1994: 225)

In *Ghost Story of Yotsuya*, Iemon's personal ambitions are situated as threatening to the very structures of Japanese society according to which the individual should put duty and obedience before personal desire. Further, as in *Tales of Ugetsu*, *Ghost Story of Yotsuya* meditates on the socio-economic pressures that cause men to sink into brutality. It is poverty and lack of status that are causational factors both in the original murder and Iemon's subsequent betrayal of Iwa. This is clearly demonstrated in the first scene in Edo, after Iemon and Iwa are married, and Iwa has given birth to their son. The gentle noise of the wind chime, between bamboo blinds on either side, symbolises the coming of summer. Open umbrellas are to be found in the corner of the right-hand side of the frame and a distant figure can be seen carrying umbrellas on his back. In the next shot, from the outside and through the bamboo blinds, we see Iemon and Iwa at work. The camera pans inside as Iwa stands up and moves away from Iemon, who is sitting working on an umbrella. The umbrellas are a significant visual trope, in that they symbolise poverty and Iemon's reduced social status. Indeed, at the time, it was common for impoverished Samurai to be employed as umbrella (*wagasa*) makers. The umbrella also functions to signify the growing distance between Iemon and Iwa. The inside (*uchi*), the domestic space, here is distinguished by its lack of human feeling (*ninjō*), as expressed visually by the physical and emotional distance between Iemon and Iwa. In addition, the use of a frame within a frame, as in the shot of Iemon standing in the doorway with the bamboo blinds casting shadows on his face, foregrounds the existence of moral darkness within Iemon, which will overtake him when he murders Iwa.

When Iemon leaves the house he hears his child cry and turns around, but after a moment's hesitation continues on his way. The juxtaposition of this scene with the following one, in which he rescues Ume from bandits, is significant, in that Iemon has already been shown as demonstrating a lack of *ninjō* (compassion) and *giri* (duty) to his wife and child. This is a pivotal turning point, in which, both literally and metaphorically, darkness overcomes light, and selfishness overcomes selflessness, and as such paves the way for Iwa's murder.

Iwa's death scene is a key sequence in all film versions and Kabuki productions of the story. Significantly, the murder happens on the night of Iemon's marriage to Ume. When Iemon leaves the house, having given Iwa the poison, he is again framed in the doorway, the bamboo shadows once again reflecting both his internal conflict and moral darkness. When Takuetsu arrives, under the pretence of giving the sickly Iwa a massage, she thinks that this is an act of compassion on the part of Iemon. However, when he makes sexual advances towards her, Iwa is horrified, refusing to believe that Iemon would be capable of such deception. Meanwhile, the poison that Iemon gave Iwa, pretending that it was 'blood medicine' to help with poor circulation, begins to work. In great pain, Iwa cries out and covers her face with her hand. She goes over to a mirror that is covered by a black lid; as she slips the cover off the mirror, the camera pans in on Iwa's reflection and we see that the left-hand side of her face is covered with open weeping wounds and sores and her eye is swollen shut. Here the mirror, as iconic symbol of female vanity, is linked to the abject as it foregrounds the interplay between pollution and purity that constitutes representations of women in Japanese art and popular culture. As Iwa is dying, fireworks celebrating Iemon's nuptials create a canopy of colour in the night sky. The cross-cutting between the scene of Iwa's betrayal and death and the fireworks emphasises the horror of Iemon's crime, as well as functioning as a metonymic signifier of historical trauma, embodied within the suffering woman, who symbolises nationhood.

While Iwa's disfigurement is key to the original folktale, it can also be interpreted as a metaphorical reference to the traumatised and defeated Japan after the Second World War. This is manifest trauma as genetic scar written on the female body, as symbolic of nationhood. In *Little Boy: The Art of Japan's Exploding Subculture*, Rauer writes:

> Twenty-two years after the mass obliteration of souls, the atomic bombs dropped on Hiroshima and three days later on Nagasaki on August 9, 1945, monstrous deformities persisted in the Japanese psyche – tragically splintered by defeat, subjugation, humiliation, and inconceivable horrors – unable to command a return to a unified monolithic persona, the ordered cerebral imperative and societal dignity of pre-nuclear innocence ... World War II left indelible stains on the Japanese psyche. (2005)

Iwa's disfigured and destroyed face is just one example of the scarred protagonists found in Japanese horror cinema of the 1950s and 1960s. Another example can be found in Teshigaha's *Face of Another* (1966). The protagonist is a chemical scientist, Okuyama (Tatsuya Nakadai), whose face has been terribly burnt in an accident, so that it almost bears no resemblance at all to a human face. Okuyama's existential quest for a new face (hence the title of the film) allows a liberation of desire from the rigid constraints of Japanese patriarchy and from the trauma of history, by making the subject anew. In addition to this, Okuyama identifies with a young woman (Miki Irie) in a film that he sees, who also has a badly scarred face. Further, Okuyama's wife (Machiko Kyō) suggests that Okuyama's putting on a 'mask' to cover up his deformed face is no different from the make-up worn by women. These multiple references to the relationship between face and self, mask and make-up, further suggest that the mask 'is an increasingly universal aspect of modern capitalist society where one cannot escape the emphasis on appearance reflected in the critical mirrors of consumer society' (Napier 1996: 103).

Similarly, Shindō's *Onibaba* also makes explicit disfigurement as metonymic signifier of war trauma. Shindō had already made a number of films dealing with the impact of the nuclear bomb on Japan, including *Children of Hiroshima* (1952) and *Lucky Dragon No. 5* (1959). In *Onibaba*, an older woman's (Nobuko Otowa) jealousy of her daughter-in-law's (Jitsuko Yoshimura) beauty and her affair with a handsome young deserter, Hachi (Kei Sato), lead to her donning a *han'nya* mask (a Nō mask which is used to express inside emotions on the outside, here the sin of envy). McDonald argues that the link to the bombing of Hiroshima and Nagasaki would have been all too evident for Japanese audiences at the time (McDonald 2006: 118). And in addition, 'Shindō himself is on record as saying he "based the make-up design for the brutal unmasking scene on photographs of maimed hibakusha" [victims of atomic bombs]' (McDonald 2006: 118).

Iwa's disfigured face can be seen to condense references to the scars of the Second World War, the Shintō concept of pollution, and the perpetration of the feudal oppression of women. Her death is crucial, as Jordan points out: 'Overcome by the treachery of her husband and her hideous appearance, Oiwa is filled with resentment and anger. The poison and illness are secondary to such powerful emotions which cause her death' (1985: 22). As such, it could be argued that the representation of historical trauma as physical trauma, written on the face of Iwa in *Ghost Story of Yotsuya*, also reveals the disfigured underside to traditional conceptualisations of appropriate Japanese femininity and motherhood. Iwa's ornate comb is found later by Takuetsu, and given to Sode, who immediately realises that it is her sister's. When Iwa appears to Sode, leading her to Yomoshichi, she appears as she was in life. This is in opposition to the disfigured vengeful wraith that haunts Iemon. Barrett remarks, 'The comb symbolizes Iwa's beauty and her loss of it. It also indicates the dual aspect of Japanese spirits who appear to be vengeful only to those who wronged them' (1989: 101).

In a scene of graphic violence shocking for the time, Iemon kills Takuetsu, his sword slicing through Takuetsu's arm, the dismembered limb still twitching as it lies on the ground beside him. Together with Naosuke, Iemon crucifies the bodies on a wooden door, before disposing of them in a nearby river. Iemon marries Ume as planned, but the ghosts of Iwa and Takuetsu return to haunt him. Iemon ends up killing both Ume and Ito, as they take on the visages of the departed. And as in the folktale, Iemon 'discovers that everywhere he goes, the spirits of the dead haunt him restlessly' (Jordan 1985: 31). When the ghosts appear, red and green lighting is used to highlight their otherworldly and demonic dimension. The use of green and red lighting is linked to the colour imagery associated with *oni* (demons), who hunt for sinners, taking them back to hell. Rubin writes:

> The earth 'Oni', according to Buddhist belief, are responsible for disease and epidemics (they are dressed in red). The 'Oni' of hell (red or green bodies) hunt for sinners and take them by chariot to Emma-Hoo, the god of hell. There are invisible demons among the 'Oni' whose presence can be detected because they sing or whistle. The 'Oni' who are women are those transformed into demons after death by jealousy or violent grief. (2000)

The final act or denouement takes place at Snake Temple, where Iemon has fled in terror from the vengeful ghosts. Often referred to as the 'dream sequence' in the play, the appearance of the ghosts haunting Iemon is as likely to be an ontological signifier of Iemon's torment and guilt as real ghosts. Certainly, the colour imagery suggests that the ghosts may be external projections of guilt and inner conflict on the part of Iemon. Jordan writes, 'As with many ghost stories, Iyemon's torture in *Yotsuya Kaidan* is largely a manifestation of his own guilt' (1985: 32). Naosuke follows him to the temple, and so starts the final revenge of the ghosts.

As in Utagawa Kuniyoshi's print, *Hebiyama*, snakes drop from the ceiling of the temple. In traditional Japanese mythology, serpents are associated with both good and evil. The snakes, like the rats in the later *Illusion of Blood* (Toyoda: 1966), are linked to the feminine. This is made explicit in *Ghost Story of Yotsuya* when Iwa tells Iemon that she was born in the year of the snake. It is apt therefore that Iemon flees from the ghost to the temple at Snake Mountain. Here the snakes dropping from the ceiling are not benevolent deities, but rather 'symbols of the fearful world, the world of the dead and revenge' (Jordan 1985: 151). When Iemon stabs Naosuke, Iwa's body surfaces from a pond of red blood and is substituted for that of Naosuke as he falls to the ground. Here an association is made between blood, femininity and pollution – the pond as a womb and water as amniotic fluid. Douglas argues that 'All bodily emissions, even blood and pus from a wound, are sources of impurity' (1966: 35).

Skewed low- and high-angle shots are edited together as a visual mirror of Iemon's deteriorating state of mind as the golden statue of the Buddha at the centre of the room is replaced by glowing *hitodama* coming towards him. Iemon falls backwards on to the ground as the menacing figure of Iwa, with her child in her arms, approaches him. As the child cries, a red mosquito net floats down from the ceiling, trapping Iemon. Barrett writes, 'This recalls the summer night when Iwa, inside such a tent, dutifully drank the poison Iemon had given her' (1989: 102). Try as Iemon might, there is no escaping his inner demons, whether real ghosts or projections of guilt.

At this point, Sode and Yomoshichi enter the temple, dressed in white with swords in their hands, declaring revenge on Iemon. As they fight, the ghosts of Iwa and Takuetsu continue to haunt Iemon, impeding him. A hand rising from the ground clutches his foot, dragging him backwards; Takuetsu's head appears on a tree trunk; and the shutter Iwa and Takuetsu nailed in place swings downwards and across his face, momentarily blinding him. Finally, the ground opens up and Iwa appears from the depths of the Earth, like an *Oni*, come to take the sinner to the underworld. The tormented Iemon begins stabbing at the air, waving his sword around wildly. Iwa appears in front of him holding the baby, distracting him, and just then Sode strikes. This is a significant departure from most variations of the story up until that time, in which it is the brother-in-law who metes out the final blow.

No longer able to fight, Iemon falls to the ground and begs Iwa's forgiveness. The final shots are of Iwa, returned to her former beauty and holding her son tenderly in her arms, surrounded by bright light. The final image of mother and child is highly symbolic. This could be as, Barrett points out, a reference to Motonobu Kano's painting of *The Sad Mother Kannon* (*Hibo Kannon-zu*), as suggested by Masatoshi Ohba. At the same time, there is an obvious similarity between the Mother Kannon of Buddhist belief, the embodiment of suffering, and that of the Virgin Mary in Western religion. Barrett concludes, 'once Oiwa the Vengeful Spirit achieved her purpose, she could, like Mary, attain eternal rest, which is called *jobutsu* or nirvana in Buddhism' (1989: 102–3).

THE SACRED MATERNAL

Iwa is the prototype of the vengeful woman who can be found in many contemporary Japanese horror films. With her long dark hair and disfigured face, there can be little doubt that the figure of Iwa provided the template for Sadako in *Ring*. As with Miyagi in *Tales of Ugetsu*, Iwa dies for the sins of her husband. Before her death, her ethereal beauty represents an idealised version of femininity and a valorised image of Japanese motherhood, through its symbolic relation to the Mother Kannon. In 'Unstable Mothers: Redefining Motherhood in Contemporary Japan', McKinlay points out how the concept of *ryōsaikenbo* (good wife, wise mother) was seen as key to the establishment of Japan as a nation-state during the Meiji Period leading up to the First World War:

As the term suggests, the notion of *ryôsai kenbo* saw a re-defining of women in terms of their roles as nurturers of children and overseers of the domestic arena. At the same time, the principle of 'rich country, strong military' [*fukoku kyohei*], which saw Japan determined to establish a nation-state comparable in strength to those of the West, emphasised the importance of the family unit within the social hierarchy. (2002)

The family unit therefore acted as a microcosm of the *ie* system that functioned within Japanese society more generally. The role of women as mothers gained increased significance in light of the need to produce a strong military and nation-state within the dictates of state Shintō. Further, McKinlay also points out that this valorisation of the maternal continued, even after the so-called democratisation of Japan during the Allied Occupation:

> Although the official ideologies of *ryôsai kenbo* and *fukoku kyohei* were somewhat tarnished after 1945 by their association with the pre-war imperialist state, the discourse on women and maternity associated with them continued to influence state policy and social ideology at least until the late 1980s. (McKinlay 2002)

The final image of Iwa in *Ghost Story of Yotsuya* can be seen as a representation of the sacred maternal and its continued significance in Japanese cultural and social mythology. This valorisation of the maternal is, as we shall see, a common feature in Japanese horror. The contradictory nature of the feminine as both polluted and pure, here signified through the figure of Iwa, cannot be simply dismissed as articulating male anxieties around female sexuality, as Western psychoanalytical frameworks would suggest. Instead, this oscillation between abject and iconic mother needs to be understood by reference to the creation myth of Shintō.

The myth of Izanagi ('Male-who-invites' or 'August Male') and Izanami ('Female-who-invites' or 'August Female') is told in the oldest Japanese texts, the *Kojiki* (712 CE, Ono Yasumaro) and *Nihonshoki* (720 CE, by a committee of scholars). Izanagi and Izanami, two deities (or *kami*), were brother and sister, according to legend. They descended from Heaven to an island, Onogoro ('Spontaneously-congeal-island'), which they created and they became man and wife.

After their marriage, Izanami gave birth to a number of seas, islands, rivers and trees (Hadland Davis 1992: 22). However, the couple's firstborn was a monstrous 'leech child' (Littleton 2002: 41). Following this and with help from the older *kami*, Izanami gave birth to Amaterasu (the Sun Goddess, from whom the emperor was said to be descended), Tsukiyumi (the Moon God), Susano (the 'Raging Male') and Kagutsuchi (the Fire God). Izanami died from burns, after the birth of Kagutsuchi, and left the Earth, descending to the Land of Yomi (the Land of the Dead). The Land of the Dead is associated with pollution, decay and death. Unable to live without her, Izanagi followed her to Yomi. When Izanagi came across her at last, Izanami pleaded with him not to look at her. However, consumed with desire to see her, Izanagi broke a piece off his many-toothed comb and lit it in order to set eyes on his beloved wife:

> The sight that greeted him was ghastly and horrible in the extreme. His once beautiful wife had now become a swollen and festering creature. Eight varieties of Thunder Gods rested upon her. The Thunder of the Fire, Earth, and Mountain were all there leering upon him, and roaring with their great voices. (Hadland Davis 1992: 24)

Izanagi managed to escape from the wrath of Izanami and the Eight Ugly Females of Yomi that she sent after him. Reaching the exit, he asked his wife for a divorce, to which she responded that she would kill a thousand people a day. Izanagi replied that he would then cause to be born fifteen hundred to replace those that she killed. This is affirmative of the Shintō belief in the power of life over death and the optimism that underlies that religion. Having escaped from the Land of Yomi, Izanagi blocked off the entrance with a large rock. Contact with pollution meant that Izanagi had to participate in rites of purification, through which numerous *kami* were born. These rites, or *O-hara*, remain fundamental to Shintō. Izanagi built himself 'an abode of gloom in the island of Ahaji, where he dwelt forever in silence and concealment' (Hadland Davis 1992: 25).

In her discussion of the cultural differences between Western and Japanese fairy tales, Kawai points out that the injunction not to look, a common feature of many fairy tales, comes from the female character in Japan as in 'The Bush Warbler's Home', unlike the typical male prohibitor in Western fairy tales such as 'Bluebeard' (France) and 'Faithful John' (Germany). As we have seen in the Shintō creation myth, it is Izanami that prohibits, and Izanagi who breaks the prohibition. Further, Kawai points out that often the prohibitor suffers more than the male character who breaks the prohibition. In 'The Bush Warbler's Home' for example, a woodcutter comes across a beautiful woman in a strange mansion. She leaves for town and tells him that under no circumstances should he look in the next room. As soon as she is gone, he breaks the injunction and finds riches and treasures in the room; in the process he breaks three eggs in a bird nest. When the woman returns, she berates the woodcutter, who unwittingly caused the death of her three daughters by breaking the eggs; she turns into a bush warbler and flies away (Kawai 1996: 1–2). In this tale, as in others, the woman disappears, leaving the woodcutter alone once more. Very rarely in Japanese fairy tales are those who break injunctions punished (as in, for instance 'Red Riding Hood'). Instead, the woman disappears, in a similar way to Iwa, leaving the reader/viewer with a sense of *mono-no-aware* and an impression of the strong function of nothingness in Japanese thought.

In *Ghost Story of Yotsuya*, both tale and films, it is made clear that the vengeful ghosts may indeed be projections of Iemon's guilt rather than ontological entities. Further, the ghost of Iwa can only materialise and gain human shape if her image momentarily possesses another. This prototype of the vengeful female wraith in Japanese cultural thought can be traced back to the figure of Lady Royoko in *The Tale of the Genji*. In this sense, Iemon dies at his own hand – made clear in the later *Illusion of Blood* (Toyoda: 1966), when Iemon, in a fitting end, falls on to his own sword. Although Iwa is more sinned against than sinning, like the woman in the bush warbler's tale, she also ends up disappearing from the narrative world as a consequence of the actions of the male protagonist.

WRONGED WOMEN

A heightened interest in ... supernatural beings occurred during the Edo period, although tales of ghosts had been circulated in Japan for centuries. The common theme that runs throughout these stories is that of the wronged or jealous woman. (Jordan 1985: 26)

Along with the tale of the tragic suffering Oiwa, the tale of Okiku is the other most important influence on the archetypical wronged woman who appears in both early and contemporary Japanese horror film. In the story, Okiku is a maid, who works for a Samurai called Aoyama Tessan. Aoyama makes sexual advances towards Okiku, which she rejects. In anger, he hides one of a set of ten plates, given to him by Dutch visitors, and then asks her to fetch the plates and count them in front of him. Of course, there are only nine plates, and Aoyama blames the loss of the plate on Okiku in order to try to convince her to become his mistress. Okiku refuses again and Aoyama kills her, disposing of her body down a well. The story goes that, each night, Okiku can be heard from the depths of the well, counting from one to nine, after which she gives a heartrending wail. In some versions of the story, Okiku drives Aoyama to madness and death; in another, Okiku is hung upside down in the well; whilst in another, the ghost of Okiku is vanquished by a neighbour of Aoyama, who, when she finishes counting to nine, cries out 'ten'. Jordan writes, 'and the ghost with a scream disappeared' (1985: 26).

Another example of Edo Gothic is Ishikawa's *The Ghost Cat of Otama Pond* (1960). It is set in the present. Tadahiko (Shozaburo Date) and Keiko (Kitazawa Noriko), a young couple in love, become lost in the woods by an old dirty pond. Try as they may, they cannot seem to find their way out of the forest; instead, they keep on coming back to the pond, which changes colour every time they find themselves back there. Here we have an example of Freud's concept of the uncanny (*unheimlich*), as that which should be familiar becomes instead strange and frightening, or unfamiliar. In his essay on 'The Uncanny' [1919] (1990), Freud writes of a time in Italy when, having gone for a walk, he finds himself lost in an unknown street. When he tries to find his way back to a familiar street, Freud is surprised to find himself, on two further occasions, back at this unknown French quarter, at which, Freud writes, 'a feeling overcame me which I can only describe as uncanny, and I was glad enough to find myself back in the piazza I had left a short while before, without any further voyages of discovery' (1919: 359). The uncanny evokes a sense of fear, and in *The Ghost Cat of Otama Pond* functions as a portent of doom.

Eventually, the couple give up trying to find their way home, and when they come upon an old deserted house, they seek shelter from a storm. Keiko is cursed when she catches sight of the ghostly form of an old woman in the house and falls into a coma. Tadahiko finds her unconscious and carries her into the old building. As she sleeps, she is bathed in red light, symbolising the nearness of death. The old woman is a *bakeneko*, or ghost cat. Slantchev offers the following definition:

> It is believed that if a cat's owner is killed and it licks its blood, the creature will become a cat monster, or *kaibyo* (also known as *bakeneko*) that could possess people and control malevolent spirits. As a metaphor of all those people who died violently and were never properly buried (as in the recent war), the cat spirit embodies the search for retribution that would let the dead rest in peace. (2006)

The next day the young couple proceed to Tadahiko's home, where a priest (who can be thought of as the *waki* that we find in Nō theatre, as discussed in Chapter 1) tells him that Keiko is cursed and it will be necessary to perform an exorcism. During the exorcism, the priest relates the story of how the curse came to be. Past and present are connected as the camera moves outside, over trees and over the pond, returning to the house as the narrative of the past begins. The use of the mobile shot here, linking past to present, is comparable to the revolving stage (*kabuki no butai*) used in Kabuki. Like other examples of Edo Gothic, the subsequent narrative, set in the Edo Period, tells of doomed love in a society in which desire for wealth and sexual desire lead directly to murder, tragedy and a dreadful retribution.

The lovers are Yachimaru (Shozaburo Date), the son of Shinbei, who is the headman in the village, and Kozasa (Kitawaza Noriko), the daughter of Gensai (Numata Yoichi), an infamous villain. The two houses are sworn enemies, which means that in line with *giri* (or duty), the lovers cannot marry. Again *giri* comes into conflict with *ninjō* (human feeling). Yachimaru leaves for the city, promising Kozasa that he will return for her. In his absence, the magistrate plots with Gensai and Goroto (who is in love with Kozasa) to get rid of Shinbei, as the magistrate desires Yachimaru's sister, Akino. Before we meet the three main antagonists for the first time, a wide shot of a Samurai sword against a red background fills the frame, signifying the murderous natures of the men. When Shinbei goes to see the magistrate on the part of the villagers, who are complaining about high land taxes, even though to question a superior would more often than not result in death, the perfect opportunity arises to get rid of him. However, unlike Serizawa's sacrifice in *Godzilla*, Shinbei's self-sacrifice for the benefit of the community does not restore harmony to society. The three men kill him as he is on his way home, and throw his body into Otama Pond; as they do so, the pond turns blood-red. They proceed to Yachimaru's family home and kidnap Akino, killing the grandmother (Satsuke Fuji) and her servant. As the old woman dies, surrounded by flames, her face is covered in red, raw burns, obscuring her features. Again we have bodily trauma as a visual reference to historical trauma, which is by now a significant component of Japanese horror film. Rather than suffer disgrace, or indeed be 'shamed', Akino commits suicide using one of her hair ornaments, and her dead body is placed out of sight down a well. In Yachimaru's absence, Kozasa is engaged to Goroto in accordance with her father's wishes. Yachimaru returns to the village when his ghostly sister, Akino, appears to him, but also falls victim to the avaricious magistrate and his retainers; his body joins that of Shinbei in Otama Pond. Immediately after this we see the family cat, Toma, licking the blood spilled by Yachimaru during the fight.

Scenes of Kozasa surrounded by flowers, either at home or in the field where she used to meet Yachimaru, signify the transient nature of life and articulate the fatalism implicit in *mono-no-aware*. The film enters the denouement with the revenge of the ghosts. Blood imagery is used to signify the presence of vengeful ghosts, from spots of blood on Kozasa's wedding kimono; water turned into blood in Gensai's sake cup; drops of blood leading to Akino's hairpin; and the red light that floods Gensai's house just after the fire bell rings.

When Gensai discovers the dead body of O'Ban (his mistress), the ghost of Akino, lit in green, appears behind him. Gensai kills his wife when the ghostly Akino appears in her place. Similarly Goroto kills Kozasa by mistake. The moment Kozasa dies, she returns to life as a *bakeneko*, sitting on the roof, watching and orchestrating the three men's demise. Surrounded by the ghosts of the dead, the magistrate, Goroto and Gensai come to their timely end, and their bodies join those of their victims in Otama Pond. As the narrative from the past ends, the camera once again circles round the forest and back to the house in the present, where we discover that Tadahiko and Keiko are both descended from the warring houses. The curse is broken once the cat is laid to rest and appropriate rituals are said; the lovers in the present are now free to marry, unlike those in the past who can be together only in death.

Whilst the films discussed up until this point are not well known in the West, the figures of the wronged woman and deceitful Samurai can also be found in the 'Black Hair' segment of the award-winning *Kwaidan* (1964). In 'Black Hair' a young Samurai (Rentaro Mikuni) who is down on his luck divorces his devoted wife (Michiyo Aratama) in order to marry the daughter (Misako Watanabe) of a rich lord. He soon comes to regret his decision, as his new wife turns out to be vain and selfish, the opposite to his old wife. The contrast between the two is connoted visually through the use of cross-cutting between his vain second wife idling away her time and his first wife working. Whilst his second wife is lazy and pampered, his first wife sits at the spindle all day making cloth. He lets the second wife go home, no longer able to put up with her spoiled behaviour. Finally, when his term of service is up, he returns back to his old home and his first wife.

The village is deserted, and his old home is both depilated and empty. Rotting boards crumble under his feet as he walks through the house, but surprisingly enough he discovers his wife as he left her, at the spinning wheel, the room in which she sits apparently unmarked by time. She is happy to see him and accepts his apologies, seemingly understanding of why he left her in the first place. They spend the night together, but the Samurai awakes the next morning to discover he has slept with a rotted skeleton with white hair. This tale of romance becomes one of terror, as the white hair turns to black and flings itself around the Samurai's throat. Hair as a source of pollution and fear is also a constant trope in Japanese horror. Ebersole writes, 'In Japan, human hair was employed in purification rituals, but it was also a potential source of pollution and danger' (1998: 86). Like the bodies of the dead, in the absence of proper funeral rites, it was believed that hair could become possessed by a vengeful *kami*. The cultural resonance of hair taking on a life of its own is also related to beliefs that female hair was associated with 'life force, sexual energy, growth, and fertility' (Ebersole 1998: 85). Ebersole elucidates, 'the long hair of young women was believed to have the power to attract *kamis* or divinities, who would descend into it and temporarily reside there' (1998: 85). Hearn points to the similarity between Japanese superstitions around female hair and the myth of Medusa. He writes, 'the subject of such tales [is] always some wondrously beautiful girl, whose hair turns to snakes only at night; and who is discovered at last to be either a dragon or a dragon's daughter' ([1932] 2006: 44). Further, Hearn asserts that other tales based around the relationship between wives (*okusama*) and concubine (*mekeke* or *ashio*) also feature hair as demonic. Forced to live together, their apparent harmony would be disturbed at night when 'The long black tresses of each would uncoil and hiss and strive to devour those of the other' (Hearn [1932] 2006: 44).

Terrified, the Samurai flees the house, chased by his dead wife's hair. The next morning, he discovers that his wife died soon after he left, and that his home has been abandoned for a number of years. This is reminiscent of the story in *Tales of Ugetsu*, with the Samurai discovering that, in abandoning his devoted first wife for riches and wealth, he has ended up with nothing. The moral of the story, central to Edo Gothic, is that wealth is an illusion that cannot make man happy.

CONVENTIONS OF EDO GOTHIC

Writing about Hirorshi Inagaki's Samurai trilogy, McDonald argues that there are two routes available for the Samurai in his quest for identity:

> opportunism versus integrity. The opportunist is content with an animal-like existence. His progress is regress, defined by images of stagnation, decline, confinement and chaos. Integrity is the hard-won choice, requiring stern commitment to the tenets of bushidō, the samurai code of conduct. This choice is associated with images of flow, ascent, openness and cleanliness. (2006: 69)

In Edo Gothic, the Samurai usually follows the first path of opportunism and regress; visual images of corruption, blood and confinement (frames within frames, shots through barred windows and doors) dominate the mise-en-scène. In a similar manner to film noir, low-key lighting, distorted camera angles and extreme long shots are used to externalise the inner corruption, and foreground the interplay between good and evil. The use of water imagery (rain, ponds, lakes) can be interpreted as both a signifier of corruption and, at the same time, a reference to the sacred maternal.

The constant references to the vengeful ghost of both Iwa and Okiku function not only as symbols of female oppression, but also as allegorical signifiers of the persistence of historical trauma. We have also seen the continuance of the valorisation of the maternal, most explicitly in the iconic image of mother and child at the end of *Ghost Story of Yotsuya* and the reaffirmation of traditional values, which privilege frugality, honesty and filial duty. A sense of *mono-no-aware*, or the transitory nature of life, and fatalism, is a dominant theme in Edo Gothic, as it is in Japanese fairy tales and horror cinema. Iwasaka and Toelken argue that the lack of demarcation between the land of the living and that of the dead is central to Japanese folklore, and that the 'fields of illusion and reality overlap and interact, and may indeed not be distinguishable', resulting in 'a kind of ambiguity and simultaneity which can thrive on anxiety and guilt … and which can create the most stunning of tragedies' (1994: 38). Further, they argue that Japanese popular cinema allows the expression of emotions not permitted by the strict dictates of Japanese society: 'in the actions of an angry ghost, feelings of guilt, selfishness, jealousy, and betrayal can be acted out in metaphorical tableau scenes which would be repressed in everyday life' (1994: 38). Edo Gothic allows this expression of emotions through the figure of the vengeful ghost as wronged woman and the situation of the narratives in the (feudal) past, where personal desire takes precedence over societal dictates and the present is structured as always in thrall to the past. Edmundson writes:

> Gothic is the art of haunting, and in two senses. Gothic shows time and time again that life, even at its most ostensibly innocent, is possessed, and the present is in thrall of the past. All are guilty. All must, in time, pay out. And Gothic also sets out to haunt its audience, possess them so that they can think of nothing else. (1997: 5)

CHAPTER 4

Ghosts of Desire:
Kaidan pinku eiga

These days the more cheaply produced AV (adult video) has largely taken over from the soft-core Japanese independent film known as pink film or *pinku eiga* and its mainstream studio-produced equivalent, *roman porno* (romantic pornography). Recently, *pinku eiga* has been making a comeback, with films such as *The Bedroom* (Sato: 1992), *Tandem* (Sato: 1994), *The Woman in Black Underwear* (Zeze: 1997) and *Lunchbox* (Imaoka: 2004). However, before the Allied Occupation, the only way to see sexually explicit films was either to visit the city and purchase a *burumubi* (blue movie) from an *eroto-gushi* ('smut peddler') or to attend an underground screening of domestically produced 'stag' films (Macias 2001: 172).

In 1949, EIRIN (Administration Commission of Motion Picture Code of Ethics) was set up to police violent and sexually explicit films. With a similar role to the MPAA (Motion Picture Association of America) in the United States and the BBFC (British Board of Film Classification) in the United Kingdom, EIRIN's guidelines in relation to sex and violence were considerably more open to interpretation. In terms of obscenity, EIRIN defined three specific areas as not suitable for public consumption: (1) genitalia, (2) pubic hair and (3) penetration shots. While similar restrictions around penetration shots and genitalia operated elsewhere, the restriction on pubic hair, as we have already seen, means that sexual violence and extreme sadomasochism, unacceptable in the West, managed to get through EIRIN as long as there was no sign of female pubic hair. This meant that Japanese pink cinema could never truly be considered 'hard-core', as it was constrained by censorship regulations, which either required fogging or, more commonly, the careful positioning of objects within the frame, such as vases and bottles, so that the genital area was obscured from view.

In contrast to the humanistic dramas of canonical Japanese directors such as Kurosawa and Mizoguchi, stood the politically informed films of the Japanese

New Wave, concerned with transgression and subversion and associated with directors such as Ōshima. Standish argues that the Japanese New Wave:

> challenged humanism by exposing it to the ideological constructedness of reified romantic love by subverting it to carnal desire and taking it through consummation, perversion, crime and punitive acts of violence. (2005: 223)

Produced by Shōchiku Studios, Takechi's *Daydream* (1964), with its surrealistic mixture of dentistry, torture and rape, is often cited as the first pink film. Hunter argues that *Daydream* was the first of the Japanese New Wave to 'present a blatantly erotic storyline'. Takechi would go on to be known as the 'Godfather of Japanese porno cinema' (Hunter 1998: 7). The term pink film, or *pinku eiga*, was of American origin and was originally applied to low-budget and low-profile 'stag' films (Hunter 1988: 26). Takechi followed *Daydream* with *Black Snow* in 1965, its combination of sex and violence so provocative that it led to Takechi being arrested on charges of obscenity. Like Ōshima later on, Takechi was eventually found innocent of the charges. In a time of dwindling box-office receipts in the face of the challenge from television, the success of films such as *Market of Flesh* (Kobayashi: 1962) and *Daydream* clearly demonstrated to the studios that there was a substantial market for erotic cinema. These soft-core pornographic dramas were to be the saviour of studios such as Shōchiku, Nikkatsu and Tōei, each of which would produce their own type of erotic film. Hunter writes, '*Roman porno* saved Nikkatsu, and some critics have suggested it may have even saved the entire Japanese film industry from imminent disaster' (1998: 23).

Grossman contends that, whilst the *pinku eiga* was ostensibly fuelled by the sort of left-wing politics and cinematic experimentation associated with key directors of the Japanese New Wave in the 1960s such as Imamura, Ōshima and Yoshida, its use of sex as a political tool was nothing if not problematic (2002). One of the key figures associated with low-budget independent pink cinema is Kōji Wakamatsu, noted for films such as *Violated Angels* (1967), *Go Go Second Time Virgin* (1969) and *The Embryo Hunts in Secret* (1966). Wakamatsu's angry films utilised sexual violence as a mechanism of questioning the body politic. In *Violated Angels*, the mutilated and bloody bodies of young nurses are laid in a circle on a white sheet, forming a visual parody of the Japanese flag in which the emergence of the national state is explicitly linked to violence towards the colonial Other (in the real story on which it is based, the nurses are Filipino), through which the body of the woman functions as signifier of the body politic. In *The Embryo Hunts in Secret*, the film's story concerns a young woman who is imprisoned by her lover and subjected to increasingly violent acts of sadism, a common theme in pink cinema. Take, for example, Masumura's *Blind Beast*

(1969), based upon a story by Rampo, where a blind painter traps a beautiful model in his studio and they enter into an increasingly violent relationship, culminating in both their deaths.

The first wave of pink cinema (1964–72) came from mainly independent studios such as Okra, Kanta and Wakamatsu (Weisser and Weisser 1998: 20). The second wave (1971–82) began when Nikkatsu abandoned its usual action genre for *roman porno* or mainstream romantic pornography. Tōei would follow suit with its *shigeki rosen* (sensational line) and became known for its sexually violent films, known colloquially as 'pinky violence' genre.

One sub-genre of *pinku eiga* was the erotic ghost story. Influenced by Kabuki and Nō, the erotic ghost story is less sexually explicit than pink cinema. Like Edo Gothic, the ghost story provides a mechanism of articulating cultural anxieties at a time of rapid transformation in Japan's socio-economic structure. Napier contends that the theme of metamorphosis is an integral component of Japanese belief systems. Whilst Shintō emphasises that all animate and inanimate things can be inhabited by *kami*, Buddhism, according to Napier, takes things one step further: 'with its notion of a karmic cycle suggesting a potential bestiality in humans and potential humanity in animals'. This transformation, she contends, is largely affirmative: 'From this point of view, the notion of metamorphosis is a largely positive one, suggesting a philosophical acceptance of a universe where boundaries between the human and the natural are constantly fluctuating' (1996: 109).

The wronged woman, a convention of Edo Gothic, as we have seen, continues to figure prominently in the erotic ghost story, as can be seen in the vengeful ghostly cat women of *Kuroneko* (1968) and the virgin bride seeking love after death in Sone's retelling of the folktale of 'The Peony Lantern', *Hellish Love*, in 1972. Another variation on the wronged woman theme can be found in the beautiful suicide ghost of *The Discarnates* (1988). Her counterpart, the less common wronged man or cuckolded husband, is the vengeful ghost in Ōshima's *Empire of Passion* (1978).

VENGEFUL CAT WOMEN

Like *The Ghost Cat of Otama Pond*, *Kuroneko* is based upon the folktale of the shape-shifting figure of the *bakeneko*, or ghost/vampire cat. According to myth, unless their tails are cut off when they are young, cats can grow into *nekomata* (goblin cats with twin tails said to possess the power of death). Addis writes of Japanese folklore, 'Beliefs in supernatural creatures and events have helped people to understand and accept the mysterious and imponderable elements in the universe by making them accountable' (1985: 177).

The number and popularity of tales about ghost cats and goblin cats led to the creation of a sub-genre known as *bakeneko mono* or monster-cat tales. As we saw in *The Ghost Cat of Otama Pond*, it is women that turn into *bakeneko*, suggesting a causal link between femininity, shape-shifting and death. In *Kuroneko,* the ghost cat takes the shape of beautiful and seductive women, who entrance and entrap their prey, draining them of blood. The films are shot in black and white, and low-key lighting with its play of shadows is used to emphasise the feline qualities and transformative nature of the *bakeneko* women. Napier suggests it is the very stratified nature of Japanese society, built upon the denigration of women, which leads to this fascination with transformation and metamorphosis. She writes, 'the very strength and fearsomeness of the powers attributed to these monstrous women attests to the low status of women in real life' (1996: 100). The discourse of respectability and filial duty that underpins constructions of women, encapsulated within the discourse of *ryōsaikenbo* (good wife, wise mother) from pre-feudal times onwards, emphasises their secondary status in Japan: 'A respectable woman's life was governed by "three submissions" – to her father, to her husband and to her eldest son' (Buisson 2003: 57).

Unlike Napier, Richie sees the transformative and sometimes bestial female ghost simply as a construction of male anxiety and desire. He comments, 'The Japanese ghost is constructed by males for males' (cited in Napier 1996: 100). Similarly, Creed, in her exploration of female monstrosity in cinema, denies any sense of empowerment contained within the figure of the transgressive female in horror cinema, arguing that 'The presence of the monstrous-feminine in the popular horror film speaks to us more about male fears than about female desire or feminine subjectivity' (1993: 7). In these terms, both Richie and Creed view representations of female monstrosity as nothing more than constructions of male desire and anxiety.

However, unlike the rape victim in the more typical erotic film of the time, female ghosts do have an agency that can be read as subversive and politically informed. Linda Ruth Williams, in her discussion of J. Sheridan Le Fanu's lesbian vampire novella *Carmilla* (1872), writes that the realm of the undead constitutes 'a liminal space within which the subject shifts into another gear, and ceases to define itself according to the either/or choices of the binary, waking world' (1995: 96). Williams suggests that Carmilla, the lesbian vampire of the title, can be interpreted as 'offer[ing] a feminist version of the death drive' (1995: 96). Freud's theory of the death-drive was constructed in the aftermath of the First World War, as an explanation of the repetition of traumatic events within an individual for which there seemed to be no resolution. Freud came to the conclusion that desire not only was a consequence of the need of the organism to preserve its life, but also represented a desire (the death drive) to return to a state of undifferentiation and extinction, associated with the ever-present archaic mother (Freud [1920] 1995: 594–628).

Williams argues that the death drive is an expression of desire, 'desire which wants its discharges, which returns to itself in order to extinguish itself' (1995: 160). In these terms, the vampiric or transformative self functions to subvert gender power relations and identification, 'since it betrays the possibility that pleasure is dangerous, and our victims might also be our violators' (Williams 1995: 176). In these terms, the female ghosts of the erotic ghost story, as embodied most evidently within the ghost cats in *Kuroneko*, might well be symbols of male desire and projections of male anxiety, but at the same time they offer a mode of empowerment outside traditional binaries. They no longer simply accept their fate, as in *Tales of Ugetsu*, but are active agents who call into question the discourses around femininity, respectability and passivity.

Kuroneko is set during the Sengoku Period, also known as 'Warring States' Period, which lasted from the Ōnin War (1467–77) until the unification of the country by the Shogun Tokugawa Ieyasu in 1615. The Sengoku Period is notable as a time of total breakdown in social order and consequently one of the most violent periods in Japanese history. The Ōnin War, which devastated Kyoto, then the capital of Japan, was marked by bitter territorial battles between competing *Daimyo* (military leaders). It was a period of social mobility, in which even the lowest peasant farmer could become a Samurai if he proved his mettle as a warrior.

In *Kuroneko*, the ghostly *bakeneko* function as a symbol of an identity in transition, through their ability to shape-shift across both gender and class boundaries. At the same time, the locating of the action in the spaces linked by Rajomon Gate is significant. Similarly to *Rashōmon*, Rajomon Gate's towering presence provides both dramatic and historical symbolism that mirrors the main narrative trajectory. This gate functions as both metaphorical device and an organisational structure around which the narrative of the film takes place, separating both literally and metaphorically the inside and the outside, the *Daimyo* and their Samurai, and the farmers and their land. As such, the gate is both connective and divisive; it both joins and separates the two narrative arenas in which the main events of the film take place. Historically, the Rajomon Gate was built in the eighth century as a symbol of strength and aesthetic beauty; however, by the time in which the film is set, it had fallen into a state of disrepair and had, as Cummings points out, 'become a haven for thieves, brigands, and various sordid activities' (2005: 5).

The film begins with the brutal assault, rape and murder of two women, Yone (Nobuko Otawa) and her mother-in-law, Shige (Kiwako Taichi). Yone and Sjige have been forced to eke out a meagre existence in the absence of Gintoki (Kichiemon Nakamura), Shige's son and Yone's husband. Gintoki, we discover later, has been forcibly conscripted into the army. It is this abandonment of the women, albeit not intentionally, which is the causational factor in the violence that erupts at the beginning of the film, reflecting again the fact that tension between *ninjō* and *giri* often leads to violence.

The scene of the two women's brutalisation is shot in graphic and unremitting detail; the animal-like behaviour, the lack of extraneous extra-diegetic sound and the use of close-ups on the men's faces as they watch the women being raped, all the time greedily devouring the women's food, suggest a reversion to a primitive state dictated by pure instincts. The period setting of *Kuroneko*, which is one distinguished by its factional fighting and lack of leadership, mirrors that of contemporary Japan in the 1960s. Ōshima comments:

> Our generation is a fatherless generation. When I look at our fathers' generation, who defeated in war did not accept responsibility and who in the post-war period continued with the lies, I feel that we are a generation of orphans. (cited in Standish 2005: 230)

As a consequence of their violent and untimely deaths, Shige and Yone are transformed into vengeful spirits or *bakeneko*, beautiful cat-like women, after their cat feasts on their dead and charred bodies. Unlike in the traditional wronged woman trope, the women's vengeance is not restricted just to those who harmed them; instead, all Samurai are subject to their wrath. As such, *Kuroneko* sets the trend for contemporary Japanese horror cinema, in that the revenge of the wronged women is not just contained to those that have committed the offence against them, but is taken more generally against Japanese paternalism as a whole.

The two women's transformation cuts across boundaries not just between animal and the human, but also between the working (peasant) classes and the upper classes. Sumptuous kimonos replace their tattered clothes, while their make-up is highly stylised in the manner of noblewomen of the time, with raised short blackened eyebrows, painted faces and accentuated lips. Ornate hairpieces are used to pin up their lustrous black hair, and they float rather than walk. It is this metamorphosis across the class divide that allows the women, like cats, to entice, snare and then take home their prey to devour and kill. At the same time, this shape-shifting signals the transitional nature of identity and, by association, 'Japaneseness'. Jackson comments: 'If form is taken as a determinant of identity, then it is hardly surprising that a cultural preoccupation with metamorphosis should surface at times of deep social transitions' (cited in Williams 1995: 108–9).

The montage of shots that accompanies the first revenge sequence provides the template for subsequent attacks, creating a series of associations between the Rajomon Gate, the outside and the inside, the wronged women, their now demonic state and their brutalisers. The scene begins with a close-up of the name of the gate, highlighting its symbolic and metaphorical significance. From

Fig. 4.1 Victim as violator: Yone (Nobuko Otawa) in *Kuroneko* (Kaneto Shindō, 1968, Tōhō / The Kobal Collection)

below, the ghostly Yone is seen as she floats across the bridge. Immediately following this, a tracking shot follows the figure of a Samurai on horseback (the leader of the gang that killed the women), returning to Kyoto. A close-up of a black cat on the bridge, yowling, acts as a portent of doom. Then the spectral figure floats over the Samurai and Yone suddenly appears in front of him. Though on one level he recognises that she is in fact a ghost – in fact he asks her if she is a spectre – his vanity and desire get in the way and he agrees to see her home. Cummings comments, 'significantly, the ghosts lure the samurai by their appetites (comfort, sake, sex) rather than attack them outright, making the same gluttony that brutalized the women now spell their own demise' (2005: 8).

Once back at the women's home, the Samurai is plied with sake brought to him by Shige and served to him by the beautiful Yone. Shige dances in the background in a manner reminiscent of Nō performances, as Yone seduces the Samurai. The savagery of their lovemaking, in which sex turns into violence and death, is significant in that it will later be juxtaposed with the lovemaking between Yone and her husband, Gintoki. Like the kimono that both conceals and reveals, the true identity of the women is hinted at but never fully realised visually; instead, the female body is always in transition, never fixed and static, suggesting an inherent instability in subjectivity. Kawai writes that the multiplicity of female characters found in Japanese fairy tales should be 'recognized as always changing positions, not as development stages. These protean female figures express the Japanese mind: multiple layers creating a beautiful totality' (1996: 189).

The next day, the body of the Samurai is discovered in the burnt-out ruins of the women's former home, where the poor plunder the corpse for clothes and armour to sell. Cummings writes that this scene, and similar ones, have a broader context than a simple revenge narrative; he contends that 'the ghosts represent the poor who exact justice against those who abuse them' (2005: 9). The wronged women, therefore, not only subvert gender norms but also function as metaphorical signifiers of class oppression.

Subsequent killings follow the same sequence of events. The ghostly Yone appears to a Samurai; she invites him to accompany her home, where she seduces him and then kills him. Cummings notes: 'each mini-narrative [is] seen in fewer and more fragmented pieces, emphasizing the ritualistic and serial nature of the ghosts' onslaught' (2005: 9). The rhythmic nature of the women's revenge is broken up by the reappearance of Yone's long-lost husband, Gintoki, now a respected and powerful Samurai, who is given the task of defeating the demonic vengeful female ghosts by the cowardly Mikado (Hideo Kanze). This marks a pivotal point in the narrative, in which the film becomes a tale of 'tragic lovers' (*kitagawa utamaro*), rather than merely a revenge narrative. Gintoki soon realises that the ghosts he has been sent to vanquish are those of his beloved wife and mother. As is typical in Japanese horror film, the protagonist becomes caught in the classic *ninjō* and *giri* conflict. Whilst *giri* requires obedience to one's superiors, necessitating that he defeat the women, *ninjō* – compassion, emotion and love – prevents him from doing so. Ultimately, the only solution to this conflict is death for Gintoki.

The implicit eroticism in the scenes in which Gintoki makes love to Yone is the opposite of that seen in the revenge sequences of the narrative. The lyricalism of these scenes is expressed through the highly stylised mise-en-scène of eroticism in which gauze curtains conceal the bodies of the lovers. Romantic music accompanies their lovemaking, emphasising the lovers' ecstasy and commitment to each other. At the same time, as Cummings contends, the cold visuals, highlighted through the use of black and white, and the audience's foreknowledge that the couple's love is doomed give the sequences a 'significant degree of melancholy' (2005: 12). This is emphasised on the eighth day, when Gintoki discovers that Yone has sacrificed herself for him by choosing love over eternal life. In the well-worn archetype of the self-sacrificing woman, *Kuroneko* seems to emphasise traditional Japanese paternalistic values rather than transgressing them. Yone fits the archetype of what Barrett terms the 'All-Suffering Female', who because of her romantic attachments to the earthly world is 'denied rebirth' and instead 'forced to undergo the torments of hell'

Fig. 4.2 The monstrous mother: Shige (Kiwako Taichi), *Kuroneko* (Kaneto Shindō, 1968, Tōhō / The Kobal Collection)

(1989: 122). By giving up her demonic guise, Yone is fulfilling societal dictates of appropriate femininity, or within a Japanese context, respectability as articulated within the discourse of *ryōsaikenbo*.

But the daughter's sacrifice is situated against the monstrousness of the archaic mother figure, who continues on her vengeful quest, undeterred by her maternal obligation towards Gintoki. It would seem that in her monstrous maternity Shige is simply a repository of male anxieties, or an embodiment of Creed's 'monstrous feminine' (1993: 88–104). Certainly, the scene in which Gintoki cuts off her arm, rendering her powerless and unable to feed and continue her revenge, seems to imply male anxiety over both maternal and female empowerment. In addition, Shige's pox-ridden face, when she attempts to retrieve her arm from Gintoki, suggests inner decay, impurity and corruption. As such, this monstrous mother is the opposite of traditional representations in the *hahamono* genre, which celebrates the sacrificing and suffering maternal. As the conventions of the Japanese ghost story at the time necessitated, the film ends with the death of Gintoki, who is unable to defeat his monstrous mother. Similar to the rape-revenge film discussed in the next chapter, *Kuroneko* is a tale of tragic love. At the same time, the inability of the son to defeat his monstrous mother can be interpreted as a feminist protest against the restrictive definitions of maternity in Japanese society.

TRAGIC LOVERS (*KITAGAWA UTAMARO*) AND THE VIRGIN BRIDE

The story of tragic lovers (*kitagawa utamaro*) has proved to be a mainstay of Japanese cultural artefacts including printmaking (*ukiyo-e*), literature, poetry and theatre. Once again, the conflict between social obligations (*giri*) and personal emotions (*ninjō*) drove stories of doomed love. At the heart of such stories was the concept of *shinjū*, which translates as 'inside the heart' but also means double suicide. Whilst ostensively a tale of female revenge, *Kuroneko* is ultimately a story of doomed love, in which both the lovers die in similar circumstances. One of the archetypical stories of doomed love is the folktale of 'The Peony Lantern', which, along with 'The Ghost Story of Yotsuya', is one of the Japanese folktales most frequently adapted for the screen. Based upon a Chinese legend, it was introduced to Japan by Sanyutei Encho (1839–1900) in the form of *Rakugo* (a traditional Japanese type of comic storytelling).

Subsequently adapted for Kabuki, with the title *Kaidan Botan Dōrō*, it was performed at the Kabuki-za in July 1892. It was the first Japanese ghost story on film in 1921, and has been filmed numerous times since: as *The Bride from Hell*, directed by Yamamoto in 1968, and more recently as *Haunted Lantern*, by Tsushima in 1998, amongst others. 'The Tale of the Peony Lantern' is a story of star-crossed lovers who are unable to be together because of class differences. The young woman in the story belongs to an upper-class household, whilst her would-be lover is a masterless Samurai or *rōnin*. Prevented from seeing the Samurai, the young woman dies of a broken heart, only to return from the land of the dead to consummate their relationship. The Samurai becomes cursed, and dies enclosed in the skeletal arms of his dead love. The lovers, unable to be together in life, are finally united in death, their bodies buried side by side (Hadland Davis 1992: 228–30 and Ross 1996: 144–54).

Set during the Tokugawa Period, *Hellish Love* features a young masterless Samurai called Shinzaburō (Hajime Tanimoto), who is forced to make a living as an umbrella (*wagasa*) maker, and therefore is not a suitable match for the daughter of a nobleman, the beautiful but sickly Otsuyu (Setsuko Ogawa). The fact that their love is doomed is foregrounded in the first encounter between Shinzaburō and Otsuyu, which takes place at the opening of the film. Caught in a ferocious thunderstorm, Otsuyu and her maid, Oyoné, take shelter. Rain functions as both a potent of doom and a projection of interior emotions in conflict with with societal duties and obligations that define the relations between men and women. It is here that the two would-be lovers meet. Shinzaburō offers Otsuyu one of his umbrellas, which she accepts reluctantly. The umbrella, as status symbol, foregrounds the impenetrable class barriers between the two, as well as functioning as a signifier of doomed love. The symbolic importance of the umbrella is solidified in a later scene, in which Otsuyu asks Oyoné, 'If I die, can my soul fly where it wants?' The next shot is of umbrellas drifting upwards, in slow motion, as they slip through Shinzaburō's grasp. The sharing of an umbrella (*aiaigasa*) by a couple formed a central trope in 'tales of tragic lovers' and functioned to establish their love in the face of societal opposition (sharing an umbrella was a metaphor for the positioning of the couple outside traditional societal mores and dictates). In Japanese horror cinema, the umbrella as a prop is both a symbol of status and a signifier of doomed love. Shinzaburō and Otsuyu fit into what Barrett terms the archetypes of the 'weak passive male' and the 'all-suffering female'. Barrett contends that, whilst the nature of doomed love is to reinforce society's boundaries, stories of tragic lovers contain an element of social protest:

> Still, the archetypes of the All Suffering Female and the Weak Passive Male are problematic, for stories about tragic lovers can be considered a protest against the society that would not permit their love. (1989: 120)

In *Hellish Love*, Shinzaburō's and Otsuyu's love is doomed because of the rigidity of class barriers in Japanese society. In accordance with *giri*, Shinzaburō's lack of status means that he and Otsuyu cannot be together. Barrett writes that, in such cases, duty required that 'The young man should obey and passively let love slip through his fingers' (1989: 125).

In a montage of short scenes, the theme of doomed love is foregrounded through the careful placing of props, as is the archetypical nature of the characters. In the first scene, Shinzaburō takes up his sword and swings it. As he thrusts the sword into the ground, he says, 'I make umbrellas; her father's a rich Hatamoto Samurai.' Falling to the ground, with his head bowed in defeat, he cries out, 'How can I escape from these feelings that torment me?' In the background, an open umbrella is placed carefully against the right-hand wall. In the next scene, the camera pans across a grassy field leading to a lake. The use of a brown filter evokes the imagery of traditional Japanese prints (or *ukiyo-e*), as the camera zooms in on Otsuyu, who is standing at the end of a short pier by a lake. The camera pauses for a brief moment, and we can hear the sound of wind chimes in the distance. The next shot is a close-up of the face of Okuni, maid of the household, as she stands staring directly in front of Otsuyu; this is followed by a cut to Otsuyu's body lying on the ground, holding a cup in her left hand, a pool of blood by her head. The camera returns to Shinzaburō, who looks into space, distracted, as he works.

This montage is significant in that it situates Shinzaburō as the archetypical passive male and Otsuyu as the all-suffering female. Barrett writes about the role of the passive male in Kabuki: 'In Kabuki the peaceable lover was further weakened by being in the lower rungs of the merchant class. Lack of funds often precipitated his tragedy' (1989: 125). Shinzaburō's passivity is signalled through the montage of shots which show him idling away his time as Otsuyu is murdered. The significance of the bridge where Otsuyu is standing is also a conventional trope of stories of doomed love; the bridge is a typical meeting place for lovers in tales of romantic passion and tragic love (Barrett 1989: 119).

In a dream sequence, Shinzaburō goes to meet Otsuyu. They go back to her house, where they make love. When Otsuyu drops her robe, soft focus is used to blur the bodies of the lovers. In the scenes between them, passion is externalised on to the mise-en-scène. As in *Kuroneko*, the romantic passion of the doomed lovers is expressed lyrically. As the camera slowly tracks forwards and backwards along the horizontal axis, and along a screen that separates the lovers' bodies from the spectator's gaze, the screen gradually transforms from green into red as an external signifier of passion. Otsuyu lets her hair down, signifying a break with familial and societal ties, and gives Shinzaburō a lock of her hair, promising that she will come for him on 13 August. As Ebersole writes, 'For a woman, to let her hair down in the presence of a man was a sign of intimacy' (1998: 194). Just then, Otsuyu's father, Ijima, bursts into the room; attempting to kill Shinzaburō, he fatally stabs his daughter instead. Shinzaburō wakes up in the boat where he is fishing with his servant, with a lock of black hair clutched in his hand. This dream functions as a signifier of the instability between reality and illusion, a crucial component of Japanese ghost stories.

The scenes of romantic passion are, as in *Kuroneko*, juxtaposed with scenes of carnal desire. These scenes show Okuni and Ijima, and later, Okuni with Genjiro, her lover. Okuni has been having an affair with Ijima since his wife's death. Motivated by greed, Okuni conspires with Genjiro to murder Ijima and Otsuyu. The evident carnality of Okuni, who uses her sexuality to get what she wants, is situated in opposition to the passive and virginal behaviour of Otsuyu. In the scenes between Shinzaburō and Otsuyu, soft lighting and romantic music are used to emphasise their love for each other, and add to the emotional impact of the scenes. The voyeuristic gaze is impeded by barriers, which conceal the bodies of the lovers from view. In the first scene between the lovers, a screen obstructs the spectatorial gaze, and in the final love scene, a high-angled shot looking down at the lovers again impedes the operation of an omniscient point-of-view. The overt exhibitionism and animalistic passion of the scenes of carnal desire between Okuni and Genjiro, shot in medium and close-up, are thus a direct contrast to the love scenes between Shinzaburō and Otsuyu. The relationship between Shinzaburō's servant, Tomozo, and his wife, Ominé (Hidemi Hara), parallels that of Genjiro and Okuni. Not only are sex scenes filmed in the same direct style, but also both couples transgress their *giri* or duty to their superiors as a consequence of unrestrained appetites, both fleshly and monetary. Here, as elsewhere, commodification and consumerism associated with Westernisation are situated as responsible for the development of the individual as antithetical to the community and the wider system, or *ie*, which defines one's subjectivity in relation to the whole. Hamabata writes: 'The social should take primacy over the emotional, durable form over transient feeling. The *uchi* should be sacrificed for the sake of the *ie*' (1994: 206). Failure to do so puts the very foundations of society at risk, and the continuance of the *ie* as a durable form of class and gender relations.

As in the folktale, Tomozo peers through a gap in the wall of Shinzaburō's house and sees the leg of a skeleton entwined with Shinzaburō's. A priest is called and rituals and mantras are said to keep his ghost bride away. The greedy Tomozo and Ominé accept 100 ryos from Oyoné to remove the protection, thus leaving Shinzaburō exposed. For their transgression of the social codes of behaviour, Okuni and Genjiro and Tomozo and Ominé must be and are justly punished. Both the couples die after fighting with each other about money, the very root of their transgressions. Okuni, discovering that the 100 ryos have disappeared, blames Genjiro. They pick up swords and fight. Outside the house, Okuni slips on a pool of blood and is accidentally stabbed by Genjiro, who falls backwards on his own sword. Ominé poisons the drinking water in an attempt to steal the money from Tomozo. However, he murders her when he discovers her with the money, which she swallows in order to prevent him from taking it from her. But, having retrieved the money and with Ominé dead, he drinks a cup of water, which leads in turn to his death. The film ends, as with all stories of tragic lovers, with Shinzaburō also dead. Ross writes, 'His hair matted, and with long unkempt beard, he looked like an old, sick man, emaciated and sucked dry. Yet, when Yusai looked closer, he thought he could see a trace of a smile around Shinzaburo's lips' (1996: 154). The final shot is of the three ghosts moving into a sea of fog and disappearing into the distance as the festival of *Obon* ends.

THE CUCKOLDED HUSBAND

Much can be read into the fact that Japanese ghosts tend to be almost exclusively female. Is it a national guilt projected and transformed into fear because of the violently subordinate place women had in the traditional Japanese society? Is it a way of admitting that the wronged ones (those most eager to avenge themselves) tended to be mostly – women? Whatever the case may be, there are much fewer stories and films about male ghosts (when they appeared, they were mostly warriors haunting their last battlefield). (Ognjanovic 2006a)

Vengeful spirits, or *yūrei*, in Japanese horror cinema are mainly, as we have seen, female. Ognjanovic suggests, as does Napier, that one way of interpreting the primacy of female ghosts in Japanese society is a result of women's subordinate role. However, whilst not so prolific or iconic, male ghosts seeking revenge do feature in Japanese horror cinema. In the last chapter, we saw the archetypical male ghost in the vengeful unquiet spirit of Yachimaru with his unkempt hair, white robe and make-up in *The Ghost Cat of Otama Pond*. In addition, Secor and Addis point out, 'Male ghosts became among the most popular figures in later kabuki plays' (1985: 49). But in Japanese horror film, male ghosts tend to be secondary figures to the vengeful female *yūrei*, or else ghosts of warriors long dead, as in the 'Hoichi the Earless' segment of *Kwaidan*. At the same time, whilst the figure of the cuckolded husband or lover is a prominent feature in both Edo Gothic and the erotic ghost story, he rarely becomes a vengeful spirit.

Ōshima's *Empire of Passion* is a tale of tragic love, and takes as its premise forbidden love between an older woman and a younger man, which culminates in the murder of the cuckolded husband and his revenge from beyond the grave. As has been noted by some critics, *Empire of Passion* bears a superficial relationship to early examples of film noir such as *The Postman Always Rings Twice* (Garnett: 1946).

Empire of Passion is set in 1895, at a pivotal turning point in Japanese history, after the restoration of the emperor, and in the aftermath of the first Sino-Japanese War, which ended China's dominance in the Far East and raised Japan to a position as a major world power. The film centres on the love triangle between Seki (Kazuko Yoshiyuki); her husband, Gisaburo (Takahiro Tamura), a rickshaw operator; and the virile, younger Toyoji (Tatsuya Fuji), an ex-soldier who has returned to the village after taking part in the Sino-Japanese War. In the figures of the two men, the tension between pre-modern values, as epitomised by the hard-working and genial Gisaburo, and the modern, based around democratic values from the West and embodied in the form of the handsome and aggressive Toyoji, is explored.

As in Ōshima's earlier and better-known *Empire of the Senses* (1976), overindulgence in earthly pleasures leads to death. Like Kichizo (Tatsuya Fuji) and Sada (Eiko Matsuda) in the aforementioned film, Seki and Gisaburo 'are victims of their own morality and the human need for intimacy marks their downfall' (Allsop 2004b: 108). The affair between Seki and Toyoji begins not with sex, but with food and the sharing of cakes and drinking of tea. The sharing of the last cake between the two symbolises the unbreakable bond between them. The repetition of this cake-sharing just before they are caught and punished, stresses the tragic nature of their love. *Empire of Passion* has been seen as a companion piece to the earlier and more explicit *Empire of the Senses*, but Seki has little in common with the sexually aggressive Sada in the latter. It is Toyoji who forces himself upon Seki, and who then shaves her pubic hair as an almost animalistic act of domination over her: an act that has to culminate in the death of Gisaburo (and most likely an implicit criticism of the Japanese censorship system). And although Seki helps Toyoji strangle her husband, she portrays an emotional depth and guilt, unlike Sada, who strangles Kichizo with his own kimono tie, signifying her total domination over him (Allsop 2004b: 109). The body of Seki's dead husband is then thrown down a well, which, as we have seen, is one of the most constant motifs in Japanese horror cinema.

The first physical encounter between Toyoji and Seki is when he forces himself on the reluctant woman. Buruma writes, 'Before sexuality can be purified it must first manifest itself. In Japanese pornography this usually means rape' (1984: 59). Having once experienced forbidden pleasures, Seki gradually takes a more dominant role in the sexual relationship, initiating sex on a number of occasions, when it is Toyoji who is reluctant. As Buruma argues, 'They become addicted to the forbidden fruit. They are polluted, or rather, their inherent impurity manifests itself' (1984: 60). This is also the main theme of *Empire of the Senses*, in which Sada's unrestrained desire makes her ever more demonic and demanding as the narrative draws to its bloody end. In *Empire of Passion*, not only does Toyoji's passion make manifest Seki's inherent impurity, as her unleashed desire seems to attest to, but also the well down which they throw Gisaburo's body can be interpreted as a representation of the archaic maternal figure associated with Shintō, especially as wells in Japanese mythology are connected to the Underworld, where Izanami fled. This is clearly shown when Seki and Toyoji attempt to retrieve Gisaburo's body from the well, after Toyoji has been seen throwing leaves down it, rather than taking them home for fuel as he should have done. The filthy water at the bottom of the well signifies pollution, and yet at the same time, healthy plants are growing down the walls of the well. As such, the well functions as a symbolic representation of the dualistic sides of the original archaic mother figure. As Seki and Toyoji desperately search in the muddy water for Gisaburo's body, his ghost appears at the top of the well looking down on his two murderers. He throws leaves and handfuls of grass at the lovers and Seki is blinded in the process. And so begins the denouement in which the lovers are captured and publicly flogged for their transgression against the community. But Seki's blinding, although functioning as symbolic punishment, allows her other senses to gain prominence, as in the final segment of *Blind Beast*.

In a similar manner to *Hellish Love*, medium shots and part-blocking are used for the erotically charged love scenes between the two antagonists throughout. Once Seki is blinded, the final lovemaking between the two takes on a ferocious brutality and desperation. In fact, the camera tracks away from the couple and remains in the centre of the room, whilst cries of passion can be heard. The viewer is positioned by the camera, in a place of blindness rather than sight, like Seki. This repeats a constant motif within the film around spectatorship, desire and sight, or indeed the lack of sight. In an earlier sequence, the almost comical figure of Inspector Hotta (Takuzo Kawatani) hides under Seki's house in an attempt to entrap the couple. However, he is unable to see anything and the visible signs of desire remain elusive, as they do for the extra-diegetic spectator. The refusal to allow a totalised vision of bodies embedded within space is one that is necessitated by censorship laws, but it also signals the tension between the pre-modern (the body) and the modern (sight). Igarashi comments on the link between modernity and sight in the early 1920s in Japan:

> During the 1920s, particularly in the urban areas such as Tokyo and Osaka, people experienced a fundamental reworking of human relationships due to the rapid transformations of the material conditions of daily life. In this process, sight emerged as a privileged sense since it helped to construct a rational, modern space ... Within this modern urban space, vision becomes the preferred trope of rationality while the other senses were relegated to a secondary status, confined to the domestic realm. (2005: 301)

By fragmenting the scene of desire into a montage of part-shots and close-ups, seen through gaps in doors, screens and floorboards, *Empire of Passion* reasserts the power of the body and the senses over that of rationality and sight. This is clearly shown through the use of chiaroscuro lighting when the police, at last, come to arrest the lovers; shafts of radiant light frame their bodies as a visual sign of transcendence. Here the clean body, as compared to the polluted one, emphasises the purity of the lovers. Barrett explains, in relation to the plays of Chikamatsu, that lovers 'become pure after they fall in love and are ready to die for it' (1989: 123). As in the films of the Japanese New Wave, the material body subverts the ideological base of romantic love and, as such, *Empire of Passion* explicitly critiques the suppression of desire by the Japanese state and the paradoxical nature of Japanese censorship laws.

Although not forgotten, Gisaburo bears many of the characteristics of the *muenbotoke*. Barrett writes: 'The thought of them arouses not only sympathy but fear because they could cause the living trouble if not appeased or pacified somehow' (1989: 81). For much of the film, Gisaburo's ghost appears as a sympathetic figure, appearing in an unthreatening manner unlike most female *yūrei* in Japanese horror cinema at the time. It is as if he has not come to terms with his death, as he sits by the fire, drinking and eating with Seki, as he did whilst he was alive. This is clearly shown in the scene where Seki, having bought sake for her dead husband, comes across Gisaburo in his rickshaw as she makes her way home. Gisaburo insists that the terrified Seki rides with him, as she did when he was alive. Against a background of gloomy fog, lit with blue light,

Gisaburo becomes increasingly distressed and disorientated, as he is unable to find his way home. The use of blue lighting as a mechanism of visually expressing a character's isolation and alienation will become a key component of the mise-en-scène of Japanese horror. In *Empire of Passion*, the vengeful ghost of Gisaburo can only be laid to rest once Seki and Toyoji have been punished for their sins against both Gisaburo and the wider community. That this is presented as a spectacle of violence, in which the pair are flogged whilst the community watches, is significant because it allows a reassertion of rationality as signified by vision and sight. Barrett writes: 'Social order is affirmed because true lovers are doomed. The audience gets a vicarious pleasure and is also admonished that such behaviour leads to death' (1989: 122–3).

SUICIDE GHOSTS

The vengeful female ghost, Kei (Yuko Natori), is at the centre of Obayashi Nohuhiko's contemporary erotic drama, *The Discarnates* (1988). One night, Kei knocks on the door of Harada (Morio Kazama), a writer of television dramas. Dressed in black with a bottle of champagne in her hands, she is rudely rejected by the self-obsessed Harada. When Harada next meets her, she is a ghost and her transition is signified visually through her white costume. For Iwamura, the visual appearance of Kei bears iconographic similarities to Regan (Linda Blair) in *The Exorcist* (1973), and she suggests that the character of Kei owes as much to the demonic Regan as it does to traditional Japanese folktales of vengeful ghosts:

> While this film displays an influence of traditional Japanese folktales, it is arguable that the female character is equally based on the demon from *The Exorcist*. This combination of traditional folktale and American filmic representations of women is possibly related to the preference of Japanese youths for American films. Japanese youth find Japanese films depressing, and are attracted to the comparatively carefree lives that American characters are represented as leading, as well as the tendency for American films to portray a happy ending. (1994)

It seems to me, however, that the representation of Kei in *The Discarnates* is more in line with traditional folkloric archetypes than Iwamura acknowledges, although the final sequences in which she is revealed as a ghost, levitating from her bed, do bear a superficial resemblance to similar ones in *The Exorcist*. In that film, Regan is the product of the breakdown in the nuclear family in America, and her embodiment by Satan can be said to articulate patriarchal fears around both female liberation and female sexuality. I would argue that

Kei is altogether a more tragic figure, a symbol of isolation and alienation in a post-modern society of rampant Westernisation and individualism, whether the ghosts in the film are interpreted as a hallucination on the part of Harada (as Iwamura suggests) or as real spirits.

Whether a projection of Harada's isolation or a real ghost, Kei functions as a symbol of Harada's callousness towards other people, demonstrating a lack of *ninjō* in a society torn between Western individualism and Japanese communalism. The past repeats in *The Discarnates* through the reappearance of Harada's dead mother and father, when he returns for a visit to his childhood home. During a *Rakugo* performance in his hometown, he comes across a man (Tsurutaro Kataoka) who is the double of his dead father. Invited back to the man's home, he finds his mother's doppelgänger (Kumiko Akiyoshi). Harada soon realises that in fact these are his parents, Hidekichi and Fusako, captured from a moment in his past, just before their deaths. It is through returning to this idealised nostalgic past that Harada finds himself once more able to connect with those that he loves in the present.

Unlike the typical erotic ghost story, in which the past is seen as violent, primitive and ultimately destructive, *The Discarnates* expresses a nostalgic longing for the past, for a time of childhood, before the restrictive burdens of Japanese paternalism confine and define the subject. The vibrant primary colours, red and yellow, of this idealised past are contrasted with the dull, grey-greenish of the present. Further, the open, welcoming domestic spaces of Harada's parents' traditional home are contrasted with the closed spaces of Harada's apartment: one of only two apartments, or living spaces, within a block dominated by work spaces, the other apartment inhabited by Kei. Unlike in his parents' traditional home, which is structured within and through the community, a pervasive atmosphere of disconnection and loneliness is articulated by new living spaces as constructed within the rarefied palate of the present. The past is associated with the (suffocating) maternal and is coded as feminine, and the present is linked to the (absent) paternal and coded as masculine. At the same time, having a living space within a work space collapses the domestic and the private, the inside and the outside, and comments on the long unsocial hours worked by Japanese men.

Tateishi points to the Meiji Restoration in 1868, which saw off the old feudal Shogunate system, marking the beginning of Japanese modernity. She comments: 'The transformation of Japanese society … was rooted in the notion of progress and development, which rhetorically signified a break from "tradition" and "the past", as in the "Enlightened Rule" of the Meiji' (2003: 295). Tateishi argues that one response to the enforced industrialisation of Japan took the form of a 'cultural nostalgia', in which there was 'an acknowledgement of what was lost, and an attempt to re-experience it' (2003: 296).

This cultural nostalgia is articulated in *The Discarnates* through the idealisation of the past and of childhood. It is significant therefore that his daily visits to his father and mother allow Harada to recover a sense of identity. In turn this allows him to reconnect with the present, as shown through his passionate affair with the ghostly Kei. Kei tells Harada that she has been badly burned in the past (her scars are actually wounds self-inflicted on the night she committed suicide), and their encounters therefore take place in the dark, with Kei's body concealed. This subverts the usual conventions of Japanese erotica in which the over-valuation of female breasts and the fetishisation of the 'covered' female crotch function as metonymic signifiers of desire, as these are the only things that can be shown directly. At the same time, Harada's relationship with his dead mother can be said to border on the incestuous. Although he is a grown man, she continues to treat him as a child. On a number of occasions, Fusako insists that Harada takes off his clothes in order to escape from the stifling heat, which can be said to function as a metaphor for the suffocating closeness of the mother/child bond in Japan, which has been the subject of much discussion in light of the increasing violence within the family in Japan. In one scene, Fusako, dressed in a flimsy slip, falls off a stool as Harada is helping her reach some ice-cream glasses on the top shelf. She slips, falling into her son's arms, initiating a brief frisson of Oedipal desire as they exchange glances. In one sense the film can be said to centre on Harada's Oedipal trajectory in that his parents can be seen as an externalisation of his 'death drive' that expresses itself in terms of a desire to return to the mother. A Freudian interpretation would argue that the early death of his parents has left Harada with an incomplete Oedipus complex, and it is this which renders him unable to attach to his wife and son in the present (Freud [1924] 1995: 661–5). But more simply, the almost suffocating closeness of the relationship between mother and son provides a means through which to comment on the breakdown of the family within contemporary Japanese society.

A key convention of the Japanese ghost story is, as we have seen, that an encounter with the dead ultimately leads to death. Harada becomes increasingly haggard as his daily visits to his dead parents and his nightly visits to his ghostly lover take their toll. On a number of occasions, Kei forces Harada to look into a mirror; the reflection that he sees looking back is one of gradual decay and disease. Like Emiko in *Godzilla*, the actions of the female principal provide a mechanism through which balance is restored:

> Then Katsura, like the archetypical vengeful spirit, not only gets revenge but also restores balance. Through her, Harada is able to transcend his sense of loss. While the vengeful spirit can lead men to destruction, then, she can also work positively as a guide. (Iwamura 1994)

However, the female ghost can only be empowered through her liminality, and is eventually forced into self-sacrifice in order to reassert a traditional Japanese masculinity.

Harada leaves the past behind, as metaphorically signified through the burning of the chopsticks from his last meal with his parents. In Buddhist death rites, chopsticks have come to have a symbolic function, both as representative of the last meal and, if improperly used, capable of attracting death (Buisson 2003: 200). The final scenes are of Harada with his son; having successfully negotiated his Oedipus complex, he is able to be a proper man and father. Thus *The Discarnates* reinforces traditional Japanese values around the sanctity of the family.

GHOSTS OF DESIRE

Suffering ghosts of desire are a central convention of the *Kaidan pinku eiga*. More often than not female, these ghosts ultimately valorise traditional Japanese conceptions of masculinity and femininity, as they end up sacrificing themselves for the good of the wider community. This is closely tied into the 'death drive', in which ghosts function as metonymic signifiers of the desire for a return to the generative mother: either metaphorically as, in *Empire of Passion*, or literally, as in *The Discarnates*. The erotic ghost story was at its height in the 1960s and 1970s, as a tangential sub-genre of the pink film; we can see this in the focus on the sexualised and desiring body. The demise of the *pinku eiga* and its replacement by AV means that the erotic ghost film no longer has such a prominent position in contemporary Japanese horror, although there have been a number of recent films dealing with ghostly desire. The seductive and sometimes demonic female ghosts, a key archetype of the genre, have transmogrified into frightening and less seductive vengeful ghosts like Sadako in *Ring* and Kayako in *Ju-On: The Grudge*. The fact that the vengeful male spirit and/or monster is an exception rather than the rule can be understood by reference to the dominance of woman in traditional Japanese fairy tales. The fact that the erotic ghost story still provides a metaphor for female empowerment, with films such as *Shikoku* (Nagasaki: 1999) and *Inugami* (Harada: 2001), implies, perhaps, that women's liberation has some way to go.

Part 2
Genre

CHAPTER 5

The Rape-Revenge Film:
From Violation to Vengeance

In *Pitfall* (Teshigahara: 1962), the middle-aged owner of a sweet shop (Sumie Sasaki), who is trapped in an almost deserted town as she waits for news from her lover, is violently raped by a policeman (Hideo Kanze). While she protests to begin with, she soon begins to participate actively in her rape, as if her violation had liberated suppressed desires.

Kurosawa's award-winning *Rashōmon* (1950) is based on a 'rape' of a woman and the subsequent murder of her husband, as told by various participants. The events unfold through the competing narratives of the dead Samurai, Takehiro (Masayuki Mori), the notorious bandit/rapist, Tajomaru (Toshiro Mifune), and the beautiful rape victim, the Samurai's wife, Masako (Machiko Kyo). However, the rape itself is only ever shown from the male perspective and the narrative is framed through the story of the woodcutter (Taksahi Shimura), the only witness of the attack outside the triangular relationship of those directly involved. The unreliability of all the narrators suggests that no objective version of the truth can ever be achieved. As Richie puts it, 'The seeming reality of each version makes us question that of the other' (2001: 139). It is not suggested that the rape did not happen; rather the stories told focus on how it happened, with each person giving a different and competing version of events. Critical readings of the film rarely explore the rape sequence or, indeed, comment on the fact that Masako goes from unwilling victim to willing lover in the short space of fifty seconds. When first attacked, she resists and struggles, staring upwards into the sky, disconnected from the on-going violation of her body. The rape ends with an eleven-second shot of the woman in Tajomaru's arms. In this medium shot, we see Masako's hand caressing Tajomaru's back, seemingly making it clear that Masako is taking pleasure from her violation.

The words of her husband, as recounted by the woodcutter, signal how little attention is paid to her. Speaking to Tajomaru, the husband says, 'Stop! Stop!

I refuse to risk my life for such a woman!' To his wife, dirty and half-naked, he spits out: 'You are a shameless whore! Why don't you kill yourself?' Turning back to the bandit, he totally devalues his wife: 'If you want her – I'll give her to you! I regret the loss of my horse more than the loss of her.' Later Masako tells the men 'Just remember ... a woman loves a real man. And when she loves – she loves madly, forgetting all else. But a woman can only be won by the strength of swords'. Masako's words can be seen as a reference to the symbolic phallus (the sword, strength, a real man) as object of female desire.

The fullest explanation of events is through Tajomaru's narrative, with which the court case begins. The woman presents her case next, but it is filled with gaps and ellipses – for example, she forgets what she did with the dagger – and her story ends when she faints. For this reason, of all the accounts given, the woman's story, surrounded by male views of the rape and its aftermath, is positioned as the least truthful. The two accounts that follow hers, that of her dead husband, speaking through a medium, and finally the woodcutter's (his second), which takes place outside the law, both undermine the veracity of her own version of events.

In 'Judgement by Film: Socio-Legal Functions of *Rashōmon*', Kamir (2004) points to the similarity between the on-screen events and the legislative framework, in which Tajomaru is presented as a prosecuting figure, Masako as the defendant, and the priest (Minoru Chiaki) and the woodcutter as rebuttal witnesses. In addition, the casting of Toshiro Mifune, already a big star by this time, in the leading role, arguably prevents the character of Tajomaru from being constructed as an unsympathetic villain. As Barrett stresses:

> The bandit played by Toshiro Mifune in *Rashōmon* (1950) is both the Untamed Male and a believable character. His sexual desire for the nobleman's wife is natural rather than perverted, and he is a likeable villain since his actions result from simply human failings. (1989: 58)

In Barrett's terms, Mifune adds an authenticity to the film and is both the point of identification for the male spectator and object of desire for the female spectator, as a consequence of which his viewpoint is privileged within the text. Kamir comments: 'The film joins its main characters in discrediting the women, inviting the implied viewer to be prejudiced against one sex in favour of the other' (2004: 128).

Indeed, the court case does not focus on the rape as a crime against the person, but instead chooses to focus rather on the murder of the husband. The fact of Masako's rape thus becomes incidental, although it is pivotal to the plot. As such, it works within patriarchal male rape fantasies, solidified in Japan as a cultural myth, which implies, of necessity, that there is no such thing as rape. Kamir expands on this:

Consequently women, especially sexual women, and particularly women complaining of sexual assault, are impure, provocative, and untrustworthy; wishing and encouraging sexual encounters, they fabricate false accusations, faking virtue and harming their sexual partners. They are unreliable witnesses, not to be trusted. (2004: 130)

The location of the narrative in the past is also significant. At this time in history, a Samurai's wife had an absolute duty to maintain her virtue and to obey strict moral guidelines of behaviour to ensure that such an event as the 'rape' within the narrative does not occur. In this sense, the blame for the rape in *Rashōmon* lies with the woman; she uncovers her face when she and her husband stop briefly, and it is this that draws Tajomaru to her. Then, having been violated, it should have been her duty to take her life – hence the symbolism of the dagger within the narrative – rather than live with the shame and bring dishonour on her husband. Kamir writes: 'Her choice to live, her survival, her life itself, constitute grave, offensive, rebellious sins against the social order and its most sacred of values' (2004: 140).

VICTIMISATION

The manner in which *Rashōmon* deals with rape can be considered typical of Japanese cultural mythology, in which rape has not, until very recently, been considered a crime. This is highlighted by the recent comment, in 2003, by a leading Japanese politician, Seiichi Ota, a member of the ruling Liberal Democratic Party (LDP), who said, at a symposium on Japan's declining birth rates: 'Gang rape shows the people who do it are still vigorous, and that is OK. I think that might make them close to normal' (BBC News Online: 2003). Whilst the response of the Prime Minister, Junichiro Koizumi, was to criticise Ota's remarks, the vice-chairman of Japan's Bar Association, Yasuyuki Takia, 'said that Mr Ota's remarks were indicative of Japanese society's passive attitude to rape, which often goes unreported'. And in terms of marital rape, 'the idea that forced sex when married constitutes violence is still relatively new in Japan' (Nakamura 2003: 163).

It would be too easy to say that the ubiquity of rape in Japanese cultural art forms, including but not restricted to cinema, has a direct correlation with the 'real' world, especially, after all, as we have seen that Japanese society is predicated on female obedience and submission. Further, not only is rape a central feature of early independent pink cinema, but it also formed a dominant motif in mainstream cinema in the 1970s and 1980s with titles such as *Rape!* (Hasebe: 1976) and *Please Rape me Again* (Nishihara: 1976). More recently, the notorious *Rapeman* series of films, directed by Takao Nagaishi and beginning in 1990, have proved 'popular mainstream entertainment in Japan' (Hunter 1998: 87). Hunter argues that the manner in which some of the films seem to condone rape may indeed be problematic:

> It is not just the frequency with which violent rape of women occurs in these films, but in particular its apparent condoning, which confuses/offends. Generally speaking, the women in pink films fall in love with their rapists, and end up begging for more; the victims are stereotypical innocents such as schoolgirls, nurses, nuns, young brides etc. (1998: 81)

While the debates surrounding the relationship between images of sexual violence and its reality are largely beyond the scope of this book, it is still necessary to sketch them out in order to understood the cultural meanings of these violent expressions of (male) desire, rather than simply dismissing the films as inherently misogynist. These debates can be situated within the anti-pornography movement associated with Second Wave Feminism (usually dated from the late 1960s or early 1970s). Radical and polemical feminists and writers such as Dworkin (1946–2005) and MacKinnon believed that pornography was responsible for the sexual oppression of women and that pornographic representations were closely linked to real sexual violence. In *Pornography: Men Possessing Women*, Dworkin writes:

> Pornography is the essential sexuality of male power: of hate, of ownership, of hierarchy; of sadism, of dominance. The premises of pornography are controlling in every rape and every rape case, whenever a woman is battered or prostituted, in incest. (1989)

In 1978 Dworkin and MacKinnon formed 'Women against Pornography', a radical feminist group which argued that sexual liberation had little to do with female rights; instead it perpetuated inequality and female subjugation. Pornography was associated with male violence, and rape became the key word for expressing this relation. In the words of Robin Morgan: 'Pornography is the theory, rape is the practice' (cited in Horeck 2004: 79). At the other end of the spectrum are the liberal and pro-pornography feminists who defend pornography in terms of free choice – in America this took the form of citing the freedom guaranteed by the First Amendment – while not necessarily condoning pornography. As Boyle writes, 'anti-censorship feminists often agree with anti-pornography feminists that much pornography is both sexist and misogynist' (2005: 29–30).

Take, for example, Williams, who in *Hard Core*, identifies pornography in terms of generic and iconographic features, comparing it to the Hollywood musical, and argues that it works within mainstream conventions in terms of the male/female opposition that structures the narrative (2006: 60–87); or Kipnis, who proposes that pornography 'is both a legitimate form of culture and a fictional, fantastical, even allegorical realm; it neither simply reflects the real world nor is it some hypnotizing call to action' (2006: 119). Here pornography either is just another genre or is inherently transgressive as a medium of cultural expression. But this is insufficient and too reminiscent of similar debates around horror cinema: 'Feminist anti-violence activists have also sought to connect violence against women in film – and in pornography and "gorenography" in particular – to real world violence' (Boyle 2005: 124). And while it might be difficult to prove a causal link between the two, the exploitation of women and children in pornography is not so simply dismissed. As Kelly writes, 'Child sexual abuse is not caused by child pornography, rather the pornography is a record of abuse which has already taken place' (cited in Boyle 2005: 31).

Media effects theory (Gauntlett 2006: 54–65), which has proposed an unproblematic reality between texts and their consumption, offers little data to justify the anti-porn or other anti-violence campaigners. Indeed, a recent survey into the relationship between rape and the prevalence of sexually explicit materials in Japan between 1972 and 1995 suggests the opposite. Diamond writes: 'The incidence of rape has progressively declined from 4677 reported cases with 5464 offenders in 1972 to the 1995 incidence of 1500 cases with 1160 offenders' (1999). However, other research shows a significant rise in sexual violence within the family as a response to the bursting of Japan's bubble economy in the late 1980s (Nakamura 2003: 162–5).

Other theorists have foregrounded the centrality of fantasy in pornography and sexually violent materials. While the term fantasy may be more profitable to use in terms of discussing sexually violent and explicit materials, it is not without its problems. Horeck points out that feminist discourse has utilised fantasy in terms of rape in two main ways: 'In the first instance, "rape fantasy" refers to lurid male fantasies of violating helpless woman. In the second instance, the terms refers to the troubling "female rape fantasy", in which women fantasize about being sexually violated by men' (2004: 4). While to suggest that all women have rape fantasies is inherently problematic, an understanding of the relationship between fantasy and reality can help us understand how rape and revenge operate cinematically in Japanese cinema from the 1970s in order to explore how 'the enduring force and intensity of public fantasies of rape can help us better understand the depth and the extent of that violence' (Horeck 2004: 13). Indeed, as we shall see, the *Angel Guts* series of films, as a paradigmatic example of representations of rape in Japanese cinema, deliberately critique any simple causal relationship between representation and societal violence and as such pave the way for the recent rape-revenge films, such as *Audition* (Miike: 1999) and *Freeze Me* (Ishii: 2000).

VIOLATION

In his case study of *Freeze Me*, Lafond compares the film to the original cycle of rape-revenge works such as *I Spit on Your Grave* (Zarchi: 1978) and *Ms 45* (Ferrara: 1981) in order to stress 'the film's specific cultural social concerns' (Lafond 2005: 78). While Lafond correctly sees *Freeze Me* as a condemnation of male violence in contemporary Japanese society (2005: 84), he perfunctorily dismisses the director Takashi Ishii's previous involvement with the notorious *Angel Guts* films, based upon his adult manga of the same time. As a result, Lafond constructs a binary distinction between the vengeful Chihiro in *Freeze Me* and the character of Nami, as violated woman, in the *Angel Guts* films, stating that: 'His first films depict nothing but sexual stereotypes' (2005: 77).

In Hantke's discussion of *Audition* he refers to the positive critical reception of the film in the West and asks, 'Does *Audition* lack cultural specificity, or is there something specifically "global" about the film that has allowed it to work so well transnationally?' (2005: 55). Hantke suggests that Asami, the avenging angel of *Audition*, can be best understood as a reincarnation of the specifically Japanese pre-modern archetype of the wronged woman, 'which makes visible the social areas, such as the domestic incarceration of women, over which modernisation seems to have passed without leaving a trace.' Hantke goes on to suggest that Western audiences may well perceive the film differently, in the form of a patriarchal backlash against 1960s feminism (2005: 61).

Whilst both Lafond and Hantke offer interesting readings of the contemporary Japanese rape-revenge film, neither locates the emergence of the female avenger as a logical outcome of the oppressed, violated and open body of the woman in mainstream romantic pornography during the 1970s and 1980s. In order to understand the complexities of the contemporary rape-revenge film, it is necessary first to interrogate the representation of rape in Japanese cinema. As the *Angel Guts* series provides a direct link to the rape-revenge film, through Ishii, it seems appropriate to begin by considering the complexity of the representation of rape within these films, and by exploring both their cultural context and possible political subtext.

There has not been any sustained critical discussion of the *Angel Guts* series. Instead their misogyny tends to be taken for granted. The series consists of five 'official' films made between 1978 and 1988 by noted directors such as Sone (*Angel Guts: High School Co-Ed* (1978) and *Angel Guts: Red Classroom* (1979)) and Tanaka (*Angels Guts: Nami* (1979)). The last two films in the series are the directorial debuts of Ikeda (*Angel Guts: Red Porno* (1981)) and Ishii (*Angel Guts: Red Dizziness* (1988)). Two unofficial films followed, both directed by Ishii, called *Original Sin* (1992) and *Angel Guts: Red Lightning* (1994).

Having had to leave Nikkatsu, where he was working as an assistant director, due to poor health, Ishii wrote the groundbreaking adult manga on which the films are based in 1977. The success of the manga led Ishii back to Nikkatsu, first as a writer and then eventually a director. The *Angel Guts* films deal directly, and sometimes unpleasantly, with the relationships between men and women in a society dominated by oppression and domination, force and submission. This is foregrounded through the use of the same central characters, Nami and Muraki, throughout the series.

With its biker gangs, disenfranchised masculinity and gang rape, Sone's *High School Co-Ed* bears similarities to Craven's *The Last House on the Left* (1972) – although rape does not lead to revenge in the former – and Italian director Bava's nihilistic *Rabid Dogs* (1974). It is clear that the representation of acts of violence towards women by men in cinema in the 1970s was not something specific to Japan. Sharp points out, in the commentary to *High School Co-Ed*, 'macho rape fantasies of this type were fairly common within European Exploitation Cinema' (2005).

In *High School Co-Ed*, Nami (Machiko Ohtani), is the archetypical victim, an innocent young schoolgirl who is subject to the unwanted attentions of a group of aggressive young bikers (*bōsōzoku*), made up of Kajima (Kenji Kasai), the gang leader, Tetsurō Kawashima (Sansho Shinsui), the protagonist, and Sadakuni (Tatsuma Higuchi). In the first film, Nami does not play a significant narrative role, but functions as an object of desire and exchange within the male group. Here, as in *I Spit on Your Grave* and *Last House on the Left*, the rapes 'are presented as almost sexless acts of cruelty that the men seem to commit more for each other's edification than for their own physical pleasure' (Clover 1992: 118).

This is clear from the opening sequences, in which the gang force a yellow car off the road and terrorise the young couple travelling in it. The fact that we have not been introduced to either the male rapists or the couple in the car makes the following rape sequence disturbing. Wearing a virginal white dress, the woman is raped first by Tetsurō and then passed over to Kajima. During the rape, the motorbikes are strategically placed as to ensure that the actual act itself remains hidden, as necessitated by Japanese censorship regulations at the time. Both men keep their motorcycle helmets on during the rape, which means that there is no point of identification for the spectator.

The motorcycle helmets also work to set Tetsurō and Kajima apart from Sadakuni visually. Sadakuni wears sunglasses instead. This is significant, because as it transpires, Sadakuni is not able to participate in the gang rape, although he does join in with the two men, as they talk and joke over the woman's raped body, making gestures at each other and even discussing Sadakuni's mother. Once Kajima is finished he offers her to Sadakuni, but Sadakuni becomes violent and brings out a knife with which to cut the woman rather than rape her. Sadakuni's impotency seems to suggest that rape is a type of homosocial, if not homosexual, bonding ritual. This is very reminiscent of

the rape of Jennifer in *I Spit on Your Grave*, when Matthew is unable to participate in the violation. Clover remarks, '[It] is against his failed performance
that the others can define their own as successful.' She continues, 'For *I Spit
on Your Grave*, at least, gang rape has first and foremost to do with male sport
and male pecking order and only secondarily to do with sex' (1992: 122).

And whilst Sadakuni and Kajima are constructed as fundamentally
unsympathetic and increasingly unstable characters, Tetsurō's role outside the
group, as protector, brother and surrogate father of his sister, Megu (Megu
Kawashima), provides a more empathetic point of identification. At the same
time, socio-economic conditions are posited as a possible explanation, but not
excuse, for the gang's brutalisation of women. Tetsurō lives in some anonymous
manufacturing suburb of Japan, and the backdrop to the events is a bleak,
steel-grey industrial landscape. The male group is presented as marginalised,
disconnected from wider society and fundamentally alienated in their relation
to the new changing landscape of Japan. As Clover remarks, in relation to *I
Spit on Your Grave*:

> The 'explanation' that *I Spit on Your Grave* presents on the gender axis
> is thus one having to do not with the male sexual nature per se (that is,
> the individual male's sexual appetite) but with male social nature, or male
> sexual nature as it is constituted by group dynamics. (1992: 123)

The formation of the group identity over the traumatised bodies of women
is particularly resonant in terms of Japanese societal structures, in which to be
part of the in-group (*uchi*) is seen as preferable to being an outsider (*soto*). The
increasing tension and struggle for power between Tetsurō and Kajima is first
seen when Tetsurō prevents Kajima from assaulting a young schoolgirl, Nami,
who comes to play a pivotal role later on. As a consequence, Kagami threatens
Megu, which suggests that 'the woman's body only serves as a mediator for
these same sex fantasies, the channels through which the characters relate to
one another' (Sharp 2005).

The rape of Nami is central in *High School Co-Ed*, as it is in all the *Angel
Guts* films. At first Tetsurō is reluctant to rape Nami as she reminds him of his
sister, Megu, but he is forced into it by the male group. The scene in which
Tetsurō rapes Nami sets the standard for similar set-pieces in the next four
films in the series. The gang waits until Nami is forced to walk home in the
rain after school, before chasing her and eventually cornering her in a deserted
train yard. There is a coldness captured by the dingy blue narrow interior
spaces between trains in which the attack takes place. Tetsurō treats Nami
violently, putting on a show for the other two men who are watching. He hits
her, drags her along the ground, and with his hands around her throat begins
to strangle her, at which point Nami goes limp, her resistance gone. In the rape

scene, Tetsurō treats Nami as if she was his lover, tenderly caressing her, his gentleness in direct opposition to his earlier brutality.

In opposition to the rape sequences in the remainder of the series, this scene is notable for its unflinching camera work, panned in on the face of the victim as she is violated. In contrast to the absence of sound during the rape sequences in *I Spit on Your Grave*, low romantic music can be heard as the rain falls on the face of Nami as she raped. This unfamiliar juxtaposition between romantic love and sexual violence foregrounds a theme which is found in all the *Angel Guts* films, in which the fantasy of rape is contradicted by the reality of the act itself. At the same time, the driving rain in which Nami washes herself in the foreground, whilst the men fight over her in the background, inaugurates a dominant motif of the series, in which rain is used to signify both alienation and isolation.

Unlike in the previous group rape scene when the body of the woman was circulated between the men, Tetsurō refuses to pass Nami to Kajima. This is a pivotal moment in which Tetsurō breaks with the group. However, the fact that his sister, Megu, ends up suffering for his actions when she is herself raped by Kajima, is typical of Japanese cinema at the time. The film ends with Tetsurō's violent act of self-annihilation, when he brutally murders a Yakuza and is subsequently captured by the police.

Although rape is important in this first film in the *Angel Guts* series, it is only significant within the main narrative theme of male alienation in modern industrial Japan. Here 'Representations of rape, and the figure of the raped women ... operate as the ground over which the terms of the social – and the sexual – contract are secured' (Horeck 2004: 9). The next four films in the *Angel Guts* series portray rape in a very different manner and fantasy takes over from reality. With the introduction of Muraki as the male protagonist, and the focalisation of the narrative mainly through Nami's point of view, *Angel Guts: Red Classroom* sets the trend for the remaining films in the series. It is on the relationship between Muraki and Nami, as somehow symbolic of relationships between men and women more generally, that these later films focus.

The opening sequences of *Red Classroom* show a young schoolgirl being gang-raped, before self-reflexively the camera pulls back to show that this is in fact a film being shown to a small group of men, in an underground cinema. One of the men, Muraki (Keizo Kanie), a photographer for an adult magazine, becomes obsessed with the woman in the film, whom we learn is Nami (Yuuki Mizuhara), and sets about trying to find her. When he eventually tracks her down, he is disturbed to discover that the original rape in the film was not a performance, but rather the real thing. Again, as in *High School Co-Ed*, rape as patriarchal fantasy is exposed as being predicated on the exploited female body. This revelation provides a moment of subversion against the eroticism of the raped female body in the opening sequence by undermining its fantasy value.

Nami takes Muraki to a 'love hotel' (love hotels are dedicated to couples, and are in demand as space is at a premium in Japanese households), as experience has taught her that this is what any man or all men want from her. Seeing himself as a 'knight in shining armour' and Nami as 'a damsel in distress', Muraki proposes to do a spread in his magazine in order to help her regain her tarnished status. They set up a meeting for the next evening, but the police arrest Muraki on the charge of under-age pornography. While Muraki denies knowing the age of the young girl that he photographed, this scene is used to imply that Muraki is no better than the group of men who raped Nami.

Three years later, Muraki is a husband and father, but remains obsessed with Nami, in her absence constructing her as some sort of Confucian ideal of womanhood. This introduces the theme of the *Otaku* to the series, played out through the increasingly alienated and isolated male protagonist, whose subjectivity is constructed outside traditional social structures. The term *Otaku* was originally associated with readers of anime, but gradually came to denote an unhealthy obsession with an ideal, whilst at the same time referring to someone who never leaves the house.

Muraki in *Red Classroom* is not a yet fully-fledged *Otaku*, as his relationship with his wife and child demonstrates. As we shall see, in the fourth film in the series, *Red Porno*, Muraki is the very epitome of the *Otaku*, who has no life outside the room that he rents and the pornographic magazines that he uses to pleasure himself. It is clear in *Red Classroom* that the narrative, as in the remaining films in the series, is a permutation of the stories of tragic lovers that, as we have seen, are so prevalent in Japanese popular culture and art. This is expressed through mise-en-scène and cinematography. A cinematic palate of primary colours – reds, blues and yellows – and periods of torrential rain provide the background to this contemporary story of tragic love. In *Red Classroom*, this is emphasised when Muraki finally discovers Nami working as a prostitute in a seedy bar, selling her body to any man who wants it. Her total degradation is made clear in two crucial sequences. In the first we see Nami encourage her pimp to urinate on her naked body. In the second, watched by Muraki, Nami is sexually used and abused by a group of six men, before being sold to the highest bidder. Once again we have a conflict between idealised fantasy and 'real life', which self-reflexively comments on the violated female body as erotic fantasy and spectacle in Japanese popular culture. This is shown when Nami's lover brings a young schoolgirl, who has been hidden in the basement, for the sexual pleasure of the group of men. As Nami gazes over to the young girl being raped, her face remains expressionless. And so the cycle of abuse repeats itself. These two scenes of Nami's degradation make it clear, as does the subsequent scene between Muraki and Nami in the driving rain, that Nami's identity and humanity have been fully extinguished by the brutality of the men that surround her.

Nami goes from innocent schoolgirl in the first film in the series, to prostitute in the second and career-driven working woman in the third. Directed by Noboru, *Nami* (1979) is significantly more violent and brutal than Sone's first two entries in the series. The plot of *Nami* centres around a magazine reporter, the Nami (Eri Kanuma) of the title, who is doing a piece on rape for the magazine she works for, which is called 'The Woman'. Here Muraki (Takeo Chii) is also a reporter, whose sister has been a victim of a violent rape. Muraki teams up with Nami, and ends up trying but failing to save her. Whilst the purpose of the article is to explore the effect of rape on victims, and how they manage to continue with their lives, Nami becomes increasingly obsessed, and ultimately aroused by the stories that she forces the victims to relate to her in graphic detail. In one scene, while she is in the shower, Nami is shown fantasising about one of the stories she has been told. Here it is Nami, rather than Muraki, who confuses the fantasy of rape with the reality of the violent act itself. It is only when Nami interviews a nurse, a survivor of a particularly violent rape, that she discovers the reality that underlies the fantasy. In the process she becomes yet another victim and statistic of sexual violence, as the disturbed nurse attempts to act out the violence perpetrated against her by using Nami as her substitute.

At this point, the narrative disintegrates and reality and hallucination prove interchangeable as Nami becomes unhinged. Her deteriorating hold on reality is contained within the increasingly swerved angles and red filters that constitute much of the mise-en-scène for the final half-hour. She continues to have fantasies about being raped, and in one scene accuses the whole staff of the magazine of abusing her. Again Muraki tries to prevent her total annihilation but fails, as do all the variants of Muraki in all the *Angel Guts* films. The film ends when Nami, for whom all men have become potential rapists, kills Muraki.

The fourth film, *Red Porno*, directed by Ikeda, is the most explicit film in the series, and borders on hard-core pornography in places. Nami (Jun Izumi) now works in a department store. Asked one evening to stand in at a photo session for a friend, Nami discovers to her horror that it is for an S&M magazine, called *Red Porno*. She is coerced into posing for photographs and the edition in which these are published becomes a bestseller, leading to her being sacked from her job. Again, this can be seen as a comment on the contrast between the ubiquity of sadomasochistic imagery and idealised constructions of appropriate femininity in Japanese society, 'where traditional values and codes of decorum coexist with a highly organized and professional marketing of sex for consumption' (Lloyd 2002: 72).

This time Muraki (Masahiko Abe) is the very epitome of the sad isolated *Otaku* generation. He lives in a rented flat, which he rarely leaves, and spends most of his time looking out of his window. The very opening scenes of the film construct an alienated and isolated mise-en-scène of desire, which also functions to situate Nami and Muraki as doubles. The first scene shows Nami masturbating, with her legs under a *kotatsu* (a Japanese heated table). The camera zooms in until Nami's red-lit crotch fills the screen, unwavering in its direct gaze, as she brings herself to orgasm. In the following scene, Muraki is similarly shown masturbating, whilst looking at photographs of Nami. In a later sequence, Muraki watches through his window as a young schoolgirl uses everyday objects to masturbate. An egg and pencils provide her with simulacra of the male phallus. As she orgasms, the egg breaks, yellow and red juices commingling as it runs down her legs. These solitary acts of pleasure obviously function as erotic spectacles, but at the same time the visual distance between Nami and Muraki, and Muraki and the schoolgirl, seems to suggest an alienated and isolated desire, a poor substitute for an intimate relationship between two people.

Not only does Nami lose her job, but her married lover also breaks up their affair, and she becomes more and more isolated, as shown in the masturbation sequence towards the conclusion of the film where Nami uses the leg of her *kotatsu* as a substitute for the penis. Muraki eventually persuades Nami, his idealised fantasy woman, to meet up with him. However, as in the preceding films in the series, the relationship between Muraki and Nami is thwarted by circumstances beyond their control. On his way to meet Nami, the husband of a woman who takes him for a pervert and rapist shoots Muraki, whose *Otaku*-style existence has caused concern within the community. In a highly symbolic scene, Muraki falls down a flight of stairs, and his body is framed against broken mannequins, lying at the bottom of the stairs. These mannequins are women as object, stripped of her physicality, and symbolise the female body as commodity, mimicking self-reflexively the double standards by which real woman cannot compete with an idealised femininity. Muraki struggles to make it to his date with Nami and holds out a red umbrella to her, before he dies. The umbrella, as we have already seen, is a motif of tragic love, and here its colour obviously symbolises desire. At the same time, this series of scenes implies that Muraki has an idealised, romanticised vision of Nami – hence the symbolism of the passive mannequins – which is at odds with the reality of female identity and sexuality. In an interview, Takeshi Ishii (2005) argues that Nami's frigidity is a symbolic metaphor for Japan's frigidity after the Occupation.

At the same time, censorship regulations are constitutive of an 'erotics of the fetish', in which the covered crotch, as signalled through the repeated use of panty shots, is fetishised. It is not, however, just the female body that is fragmented, as a result of the need both to show desire and to conceal the actual operation of desire; the penis cannot be shown either. However, the symbolic phallus is omnipresent, displaced on to everyday domestic objects, such as a table leg, a showerhead, an egg and pencils. In addition, the centrality of the breast in sex scenes, as the only object of desire that can be shown, stands as metonymic signifier of both male and female desire.

In the first four films, Nami is not just all women or any woman, but also the eternal victim, born to be raped, abused and dominated in an unjust patriarchal society in which she has no identity beyond her objectification. However, Muraki fares no better; in his various guises, he is pornographer, stalker, fantasist and *Otaku*. The final film in the series, *Red Dizziness*, is much more a romantic melodrama than a pornographic film, even though it has the obligatory number of sex scenes required by *roman porno*. Here Nami (Mayako Katsuragi) is a nurse, who, whilst on night shift, is subjected to a violent but unsuccessful rape by two of her male patients. Fleeing back to her home and her boyfriend, a pornographic photographer, she finds him having sex with one of his models (Jun Izumi). Betrayed, she leaves the house and flees.

Muraki (Naoto Takenaka) is a stockbroker who has been embezzling money from his clients and employers. His wife has left him as a consequence of the threatening phone calls they have been receiving, and Muraki is a man on the edge. Desperate, he leaves his house and gets into his car. Not watching the road, he knocks Nami off her bicycle and, convinced she is dead, puts her body into the front seat of the car whilst he decides what to do with her. Suddenly realising that Nami is still alive, Muraki ties her up and tries to have sex with her on the front seat whilst she is unconscious. However, like Nami's male patients, Muraki is unable to penetrate her, and Nami suddenly wakes up to find, once again, an attempted violation of her body.

Nami runs away but Muraki catches her, and they end up together in a dilapidated and deserted building where Muraki again attempts and fails to rape her. Indeed, the last film in the series is about the inability rather than the ability to rape, and suggests that a relationship between a man and woman needs to be based upon mutual love and trust. The remaining narrative details the growing relationship between Nami and Muraki, both isolated and alienated characters, eventually leading to an erotic and extended sex session between the two at a 'love hotel'. But as in all *Angel Guts* films, it seems that men and women are not meant to be together. Muraki leaves to buy petrol and is shot for no apparent reason. As he promised earlier, his spirit returns to her, to the deserted building where their relationship began, as symbolised by the broken tape recorder which suddenly works again. A song of romantic love comes out of the radio, as Nami stands alone in the dark. The film ends with Nami's realisation that Muraki is not coming back.

However strong the desire may be to dismiss the *Angels Guts* series of films as pure sexploitation, in their unflinching vision of the raped, violated and abused women these films work at some level as an indictment of the oppressive nature of Japanese paternalism. It is true to say of these films that there is little in the way of positive male characterisation, and as such, this draws parallels to the original rape-revenge cycle in America, in which 'all men are presented as sexually repulsive' (Lehman 1993: 109). Lehman comments, 'The male spectator can hate rather than simply identify with these men who embody desires similar to their own' (1993: 112).

At the same time, the constant objectification of the female body, its fragmentation into a series of fetishistic body parts – breasts, legs, the covered crotch – is in a sense at odds with the underlying narrative of female oppression in Japanese society and the commodification of the female body as an object of exchange between men. And the reference to 'guts' in the title has symbolic importance as a reference to the sacred and aesthetic dimension of being which is often constrained by the rules and regulations of Japanese society. It is difficult to deny the political sub-text of the *Angel Guts* films and the implicit, if not explicit, criticism of Japanese society's oppression of woman.

ANTI-MODERNITY AND THE NATIONAL BODY

Angura is the name given to an art movement of the 1960s, which was characterised by its opposition to modernity. Matsui explores the origins of anti-modern thinking in the wake of the Meiji Government in 1867, through which 'modernization in Japan has unambiguously meant the acceptance and domestication of Western theories and aesthetics' (2002: 142). At the same time, the preservation of the *ie* system meant that Japan had, in Matsui's words:

> a self-contradictory social structure in which utilitarian competition was encouraged, while the preservation of the overprotective structure of the Japanese family by public institutions prevents the development of individualism and original thinking. (2002: 142)

This incomplete modernity as a result of the enforced modernisation of Japan through the adoption and integration of Western ideas and values sat uncomfortably with traditional Japanese ethics and paternalism. This conflict was often explored in literature and the visual arts, through the reassertion 'of the pre-modern Japanese "motherly" sensibility' against 'the influence of modern Western "patriarchal" culture' (Matsui 2002: 143). The late 1960s and the early 1970s saw the spread of anti-modern spirit, or what Matsui terms 'a return of the repressed Japanese "body"' (2002: 144). *Angura* culture also focused on the domestic spaces, rather than the public sphere. The reason for the rise of the *Angura* movement included the failure of political protest against the Japan–US Security Treaty and the repression of the students' protest movement against the authoritarian policies of Japanese universities between 1968 and 1972 (Matsui 2002: 144). This anti-modern sentiment was contained within a counter-cultural movement, which asserted the body, or *nikutai*, against the intellect. Matsui writes, 'the energy of Japanese youth ran to the production of underground dance and theatre, pornographic films and narrative comics' (2002: 144). However, in the aftermath of the United Red Army murder case in 1972, whose members were associated with the left-wing tendencies of the *Angura* movement, the meaning of *Angura* became associated more with underground comics, whose theme concerned 'lyrically depicting the details of their daily life with a sense of isolation and frustrated sexuality' (Matsui 2002: 147).

VENGEANCE

The *Angel Guts* series provides a useful position from where to start to consider the recent emergence of the rape-revenge film in Japanese horror cinema, rather than contextualising it in the light of the original American rape-revenge cycle. Certainly it becomes possible to see the figure of Chihiro (Harumi Inoue) in *Freeze Me* as another variation on the eternal female that is the key theme in Ishii's work. In these terms, Chihiro, the beautiful office worker, could as easily have been called Nami, and Nogami, her boyfriend, Muraki. The pivotal difference here is, of course, that Chihiro fights back against male oppression, unlike the various incarnations of Nami in the *Angel Guts* series. Similarly, in Miike's *Audition*, the ethereal and beautiful Asami Yamazaki (Eihi Shiina) is no longer the mutilated, violated body of traditional Japanese narratives of rape, but an avenging angel who mutilates the male body, transposing it into a series of body parts, the narrative position originally occupied by the woman.

> Portraying rape through flashback demonstrates how trauma returns and imposes itself upon the subject, but also self-consciously positions the cinema audience, calling attention to their role as spectators. (Horeck 2004: 105)

Both *Freeze Me* and *Audition* present the rape/abuse of the central character through a series of flashbacks, rather than directly. The driving rain against which the credits are set in *Freeze Me* clearly signifies the alienation and oppression of Chihiro, as the next two scenes also demonstrate. The first scene is a short sequence of Chihiro as a child, standing on a deserted pavement under a street lamp as snow flurries envelop her, whilst the sounds of a struggle are heard. In the present, Chihiro is shown as a confident, articulate and self-assured young women, exchanging banter with her workmates and her boyfriend. As she sits typing in the darkened office, she is suddenly grabbed from behind, a hand groping her breast; as this happens, the film switches to a grainy format, capturing the terrified expression on Chihiro's face. Unlike the traditional dualistic format of the rape-revenge film, *Freeze Me*, like *Audition*, embeds the events of the past within the present-time format of the narrative. In doing so, both films suggest the continued influence of past oppression on their female protagonists, as well as connotating the pre-modern body, associated with the feminine spirit, in which 'a co-existence of different historical moments attains ... a reality through individual or collective memory' (Matsui 2002: 144).

It is perhaps no coincidence, given the *Angel Guts* series of films, that it transpires that Chihiro has been gang-raped by three thoroughly unpleasant and unredeemable male characters as a child. The past seeps into the present as one of the rapists, Hirokawa, turns up on Chihiro's doorstep. Again, driving rain and snow are utilised to create an imagistic system of oppression and isolation as Chihiro flees and takes the lift back up to her apartment. Threatening her with exposure, as if somehow the rape was her fault, Hirokawa proceeds to abuse her again. As such, *Freeze Me* foregrounds the stigma of shame and loss of honour attached to a rape victim, commenting on a paternalistic society which continues to function through the oppression of women. It is society that allows men such as Hirokawa to use and abuse women as simple objects of exchange. Even Kojima, the second rapist from the past who first asks for her forgiveness, is quick to blame the rape on Chihiro, before attempting again to force himself on her. Baba, the third rapist, is the typical self-obsessed *Otaku*, playing his violent video games whilst Chihiro is forced to wait on him hand and foot. No longer is rape a mechanism through which to liberate female desire from its oppression; instead it is seen as the very basis of that oppression. As is the convention in the rape-revenge film, Chihiro takes a bloody and violent revenge against each of her attackers separately. Using close-at-hand domestic objects – a bottle filled with water, a hammer – and wrapping the bodies up in plastic, Chihiro utilises the space of the domestic (interiority) to turn the tables on the men. The corpses of the men she keeps in industrial-size freezers, finding their company much more amenable when they are simply objects. Here the male body as object subverts the traditional idealisation of the female body.

There is no happy ending for Chihiro. Earlier her boyfriend, Nogami, is repelled when Hirokawa offers to sell her to him and relates her rape in detail. Instead of 'saving her', Nogami flees. In a society predicated on female respectability, Chihiro is now 'damaged goods' and no longer marriageable. *Freeze Me* seems to be suggesting, as we saw in *Rashōmon*, that 'rape' is still constituted as somehow the responsibility of the victim, rather than the violator. Nogami returns, just as Chihiro is about to flee the country, giving her hope that she can start again. But Nogami is constructed as little better than her rapists, as Lafond points out:

In fact, Nogami's acts are clearly at variance with his declaration of intent: he pretends to be concerned about Chihiro's problem, although he is clearly more interested in her body as he keeps fondling her breasts during his whole monologue. (2005: 83)

Her one symbol of hope dies when she is forced to kill Nogami after he discovers the body of one of her rapists. As such, *Freeze Me* is no more optimistic than the earlier *Angel Guts* films in imagining an equal and equitable relationship between the sexes. The final image, which suggests that Chihiro is also dead, provides a bleak commentary on the oppression of women in Japanese society.

Miike's *Audition* also explores the gap between men and women, and similarly suggests an unbridgeable chasm between the two by utilising a variation on the rape-revenge format. Unlike Ichii's *Freeze Me*, *Audition* was marked by a general consensus of agreement as to its critical merits in the West. And

Fig. 5.1 Asami, the epitome of idealised womanhood, *Audition* (Takashi Miike, 1999, Omega / The Kobal Collection)

it was the perceived perversity of the ending sequences that, arguably, created a general buzz amongst film viewers as a whole. For most of the film, the narrative plays out as a typical romantic drama, albeit with a twist. A middle-aged widower, Aoyama (Ryo Ishibashi), seeks to find himself a new wife by duplicitous means by auditioning (hence the title of the film) for an actress for a part in a low-budget independent film with the help of his friend Yoshikawa (Jun Kunimura), who works in the film business. Unlike the typical male character in Japanese rape dramas, Aoyama is fundamentally a respectable and sympathetic character, providing a possible point of identification for the (male) spectator. Asami, a beautiful and seemingly demure young woman, seems to meet all of Aoyama's criteria; she appears to be the epitome of passive Japanese womanhood and respectability, as contained within the discourse of *ryōsaikenbo*. In his promise to Asami that he will love only her, a promise that he cannot keep, Aoyama is – the film suggests – at least partly culpable for Asami's violent revenge against him.

During a romantic weekend together, Asami disappears. The remaining narrative focuses on Aoyama's obsessive search for her. All he discovers are lies and half-truths; men who have been in contact with her are either missing or dead, and the ballet school at which she learnt to dance is boarded up and derelict. In the end it is not Aoyama who finds Asami (as, in a sense, she never really existed outside his fantasies), but Asami in her role of murderous and sadistic *fatal femme* (Pidduck 1995: 65) who finds Aoyama. In a subversion of the conventions of Japanese sadomasochistic pornography, in which the violated and open body of the woman functioned as an object of sadistic pleasure, it is now the paralysed, impotent and objectified male body that is now experimented on by Asami with her steel wire and sharp pins.

In his search for Asami, the places to which Aoyama goes are filtered through a red lens, signifying corruption, disease, sexuality and impurity. In one scene, set in the old dance school, the crippled figure of Asami's uncle and abuser (Renji Ishibashi) plays the piano, whilst next to him a bin full of bloody long sharp sticks attracts flies. Here the mise-en-scène signifies something corrupt and malevolent, something festering away at the heart of Japanese society. Similarly, the old building where Asami used to live is a place of death, bodily corruption and abjection, as Aoyama sees from the corner of his eye a palpating tongue, a symbol for the female vulva. As the final events take place, the film dips in and out of hallucination and nightmare: Asami, a pretty young girl in her ballet costume, being abused by her uncle with long hot sticks in the past; Asami, cutting off the head of her uncle in the present; Asami as a fetishised schoolgirl with her head in Aoyama's lap. While the figure of the *fatal femme* can be understood as a feminist statement, Mes suggests that *Audition* 'is about two people who misunderstand each other; and this (often unconscious) mistreatment works both ways' (2004: 204).

SEX AND VIOLENCE

> The densely populated and highly gendered space of the city is counter-balanced in Japanese visual culture that uses sex as a form of dissent, transgression or disobedience that rejects the effects of Japanese modern-ization and frequently returns to pre-modern indigenous traditions which, focussing on the raw body, became metaphors for the violation of the national psyche or body of Japan ... the uncovering of this power is a form of resistance which enables critical reflection. (Lloyd 2002: 16–17)

The aggressiveness of both the erotic and scopic drives in the *Angel Guts* films brings together Eros (life) and Thantos (Death), sex and violence, as a form of counter-cultural protest against modernity, Westernisation and commodi-fication. The libidinal and abject body, as constructed through both the violated female body and the saturated mise-en-scène of primary colours, condenses multiple traumatic events in the construction of the modern Japan. These events include Japan's colonisation of Korea and the use of Korean women as comfort women (forced to prostitute themselves for Japanese soldiers during and after the Second World War), the bombings of Hiroshima and Nagasaki, and the subsequent Allied Occupation. The *Angel Guts* series, with its emphasis on the taboo and marginalised areas of society, can most profitably be under-stood as part of this counter-cultural movement. Whether rape is a male or female fantasy, these films suggest that the reality that underlies the fantasy is brutal and has real consequences. At the same time, the films expose the contra-dictions within Japanese society, in which the commodification of sex exists uneasily side by side with traditional discourses of appropriate femininity. Further, it is possible to interpret these films as feminist, as the 'trashing of the Confucian ideal of woman as demure and submissive is one of the essentials of Japanese feminism' (Bornoff 2002: 51). And, although gendered images of violence are fundamentally unpleasant, it is necessary to tackle such images in order to challenge and change 'the meanings and rewards attached to violence in our society' (Boyle 2005: 49).

While Williams's discussion of pornography as a genre may well be appli-cable to the *Angel Guts* films, the films themselves are not paradigmatic examples of pornography. Indeed, as we have seen, these were mainstream productions, financed by Nikkatsu, one of the main studios at the time. And although it could be argued that the films eroticise rape through its visuali-sation, we are positioned through the use of the subjective shot (point-of-view) to have empathy with the female victims. Neither is it true to say that pornog-raphy is inherently transgressive, even in relation to Japanese pink cinema (either independent or mainstream); films such as *Crazy Lips* (Sasaki: 2000), which portray the repeated violation of the female body as little more than erotic spectacle, exist side by side with films that offer nuanced explorations of sexual desire such as *The Woman in Black Underwear* and *Lunchbox*. In relation to Rousseau's *Le Lévite d'Ephraïm*, Horeck writes that the substitution of a woman's body for that of a man's operates as 'an attempt to distinguish self and other through the medium of the woman as rapable object'. In doing so, the rapable female body denies the possibility of homosexual desire and constructs the male body as exempt from violation (Horeck 2004: 52). Citizenship then is made possible through the violation of the body of the woman, but at the same time, the tenuous nature of the socio-sexual bond is revealed (Horeck 2004: 65). The visual and symbolic gap between men and women in the *Angel Guts* films clearly articulates anxieties around the instability of the socio-sexual contract and can be related to the transformations in the socio-political framework of Japan at a time of unprecedented economic and social change.

While Lafond (2005) suggests that *Freeze Me* can be understood through comparison to the American rape-revenge film, the contemporary Japanese rape-revenge film is a continuation of, rather than a break with, the violated, traumatised and raped body commonly found in *roman porno*. In relation to *I Spit on Your Grave*, Boyle states that 'such self-conscious performances of rape myths arguably draw attention to their absurdity' (2005: 139). In their depiction of the gap between violent men and abused women, *Freeze Me* and *Audition* continue the themes laid down in the *Angel Guts* films. Chihiro and Asami are just one more face of the wronged women in Japanese culture. Neither of these women can find solace in the present, as the traumas of their pasts (as connotative of the historical past) cannot be forgotten; nor can they be forgiven. They are victims of repression and oppression, and only death and loneliness remain for them.

CHAPTER 6

Zombies, Cannibals
and the Living Dead

With more than 24 million sales worldwide, the *Resident Evil* video game franchise began in 1996 with *Resident Evil* for Playstation 1. The game is based upon an earlier one, only released in Japan, called *Sweet Home*, which is often compared to Hooper's *Poltergeist*. The video game series has so far spawned three films, *Resident Evil* (Anderson: 2002), *Resident Evil Apocalypse* (Witt: 2004) and *Resident Evil: Extinction* (Mulcahy: 2007).

Perhaps surprisingly, taking into account the success of the zombie-haunted spaces of the *Resident Evil* games, there are not that many Japanese zombie films. Whilst one of the alternative titles of *The Discarnates* was *Summer amongst the Zombies*, the film bears very little relation to what in the West we conceive of as a zombie film; there is very little gore and no scenes of cannibalism, and the dead return looking for love rather than as consuming revenants who threaten the world with apocalyptic destruction. Most Japanese zombie films have emerged in the wake of the success of *Resident Evil*, including *Versus* (Kitamura), *Wild Zero* (Takeuchi) and *Junk* (Muroga), all released in 2000, and *Stacy* the following year. More recently, we have *Tokyo Zombie* (2005), based upon the manga by Yūsaku Hanakuma and directed by Satō.

Satō's *Naked Blood* (1995) is one of the few cannibal films to come out of Japan. Slater writes that the film 'takes the theme of cannibalism to a new extreme' (2002: 15). A science fiction/horror hybrid, it takes as its premise a drug called 'My Son', whose purpose is to eradicate pain by producing a massive secretion of endorphins. Three women, who are taking part in a trial of new contraceptive drug, unknowingly also become test subjects for 'My Son', run by Yuki Kure (Masumi Nakao).

The first woman (Yumika Hayashi) develops a voracious appetite for human flesh, and more specifically her own. In a series of disturbingly graphic scenes, she is shown eating her fingers after having plunged them into tempura batter; cutting off her labium and devouring it as if it was a great delicacy; sawing through her breast before with relish eating her nipple; and then, after thrusting a knife into her eye, cheerfully eating it, all the time moaning in (sexual) pleasure. The second woman (Mika Kirihara) becomes a human pincushion, also feeling pleasure instead of pain as she mutilates her body with jewellery and a variety of other sharp objects. Whilst these acts of self-harm are taking place, Eiji (Sadao Abe), the seventeen-year-old son of Yuki, who is responsible for adding 'My Son' to his mother's contraceptive drug, is shown filming the results of his experiment, calling to mind comparisons with Powell's study of male voyeurism and masochism in *Peeping Tom* (1960).

The manner in which the women die, as a result of gluttony and vanity, bears a superficial resemblance to Fincher's *Se7en* (1995), in which characters meet their deaths in a manner befitting their lives. The final woman, Rika Mikami (Misa Aika), traumatised as a result of her first ever period, is an insomniac and the drug affects her differently. Instead of finding pleasure in her own pain, she finds pleasure in the pain of others. Not only does she kill the other women, including Yuki, but she also slits Eiji's throat after making love.

The apocalyptic end sequences show Rika, with her young son (whose father we presume is Eiji), in the middle of an empty and deserted landscape, determined to rid the world of all living plants; the exception is the cactus, with which she is shown communicating in previous scenes through the use of virtual reality headsets. Hunter writes:

> Mixing shock gore with cybersex, medical fetishism, video mediation, narcolepsy and Nietzschian notions of eternal return, *Naked Blood* may well be the ultimate fusion of the visceral, the psychopathological and the metaphysical, a film whose nearest analogue in Western cinema would be the work of David Cronenberg. (1998: 139)

Unlike Italian cannibal films, such as *Deep River Savages* (Lenzi: 1972) and Deodato's *Last Cannibal World* (1977) and subsequent *Cannibal Holocaust* (1979), in which members of expeditions to the Amazon Basin meet up with flesh-eating natives and rarely escape with their lives, *Naked Blood* explicitly links cannibalism with commodity fetishisation and consumerism. As such, *Naked Blood* has more similarities with the zombie film than the cannibal film.

As Slater points out, 'defining a "real" zombie movie is difficult' (2002: 15). However, he goes on to make a crucial distinction between spirits of the dead and the living dead, as in the Haitian myth (2002: 17). Further, cannibal and zombie myths have different origin stories – tribal ritualistic cannibalism as opposed to the soulless corpses of the living dead controlled by black or voodoo magic. Romero's *Night of the Living Dead* (1968) and *Dawn of the Dead* (1978) transformed the zombie and cannibal into the composite living corpse motivated purely by hunger for human flesh. Known as *Zombi* in Italy, *Dawn of the Dead* spawned hundreds of zombie films, including Fulci's *Zombie Flesh Eaters* in 1979, which was retitled *Zombi 2* in order to cash in on the success of Romero's film.

The shuffling zombies in the Japanese zombie film tend to be recycled revenants of the zombie films of the 1970s and 1970s, as in *Junk* and *Wild Zero*. At the same time, these zombies owe as much to contemporary popular culture, both American and Japanese, as they do to their earlier prototypes. *Junk* is perhaps closer to what we in the West have come to expect from a zombie film than *Wild Zero*, *Versus* or indeed *Stacy*, with its schoolgirl zombies. And whilst *Versus* does feature zombies, it would be difficult to categorise it within the generic features of the zombie film.

RESURRECTION

Kitamura's *Versus*, with its forest of resurrection and battle between immortals, is as far away from the conventions of the zombie film as it is possible to get. An escaped prisoner, KSC2–303 (Tak Sakaguchi), finds himself trapped in a menacing forest, hunted down by a Yakuza gang, hired assassins, two policeman and a mysterious man (Hideo Sakaki). A mysterious beautiful girl (Chieko Misaka), whose blood contains the power of rebirth, stands between KSC2–303 and the Man. With a nod to Stephen King's *Dark Tower* series, with its gunslingers, wastelands and mysterious man in black; Argento's *The Stendhal Syndrome* (1996); the Wachowski brothers' science fiction-defining *The Matrix* (1999); Romero's *The Night of the Living Dead* and Fulci's *Zombie Flesh Eaters*; with a plot derived from *Highlander* (Mulcahy: 1986); disembodied shot sequences that call to mind Raimi's *The Evil Dead* (1981) and its merging of Hong Kong action sequences (especially with regard to the films of John Woo) with those commonly found in traditional Samurai films; *Versus* is similar to an extended post-modern music video rather than a narrative film.

The plot itself, if in fact it can be called a plot, revolves around the battle between good and evil that has been going on since the beginning of time and will go on until the end of time. Good and evil are embodied by the two protagonists: the Dark Hero and the Man (hence the similarity to *Highlander*). Between the two stands the Girl, the archetypical self-sacrificing woman, whose blood has the power to resurrect the dead. The prologue of the film, set 500 years before, introduces us to the main characters – the Dark Hero, the Man and the Girl – and explains the meaning of the location, the Forest of Resurrection; this is the 444th portal of 666 gates, which allows those killed in it to come back to life. The prologue also introduces the key concept of the karmic cycle, which creates a temporal and spatial connection between the past, present and future. Further, the karmic cycle is an eternal cycle of rebirth, in which good (selfless) and bad (selfish) actions in this life determine our karma in the next. The Dark Hero and his nemesis, the Man, in *Versus* are forced to repeat their encounter throughout eternity. There is no escape for any of the three central characters from their karma. The Dark Hero must battle the Man, and the Girl must be the pawn passing between the men. This is true of the past, as it is of the present and of the future. The final scene is of an apocalyptic world set 99 years in the future, where, amongst the devastated landscape, the battle between the Dark Hero and the Man continues.

The battleground can be interpreted as a type of limbo, between the planes of existence, in which characters cannot die but are forced endlessly to return to life to continue their chosen paths. As the members of the Yakuza gang die one by one, they return to life as zombies, forced into a never-ending cycle of violence and death. Unlike the 1970s zombie, these fire guns, use knives and have the potential to act like sentient beings. And these zombies cannot be killed, even with a shot to the head – a common way of killing these creatures in the traditional zombie film and video games such as *Resident Evil*. When the Man thrusts his hand into the chest of the leader of the Yakuza gang (Kenji Matsuda), removing his heart, the latter does not die. *Versus* totally dispenses with the mythology of the zombie and the implicit criticism of consumerism and capitalism, as connotated by the living dead of Romero's zombie cycle, choosing instead pure kinetic thrills and a post-modern aesthetic based on speed and circulation. As Harper writes in relation to the films of Romero:

> Zombies function in *Dawn of the Dead* as a lumpenproletariat of shifting significance, walking symbols of any oppressed social group. This function is derived in part from their origins in the literature and cinema of the twentieth century, in which zombies are synonymous with oppression and slavery. (2002)

Even though the zombies are to an extent controlled by the Man in *Versus*, they do not function as revenants produced by the oppressive forces of capitalism, as in *Dawn of the Dead*. Cool replaces class, image replaces identity, and style triumphs over substance. *Versus* is representative of a trend in Japanese visual art towards what is known as the 'super-flat aesthetic', epitomised by the pop art of Murakami. Shimada writes that Murakami's 'Superflat Manifesto' proposed 'that everything exists on a flat two dimensional plane situated somewhere between traditional Japanese painting and modern anime' (2002: 188). Shimada comments on how some Western critics and curators 'see Japanese pop culture and its eradication of history and meaning as radical, futuristic and uniquely Japanese' (2002: 188). In opposition to this view stand critics such as Bornoff, who argues that 'Everything about Murakami is commercial – and derivative'

(2002: 66). Again, debates surrounding nationalism and self-orientalism are foregrounded in discussions of Japanese culture. The super-flat surfaces and MTV aesthetics of *Versus* are symptomatic of the trend in Japanese art towards trash aesthetics, which, as I argue later in this chapter, can be seen as a type of *asobi* (play) and as such challenge rather than support the status quo.

INVASION

Wild Zero seems to be more of a marketing tool for the Japanese band, Guitar Wolf, than a sustained political critique. In fact, consumerism is embraced in *Wild Zero*, rather than critiqued, as it is in *Versus*. Like *Versus*, *Wild Zero* 'borrows' from a number of zombie, science fiction and action films, including *Plan 9 from Outer Space* (Wood: 1959), *Rock and Roll High School* (Arkush: 1979) featuring the punk group The Ramones, *Mars Attacks* (Burton: 1996) and even Hitchcock's *Psycho* (1960). As in *Rock and Roll High School*, the protagonist, Ace (Masashi Endō), is a fan of the coolest band on the planet, Guitar Wolf (the band is made up of the appropriately named Guitar Wolf, Drum Wolf and Bass Wolf), with their quiffed hair, black leather trousers and jackets, and motorbikes.

Guitar Wolf's primary mission is to combat the very uncool 'J-Pop', which is in danger of taking over from rock and roll as embodied by The Captain (Makoto Inamiya), in his skin-tight Lycra shorts, who proclaims that 'Rock and Roll is Dead', leading to a shoot-out with the Group. A fan – Ace (Masashi Endō) – helps *Guitar Wolf* out, becoming a 'blood' brother in the process. The fact that they end up battling zombies from outer space, and an assortment of baddies (including a Yakuza gang), seems somehow incidental to the aesthetics of cool that runs throughout the film. Guitar Wolf is forever ensuring that his hair in his place and that he retains his 'cool' (*kakkoii*) image, even during battles with the unending deluge of zombies.

The action takes place in and around the town of Asahi-Cho, the scene of a meteor shower and for some unknown reason the site of the alien invasion. The main love interest in the film, Tobio (Kwancharu Shitichai), whom Ace rescues on more than one occasion from gangs of murderous zombies and other perverts, is anatomically male rather than female, the revelation of which recalls a similar scene in *The Crying Game* (Jordan: 1992). Gender should not, the film proclaims, stand in the way of true love or the aesthetics of cool. Writing about transgender practices in Japan, Lunsing argues that men who 'do not wish to conform to the boundaries of the construction of male gender act to undermine its rigidity' and that such practices 'transgress the typical masculinity associated in Japan with the phrase "*okoko rashiku shinsai*: behave like a man"' (2003: 33). While playful in its approach to the zombie genre, *Wild*

Zero explicitly critiques traditional ideological constructions of masculinity.

In *Wild Zero*, even turning into a zombie should not stand in the way of true love, as in the case of Toschi (one of the few who has not been turned into a zombie), who is reunited with his girlfriend even after she has become one of the living dead. The film's ending, in which Guitar Wolf hacks through the alien ship using his guitar, whilst of course retaining his cool, gives some indication of the sheer lunacy of *Wild Zero*.

However, in its depiction of Japanese youth culture, as epitomised by the casting of the members of Guitar Wolf, *Wild Zero* is continuing within the tradition of youth-orientated films, known as the Sun Tribe or *taiyozoku* films, of the 1950s and 1960s. In 'Imagining a New Japan: The Taiyozoku Films', Raine traces the term to the emergence of a new generation of post-war Japanese youth:

> Like the French term nouvelle vague, the word *taiyozoku* (Sun Tribe) referred to a postwar generation before it was applied to the cinema. It was coined to describe the rich, bored, and vicious characters populating the pages of writer Shintaro Ishihara's books, such as *Season of the Sun* (1955) and *Crazed Fruit* (1956). Those characters embodied all that Japan's postwar disillusioned youth desired, and that Japan's new conservative government feared: absent parents and an excess of money, leisure, and sex. (2005)

The tragic figure of James Dean, as eternally immortalised on celluloid in his most famous role as James Stark in *Rebel without a Cause* (Ray: 1965), along with those of Marlon Brando and Jack Palance, adorned many Japanese film magazines in the 1950s. And in 1957, Elvis Presley was, according to Raine, 'the big new "foreign" face' in Japan in what he terms 'an intensification of celebrity' and 'consumer culture' (2005). The Sun Tribe films were the predecessors of Nikkatsu's later *roman porno* genre that flooded cinemas in Japan in the 1970s and 1980s, as discussed in the last chapter. Films such as *Crazed Fruit* (Nakahira: 1956) and *Punishment Room* (Ichikawa: 1956) established a sense of 'cool' through what Raine terms 'an intimacy between character and youth audience' (2005). The same could be said of Japanese zombie films. Whilst *taiyozoku* films were successful, or perhaps because of their very success, a climate of moral panic was created by the mass media over the so-called youth delinquency that these films were seen to glamorise. Raine comments:

> In the summer of 1956, almost every week brought new cautionary tales of young hoodlums terrorizing seaside resort towns, young women forced into sexual slavery, and lewd behavior among male workers on vacation. (2005)

The pressure from government, moral pressure groups such as the PTA, and EIRIN eventually led to the demise of the *taiyozoku* genre. In a society which privileges conformity over difference, the community over individualism, and the inside over the outside, the embracing of American popular culture and its ideological link to consumerism and commodity culture allowed the youth of Japan a mechanism of expression which was not available within the rigid hierarchies of traditional Japanese paternalism. Emerging from this sub-culture in the 1980s were the *bōsōzoku* and *yankī*. The term *bōsōzoku* (translated as 'the tribe of running violently') is used to refer to motorcycle and car gangs (Standish 1998: 70), while *yankī* is the term for urban gangs or juvenile delinquents marked out by their bleached hair and Yakuza-influenced outfits. *Yankī* often become members of Yakuza gangs when they are older. According to Satō, *bōsōzoku* behaviour needs to be understood as a type of *asobi* (play), whose purpose is to function as a rite of passage from youth to adulthood (Standish 1998: 57). Standish suggests that *bōsōzoku* should be considered as an example of generational consciousness that 'poses a direct challenge to the traditional 'work ethic' and achievement-orientated ideology of the previous generation' (1998: 58).

In *Angel Guts: Red Classroom*, discussed in the last chapter, the motorcycle gang, or *bōsōzoku*, is directly related to class structures within the film. With the exception of Tetsurō, the biker gang are unemployed, and their violence is motivated by the gap between their social aspirations and their social reality. This gap is expressed within the mise-en-scène of industrialisation against which the narrative is set. However, in *Wild Zero*, the *bōsōzoku* are constructed as heroes rather than anti-heroes. Unjustified violence towards women, which formed the key conventions of Nikkatsu *roman porno* generally and the *Angel Guts* series in particular, is replaced by justified violence towards the shambling zombies that threaten to take over Japan. The homoerotic overtones of the biker gang in *Red Classroom*, never fully realised, is displaced by a questioning of normative constructions of heterosexuality in *Wild Zero* through the love story between Ace and Tobio. Indeed, the film ends with a subversion of the codes of patriarchal heterosexuality as the faces of Ace and Tobio in a heart-shaped frame provide the final defining image of the film. Even *Versus* suggests an alternative to compulsory heterosexuality in the relationship between the leader of the Yakuza gang and one of his henchmen, expressed through both costume and mise-en-scène.

COMMODIFICATION

By the standards set by *Wild Zero*, *Junk* is a relatively sane excursion into zombie territory, although once again the film features a Yakuza gang, in addition to hordes of shambling living dead. Directly referencing Romero's *The Night of the Living Dead*, Fulci's *Zombie Flesh Eaters* and O'Bannon's *The Return of the Living Dead* (1983), the zombies in *Junk* are the product of experimentation gone wrong on the part of the American military. As such, *Junk* seems to continue the implicit critique of military technologies associated with America and the West that can be traced back to the monstrous emergence of Godzilla in a post-nuclear context.

At the beginning, the typical mad scientist of the science fiction genre, Dr Kinderman, brings back to life a beautiful young woman, Kyoko (Miwa Yanagizawa), who returns the favour by immediately killing him. Take a group of jewellery thieves, including a kick-ass action heroine, Saki (Kaori Shimamura), a Yakuza gang, and hordes of hungry entrail-eating, self-cannibalising zombies (who can this time be killed by a shot to the head), led by the beautiful Kyōko, and you have the formula for a nostalgic zombie film whose roots are firmly embedded in the 1980s.

Unlike *Wild Zero* and *Versus*, *Junk* manages to retain a critique of commodity fetishisation; members of the gang of thieves and the Yakuza gang are eaten alive as they desperately battle for a bag of jewels worth one million yen. Even when dead, the leader of the Yakuza gang, Ramon (Tate Gouta), keeps a deathly hold on the bag, although he no longer has any use for it. This is similar to the manner in which the zombies in *Dawn of the Dead* are mindlessly attracted to the shopping mall – a double play on the practice of consumption and consumerism in American society, of which the shopping mall is emblematic. Saki's desire for a brand new sleek Porsche, which she intends to buy with her proceeds from the robbery, comments on the aspirational nature of the commodity in contemporary society.

At the same time echoes can be found of *Parasite Eve* (Ochiai: 1997), also a game produced by Sony in 1998; a widower, Toshiaki Nagashima (Hiroshi Mikami), seeks to bring back his dead wife, Kiyomi (Riona Hazuki), with disastrous consequences. In *Junk*, it turns out that the experiments were started by Dr Takashi Nikada (Kishimoto Yuuji), in an attempt to return his wife, Kyōko, to life after she was killed in a car crash. And in *Junk* as in *Parasite Eve*, the resulting mutation is constructed in terms of a threat to humanity. Given the conventions of Japanese horror, it should come as little surprise that Dr Nikada is forced to sacrifice himself in the service of the greater good, in order to vanquish the mutant zombies for ever; nor that Kyōko takes on the coded characteristics of the vengeful female *yūrei* before she is finally defeated by Saki. In a sequence which provides a direct visual reference to the death of the replicant Priss (Daryl Hannah) in Ridley Scott's *Blade Runner* (1982), Kyōko is shot; falling to the ground, her body convulses and she makes screeching noises, just as Priss does. But unlike Priss, bullets cannot keep Kyōko down. She gets to her feet, her hair now white and her features ghost-like, more like a traditional *yūrei* than a zombie. Replicant-like, she continues to defy death even when dismembered, the top half of her body grappling with Akira (Osamu Ebara) – the only other member of the thieves besides Saki to survive the onslaught of the living dead. It is up to Saki, as is typical of the 'final girl' (Clover: 1992) of the contemporary horror film (the last girl standing, the prototype being Laurie in Carpenter's *Halloween*), to rescue Akira by killing her nemesis, Kyōko. However, she is returned to an appropriate Japanese femininity (as is often the case with her Western counterpart, the final girl); having escaped from the zombies with Akira, who arranges for a car salesman to meet them with a car (by offering him twice the money that it is worth), she declines to drive, instead taking the passenger seat. Unlike *Versus* and *Wild Zero*, in which gender categories are subverted, it could be argued that *Junk*'s conclusion restores normative patriarchal and heterosexual values.

FEMINISATION

> The schoolgirl icon, one that even shop-worn harlots aspire to emulate, has by now been a staple in Japanese sexual iconography for 50 years. Many Japanese men are galvanized by what they call Roricon – short for 'Lolita Complex'. (Bornoff 2002: 50)

While *Versus*, *Wild Zero* and *Junk* can be seen as expressions of male sub-cultural resistance, the low-budget, digitally shot *Stacy*, with its ravenous murderous zombie schoolgirls, or Stacies, can be usefully interpreted through its engagement with *shōjo bunka* or girl's culture, the dominant force in Japanese popular culture since the 1970s. *Stacy* reworks traditional conventions around femininity, of which the virginal *shōjo* is a dominant trope, through the juxtaposition of the *shōjo* and the sexually promiscuous *kogal*: the schoolgirl before and after her transformation into a zombie.

The plot of the film, such as it is, concerns the transformation of pubescent schoolgirls into Stacies, and the inability and inadequacy of Japanese paternalism to deal with this zombification. The reason for the zombification of the schoolgirl is never made clear. Instead, it becomes the duty of fathers, brothers and boyfriends to kill their loved ones; hence the film's tagline, 'Men, kill your daughters! Be the one to kill your girlfriend!' Failing this, the 'Romero Repeat Kill Squad' (an offshoot of the military) is called in to do the job for them.

Whilst the Romero Repeat Kill Squad cut the bodies of the Stacies up into 165 pieces, Dr Inugami (Tsutsui Yasutaka) – another mad scientist – experiments on their still-thinking brains in order to try to discover what it is that brings the dead schoolgirls back to life. Despite the obvious verbal and visual references to American zombie films (such as *Dawn of the Dead*, *Day of the*

Dead and *The Evil Dead*), *Stacy* is not a simple parody of the genre that can be considered generically outside its specific cultural and historical context. Indeed, as in *Wild Zero*, the zombies are not unthinking, decaying corpses without motivation; instead, they come back to life seeking the love that was denied to them whilst alive. As such, they are comparable to the traditional *yūrei* of Japanese ghost stories, rather than the zombies of the West.

The fetishised figure of the pubescent schoolgirl in Japanese culture is a common trope of contemporary Japanese horror. With her short skirt, white shirt, blazer and coloured necktie, known as *sailor fuko* (the secondary school uniform in Japan), she can be found in films such as *Eko Eko Azarak: Wizard of Darkness*, *Cursed* (Hoshino: 2004), *Suicide Circle* and *Battle Royale*. This fetishisation of the schoolgirl is epitomised by *kawaii* (cute schoolgirls), young pop idol schoolgirls called *aidoru*, who were at the height of their popularity in the 1990s, and the cult of Lolita. The figure of the schoolgirl is also ever-present in pornography and Lolicom (Lolita Complex) anime and manga. Treat writes:

> The word most often associated with this shōjo culture is *kawaii*, or 'cute'. This aesthetic value is directly linked to the consumer role that shōjo exist to play. A *kawaii* girl is attractive, and thus valorized, but lacks libidinal agency of its own. While others may desire the shōjo – and indeed, another phenomenon in the Japan of the 1980s was the talk of the rorikon 'Lolita complex' of adult heterosexual males – the shōjo's own sexual energy, directed as it is towards stuffed animals, pink notebooks, strawberry crepes and Hello Kitty novelties, is an energy not yet deployable in the heterosexual economy of adult life in Japan. (cited in Nakamura and Matsuo 2003: 69)

Here Treat argues that the very non-sexuality of the *shōjo* can be interpreted as threatening to the dominant heterosexual economy in Japan. As Nakamura and Matsuo comment, 'Performing *shōjo* is one active and dynamic way that Japanese women can control their sexuality' (2003: 69).

The virginal *shōjo* is the counterpart of the sexually promiscuous *kogal*. Napier argues that the 'shōjo and her alter ego the *burikko* (the cute girl), is the perfect non-threatening female, the idealized daughter/younger sister whose femininity is essentially sexless' (1998: 94). But she is more than sexless; she signifies maidenly virtue, propriety and respectability. At the same time, *shōjo* is also the slang for virgin in Japanese. Her very presence is said to cause a feeling of *moe* in the male spectator. Derived from *Otaku* culture, *moe* also refers to an absence of vanity, or self-awareness, of 'cuteness' on behalf of the *shōjo*. Whilst some argue that *moe* does not have any sexual connotations, others have suggested that it can encompass elements of paedophilia. At the same time, the *shōjo*'s hyper-femininity or girlishness conforms to traditional Japanese stereotypes of appropriate femininity. Davis and Ikeno elucidate on the persistence of traditional concepts of 'woman' in contemporary Japan:

> This powerful stereotype takes many forms. First, almost all little girls have dress-up dolls called rika-chan ningyō, which have ideal proportions, reflecting the Japanese image of the feminine. Therefore, girls tend to yearn to be like these dolls and identify with them. In addition to dress-up dolls, there are various kinds of toys that symbolize woman's roles: miniature models of items such as sewing machines, kitchen appliances, and household items. (2002: 181)

In 'Those Naughty Teenage Girls: Japanese Kogals, Slang, and Media Assessments', Miller argues that the term *kogal* 'has come to denote greedy, witless shoppers' (2004: 241). Similarly, Lloyd discusses the significance of increasing economic independence and sexual freedom for teenage girls in the 1990s. She writes:

> Presented by the media as bodies to be consumed, they were also seen as consuming bodies who congregated in Tokyo's fashionable shopping centres awaiting opportunities to acquire the latest luxury goods. (2002: 78)

In a similar manner to the moral panics that accompanied other sub-cultural movements, such as *taiyozoku* and *bōsōzoku* gangs, as detailed earlier in this chapter, the Japanese and foreign media in the 1990s constructed the *kogal* lifestyle and language in terms of deviant behaviour. However, as Miller points out, the use of labels for specific sub-cultures can work first to record and then to recuperate the potential resistance within that sub-culture through redefinition. Further, Miller contends that 'Kogals symbolize the ongoing redefinition of women in late capitalism' (2004: 226).

Heavily influenced by black American culture, in particular hip-hop and soul, the *kogal* is the latest in a long line of girls and women who have resisted the norms of paternalist culture in Japan, which defines women in terms of respectability. One of the earliest types of resistant girl and woman was the *daraku jogakusei* (degenerate schoolgirl) of the Meiji Era. The *kogal*, however, is closer to the pre-war *mogal*, who, similar to the *kogal*, 'was described as decadent, hedonistic and superficial.' Miller suggests that every time these new types of resistant femininity appear, they incrementally 'destabilize and modify normative gender ideologies' (2004: 226).

The term *kogal* is thus applicable to the zombie schoolgirls in *Stacy* in that they fail to conform to the complex system of obligation that defines both familial and societal relationships in Japan, unlike the figure of the *shōjo*. At the same time, these conflicting and contradictory images of the schoolgirl function to demythologise her fetishisation, as object of the male gaze. This can be clearly seen in the first few scenes of *Stacy*.

The very first image of the film is a typical romanticised image of the schoolgirl as *shōjo*. We see Kana, dressed in the compulsory *sailor fuko*, sitting in the grass, surrounded by four young children of whom she is taking care. As the children put flowers on Kana, they refer to her as Sleeping Beauty waiting for the Prince to come. This ironic reference to Victorian fairy tales, contained within both the pastoral mise-en-scène and the dialogue, situates *Stacy* as a post-modern fairy tale. The camera pans left, to the figure of another schoolgirl, Eiko (Natsuki Kato), walking with her back to the camera and holding a wind chime. As she walks away from the camera, the mother of the children passes her. She calls out to Kana and the camera pans right, cutting to a close-up of the back of the schoolgirl as she slowly stands up.

Unlike the previous zombie films discussed, *Stacy* makes explicit the connection between consumerism and zombification. When the children ask their mother whether she has bought them anything, Kana stands up, the camera gradually revealing her transformation into a zombie. Against all dictates of maternity (*ryōsaikenbo*), Kana turns on the children and tears them to pieces with her voracious red mouth. While in the foreground Kana is consuming the bodies of the children, Eiko can be seen in the background, constructing a visual connection between the two. Holding a wind chime and bathed in bright light, she appears as a typical virginal *shōjo*: the opposite to the consuming cannibal, or *kogal*.

The opposition between the schoolgirl as *shōjo* and as *kogal* is therefore foregrounded immediately as a key theme. In 'New Year (Bon-Sai)', by the Japanese artist, Hiroshi Masuyama, a bonsai tree is placed in the centre of the frame. On either side of the bonsai tree are two prepubescent schoolgirls, one sitting and the other kneeling. Lloyd points out how the bonsai tree in the painting is used to connote 'careful nurturing and cultivation', and therefore calls the spectator's attention to the disjunction between the traditional image of the tree and that of eroticised schoolgirls. Lloyd comments:

> Masuyama's depictions of the erotized images of young girls, placed on the same level and occupying the same indeterminate space on the canvas, present the spectator with two contradictory and conflicting images which embody different values and cultural sensibilities of past and present-day Japan. (2002: 79)

The same is true of the construction of the prepubescent schoolgirl in *Stacy*, as demonstrated by the opening sequences discussed above. Through the use of deep focus, the competing and conflicting images of the *shōjo* and the *kogal*, as both demure daughter and consuming cannibal, comment on the gap between cultural mythology and lived reality for women in contemporary Japanese society. Bornoff states that the Japanese educational system was 'devised to nip individualism in the bud and discourage abstract thought' (2002: 61). However, changes in the socio-economic structure of Japan have led to radical transformations in the education system. Bornoff writes:

> In Japan, where consensus, peer pressure and the strictures of the group have reigned for too long, individualism is welcomed as a key to Utopia but, unfortunately, little understood. Still deplored as mere selfishness in the eyes of the older generations and even exalted by some of the young, individualism is producing alienation. (2002: 63)

Whilst offering the type of graphic gore that we associate with the zombie narrative, *Stacy* is also, perhaps somewhat paradoxically a love story, a variation of the tale of 'tragic lovers'. The main narrative utilises parallelism, situating the romance of Eiko and a middle-aged puppeteer, Shibu (Toshinori Omi), against that of a young member of the Romero Repeat Kill Squad, Arita, and his penfriend, Momo, who becomes a Stacy. The only explanation that the film offers for the zombie schoolgirls is a reference to a spate of killings of schoolgirls in the past. In these terms, the film seems to suggest that the Stacies are embodiments of female oppression and male aggression.

Throughout the film, Eiko's costume alternates between the typical schoolgirl uniform and the costume of the gothic Lolita: a Victorian ruffled white gown that imitates the look of Victorian porcelain dolls. The manner in which Eiko is dressed suggests a similarity between *shōjo* and *kogal*, in which both female identities subvert patriarchal language through which female identity is constructed. Buisson argues that fantasy about schoolgirls, or Lolitas, is the most pervasive male fantasy in Japan. He writes: 'With the growth of video and the internet, it makes more converts everyday, people who literally fetishise images of students in provocative poses, even secondary school girls on the threshold of puberty' (2003: 64). At the same time, the figure of the gothic Lolita has also been theorised as representing a reaction against the *kogal* sub-culture.

The transition phase between being a *shōjo* and becoming a *kogal* is called Near Death Happiness (or NDH) in the film. This phase takes place approximately a week before the transformation. As such, it is both a transition and a transitory phase of identity for the schoolgirls-cum-zombies in *Stacy*. In *Stacy*, rather than the schoolgirls becoming women and adopting their proper place in the family, their metamorphosis situates a female identity outside patriarchal and capitalist norms. Rather than turning into good wives and mothers, or *ryōsaikenbo*, as dictated by the traditional value system of Japanese society, Stacies become uncontrollable and unmanageable, thereby resisting restoration to patriarchal norms. The result of this, as suggested by the voice-over to the film, is the eventual destruction of society as a whole, as there will be no more children born.

The existence of the Drew Repeat Kill Troops, which consists of three young girls still to become Stacies, further threatens traditional construc-tions of appropriate femininity. This provides an intertextual and imagistic reference to *Charlie's Angels* (McG: 2000). As in the other zombie films discussed, American popular culture is remediated in order to provide a site of resistance to pre-modern traditions. These action girls provide an alternative to the governmental Romero Repeat Kill Squad and the concept of shame that failing to kill your own daughter or girlfriend entails. In their desire for celebrity, the girls seek to make enough money to pay for an iconic star to kill them. The girls do not, however, live to fulfil this wish; instead, they sacrifice themselves in the name of true love.

The sequences leading up to the transformation of Eiko from *shōjo* to *kogal* are significant. She spends her last day with Shibu at the botanical gardens, where she used to play with her sister as a child. Once again, the film shifts between the pastoral and the hyper-real, as it cuts between the gardens and the military camp where the schoolgirls about to become a Stacy have been sent. At the military camp, Arita finally comes across Momo, who has transformed into a Stacy. His attempt to rescue her indirectly leads to the death of the Drew Troops, who give up their mission to kill her, touched by the love that Arita shows Momo. As the girls lie dying on the floor, the film cuts between Eiko in the botanical gardens and the military camp, creating a continuity or sisterhood between the women. Dressed in her gothic Lolita outfit and flooded by brilliant white light, Eiko appears to the zombified Stacies in Dr Inugami's laboratory. Constituting an expression of female language – or *parler-femme*, a concept introduced by feminist writer Luce Irigaray linked to the idea of disruptive excess (Irigaray 1996: 44) – in opposition to patriarchal structures, the voices of the dying Drew Troops, the Stacies and Eiko become one.

The film concludes with Eiko's (unseen) death at the hands of her lover, Shibu. Once again, we have the motif of the sacrificial woman, whose death makes possible a restoration of order in the diegetic world of the film. At the same time, it is love (the love of Shibu for Eiko and the love of Arita for Momo) that enables the construction of a new future in which men and women once again become connected.

Whilst ostensively *Stacy* projects male anxieties around the erosion of patri-archal power and situates romantic love as a solution, it also critiques the ideal-isation of the figure of the *shōjo* and the over-valorisation of the attributes of hyper-femininity found in contemporary Japanese society. These misbehaving teenagers, to coin a phrase used by Miller, 'undermine patriarchal models of propriety used to evaluate and control women' (2002: 241).

CONSUMERS

It is little surprise, therefore, that most Japanese zombie films have appeared in the aftermath of the collapse of the bubble economy in 1990. The Japanese zombie film, as we have seen, is a cannibalistic genre, which not only references the traditional stereotype of the zombie, but also transgresses generic boundaries. It could be argued that Japanese zombies are vengeful *yūrei* rather than traditional zombies, as is made clear in *Junk*. And while at first glance the Japanese zombie film appears to be a matter of style over substance, as perhaps most evidently seen in the MTV aesthetics of *Versus*, the utilisation of American forms can be seen as a type of counter-cultural and sub-cultural resistance to traditional Japanese structures and cultural forms. As such, the Japanese zombie film can be considered as a logical outcome of angry youth films, such as the Sun Tribe films.

In 'New Kids on the Street: The Pan-Asian Youth Film', Desser identifies a dominant tendency in East Asian cinema as the 'rise of youth-oriented films', which share similar iconography and motifs. In terms of Japan, Desser argues that the Sun Tribe, or *taiyozoku*, films of the 1950s, together with the films of the Japanese New Wave, made 'politically cogent attacks on mainstream Japanese society through the use of youthful protagonists who reject their cultural heritage in favor of protest and rebellion' (2008). In these terms, the hyper-flat aesthetics of the Japanese zombie film should be considered as a remediation of this trend for youth protest cinema and understood as a critique of Japanese modernity and with it the Japanese preoccupation with the consumption of luxury goods (Lloyd 2002: 69). We saw how *bōsōzoku* and *yankī* gangs were associated with youthful rebellion and gave rise to associated media panics. In Napier's words: '*Bôsôzoku* have adapted and inverted images, styles and ideologies to construct an alternative identity, an identity which challenges the ideal of Japanese social and cultural homogeneity' (cited in Standish 1998: 58). Desser argues that one 'characteristic of adolescence is the struggle to define oneself against familial bonds and expectations' (2008). The zombie film articulates the adolescent struggle for identity in a society built upon knowing one's place in the larger structure; the outcome of this struggle for self-determination is often an apocalyptic future identifiable in the wastelands of *Versus* and *Naked Blood*.

CHAPTER 7

Haunted Houses and Family Melodramas

One of the dominant features of contemporary horror film is the manner in which the break-up of the nuclear family has become a source of horror. Films such as *The Amityville Horror* (Rosenberg: 1979), *Poltergeist* (Hooper: 1982), *The Shining* (Kubrick: 1980), *The Stepfather* (Ruben: 1987) and, more recently, *Hide and Seek* (Polson: 2005) and *Silent Hill* (Gans: 2006), based on the video game series, situate the threat to the family as coming from within rather than outside. These gothic narratives construe the sins of the father, as monstrous Other, as that which returns to threaten the sanctity of the bourgeois nuclear family. In Japanese horror film, however, it is the sins of the mother, and her daughter as her double, that return to threaten the home as microcosm of society, signifying the persistence of trauma, both historical and economic.

Kurosawa's *Sweet Home* not only provided the inspiration for the *Resident Evil* series of games, but also was the template for the contemporary Japanese haunted house film. With its vengeful maternal ghost, *Sweet Home* prefigures Nakata's *Dark Water* (2002) and Shimizu's *Ju-On: The Grudge*, with its sequel, *Ju-On: The Grudge 2* (2003). These films deal with anxieties around transformations in the nature of the family in Japan from the *ie* system to the Western nuclear form, using the template of the haunted, or cursed, house. While *Sweet Home* and *Carved: A Slit-Mouthed Woman* (Shiraishi: 2007) offer monstrous mothers whose horrific acts of violence subvert the ideology of *ryōsaikenbo*, *Dark Water* focuses on the vengeful foetus while *Ju-On: The Grudge* takes as its inspiration the wronged woman theme.

Barrett stresses the importance of the family in contemporary Japanese dramas, in which loyalty to one's superiors 'has been considerably de-emphasized in favor of homilies about familial and neighborly ties.' He continues: 'This indicates that, in the value system of contemporary Japanese, the family has become more important than polity' (1989: 219). At the height of the economic boom, we find the figure of the salaryman (*sararīman*), 'the featureless face of

Japanese modernity' (McLelland 2003) and in popular consciousness a 'latter-day samurai, selflessly dedicated to the national cause of economic expansion' (Stockwin 2003: xiv). Loyalty to the company was privileged over men's role in the family, as father and husband. Death by overwork, or *karoshi*, led to court cases in which companies have been forced to compensate families for the loss of their provider. Suicides by men in their forties and fifties constitute approximately forty per cent of all suicides in Japan. When the economic bubble burst, rising unemployment created a crisis in hegemonic constructions of an idealised masculinity based upon loyalty to the corporation. McLelland writes:

> There has been a fundamental shift in popular discourses about masculinity – from 'salary man' to 'family man' – a shift that has left some men of the older generation feeling stranded and many younger men feeling confused about what is expected of them. (2003)

In different ways, the films discussed in this chapter interrogate the changing shape of the family in contemporary Japan. The domestic space, *uchi*, which is connected to ideas of the sacred, becomes instead a place of horror and terror. However, unlike in *Godzilla*, in which the threat is mainly associated with the profane spaces of the outside (*soto*), the threat is now inside and knocking on the door of the last bastion of Japanese patriarchy: the family as embedded within the wider community.

MONSTROUS MOTHERS

> The mother-fixation of men, or their inability to break from their mother's influence, appears to be a common phenomenon in many cultures. However, it seems there are some characteristics particular to contemporary Japanese society that promote an extreme closeness in mother–child relationships, especially in the case of the mother–son bond. (Gössmann 2000: 209)

Gössmann argues that the closeness of the mother–child dyad in Japan, as expressed in popular cultural representations, can be seen as a result of the absent father and the competitive education system which gave rise to the *kyōiku mama* or 'education mother'; this, he suggests, explains the prevalence of the *mazo-kon* (mother complex) amongst sons of wealthy parents. Similarly, Goldberg argues that dominant Japanese ideological constructions of maternity 'have not adapted to fit the changing social landscape' (2004: 373). However, in popular culture, in opposition to this over-valorisation of the maternal, is the demonic or nightmare mother. As Goldberg writes: 'The flipside of the idealized representation of Japanese motherhood, found in the *haha-mono*, is the *bukimi'na haha*: the nightmare mother who has a special link to madness or the supernatural' (2004: 373).

In a similar vein, in his analysis of changing male and female roles in Japanese television drama, Gössmann argues that since the 1970s traditional representations of woman as either the reliable mother or the suffering woman, and in particular those associated with the cult of motherhood, have shifted in favour of the demonic mother; the latter can be found in television drama of the 1990s, the paradigmatic example of which, according to Gössmann, is *I've Always Loved You* (*Zutto Anata ga Suki Datta*). Gössmann argues that the demonic mother 'is a perverted, negative version of the strong, reliable mother', who suffers not only in the outside world 'but within the family as well' (2000: 213). However, the demonic mother is not a new archetype, as Kawai points out in her discussion of the Great Mother in Japanese fairy tales. In stories such as 'The Woman Who Eats Nothing' and 'The Two Kannons' the demonic side of the Great Mother figure is commonly represented as *Yama-uba* (*yama*: mountain, *uba*: old woman or crone). In a similar vein to Goldberg, Kawai argues that such negative images of the mother figure in Japanese culture:

> function to compensate the general trend in Japan to evaluate motherhood extraordinarily highly. It has been taboo to talk ill of or to neglect Mother. In contrast, fairy tales portray so vividly her dreadful devouring power. (1996: 33)

'The Woman Who Eats Nothing' provides the template for the monstrous cannibalistic mother in *Carved* with her slit for a mouth, while *Sweet Home*, it could be argued, is a contemporary version of 'The Two Kannons' (Kannon is a Buddhist deity). As such, it is worth sketching the fairy tales out briefly to begin. In 'The Woman Who Eats Nothing', a man marries a beautiful woman who declares to him before they are married that she eats nothing. However, one day, the husband watches his wife surreptitiously and, to his horror, discovers that the woman who eats nothing is in fact the woman who eats everything. In Kawai's words: 'This beautiful woman has a big mouth on the top of her head which devours thirty-three rice balls and three mackerel' (1996: 29). In 'The Two Kannons', which Kawai does not discuss in detail, a *Yama-uba* – the negative or demonic side of the Great Mother – is being chased and transforms herself into Kannon when she is cornered. However, 'her true nature comes out and she is killed' (1996: 34). Kawai argues that the story is interesting because 'we sense that even Kannon – the positive Great Mother – has her shadow side' (1996: 34). Rather than see Japanese fairy tales about the two sides of the Great Mother as being simply patriarchal fantasies or anxieties around female monstrosity, Kawai suggests that their collective value is 'directly connected to everyday tragedies' (1996: 36).

Finally, this duplicity of the mother figure and the oscillation between her negative and positive sides also figures in Japanese Buddhism, in which the two mothers are Kannon (positive) and Kariteimo (negative). Kariteimo is said to have originated as the Indian Goddess Hariti, the original monstrous mother who kidnapped and consumed the children of Rajagriha. When Buddha steals her eldest child, Hariti can empathise with the suffering of the woman from whom she stole the children, and is transformed into Kannon – the goddess of mercy and iconic symbol of maternal love (Balmain 2007c). As Foster points out, 'contemporary legends can encode sometimes contradictory ideologies, providing insight into the dynamics of complicity and resistance as well as into the complex sociohistorical concerns of a given moment' (2007: 700).

Sweet Home makes the relationship between the negative and positive sides of the Great Mother explicit. The monstrous Lady Mamiya haunts a decaying old mansion that a television crew go to in order to discover the rumoured last fresco of her husband, Ichiro Mamiya, a famous artist; Lady Mamiya is as tragic as she is demonic. Killing her own longed-for daughter when she accidentally turns on the furnace in which her child is playing, Lady Mamiya descends into madness. Her maternity become monstrous as she attempts to fulfil the maternal bond, even after her child's death, by providing other children to accompany her child in the afterworld. Her child has been buried outside the mansion, and mother and child are separated by death as they were in life. The television crew is comprised of Taguchi, the camera operator; Asuka, the reporter; Aki, the director, and finally, Kazuo, the producer and his daughter, Emi. On their arrival, Lady Mamiya makes her presence felt, as she lurks in the shadows and attempts to use the psychically sensitive reporter, Asuka, to return her child to her. As tendrils of black shadow fall over Asuka's face, the hidden demonic side of woman is revealed through mise-en-scène and the interplay of shadow and light. The shadows reach out and consume both Taguchi and Asuka, before Lady Mamiya captures Emi in her demonic embrace and takes her down to the basement: the room in which the angry villagers killed her when they discovered her horrific transgressions.

Seemingly opposed to Lady Mamiya is Aki, who represents the good wife and wise mother. Not only is Aki in love with Kazuo (the symbolic father figure), but her relationship with Emi is also configured in terms of the maternal dyad. This is also signalled in terms of costume; Emi's dead mother's dress provides a signifier of wise motherhood, transferred from daughter to Aki as substitute mother, who puts on the dress to fight the monstrous mother in the final confrontation.

The mansion itself is King's 'Bad Place' and Clover's 'Terrible Place'. King points out that not only are we most vulnerable in our homes, but that a good horror story about the Bad Place also 'whispers that we are not locking the world out; we are locking ourselves in ... with *them*' ([1981] 1993: 299). Clover's 'Terrible Place' similarly is a 'venerable element of horror' in which the promise of a safe haven turns into one of horror as the 'walls that promise to keep the killer out quickly become, once the killer penetrates them, the walls that hold the victim in' (1992: 31). The Mamiya mansion is a Terrible House, a variation of the Bad Place and the Terrible Place, whose walls enclose the television crew, refusing to let them go.

Not only does Lady Mamiya inhabit the mansion; she also is the mansion, both literally and symbolically. Although they have the key, the group are unable to unlock the door. Instead, they have to break through a boarded-up window; as they do so, a shaft of light illuminates an old rusted baby's pram, signalling the centrality of motherhood to the ensuing narrative. In addition, the key itself – which tries to keep them out – is slowly revealed in the opening sequences at the bottom of folds of pink fabric, visually and symbolically linked to the mother's genitalia. Gaining entry to the mansion through breaking in could thus be considered a metaphorical act of rape against the Great Mother, who has hidden for thirty years undisturbed.

The mother's duplicity is painted on the walls of the mansion. The first image that is revealed through layers of dust is an iconic one of the mother with a child cradled in her arms, similar to those found often in artistic and sculptural renditions of Kannon as a Buddhist deity. However, once the group become trapped, they uncover more paintings telling the horrific story of the mansion and showing Lady Mamiya's transformation from wise to monstrous mother. The use of fleshy pink tones in the frescos again provides a symbolic link to the monstrous mother's womb. Images of birth, death and madness associated with the maternal are solidified into abject images of bodily putrefaction when both Taguchi and Asuka are slowly and graphically killed.

In her discussion of the abject, Kristeva (1982) argues that the most abject of all things is childbirth, as the outside comes into contact with the inside, the boundaries between which give the subject a sense of their integrity. Indeed, as Creed (1993) has persuasively argued, the abject is omnipresent in horror cinema; it is encapsulated in that moment when, faced with scenes of bodily disintegration and graphic horror, the spectator chooses to look away. Yet, although the mansion is an abject rendering of the maternal womb, the reintegration of Lady Mamiya into appropriate maternity, from Kariteimo to Kannon, when reunited with her child – she is enveloped in bright white light as she floats up towards the sky – suggests the inseparability of the two sides of the Great Mother. This is also inferred through the interplay of light and shadow, made explicit when an elderly petrol station owner, Mr Yamamura (the wise old man we often find in horror cinema, whose warnings are ignored), tells Kazuo that light alone is not enough to conquer the deadly and demonic Lady

Mamiya, as light only functions to create more shadows. Once again in Japanese horror cinema, the light of modernity here is shown as causative of demons and monsters that can only be conquered by a return to traditional ways.

If the television crew represents modernity and modern ways, Mr Yamamura represents pre-modern and traditional beliefs, as he is the one who retrieves Emi from Lady Mamiya using only willpower and an old carved amulet. His self-sacrifice, in a similar manner to that of Serizawa in *Godzilla*, provides the mechanism through which traditional values and morals are asserted over those connected to modernity and Westernisation. As such, the real father, Kazuo, is displaced and replaced by both Yamamura and the mother–daughter dyad of Aki and Emi. Throughout the film, he is shown as ineffectual, unable to communicate his feelings, needing to be looked after by his daughter and eventually unable to retrieve her from Lady Mamiya. In a moment of light humour when Aki and Emi have returned to the outside, the camera pans inside, a cupboard falls open and the terrified Kazuo falls out. *Sweet Home* provides the prototype for many Japanese haunted house films, although it is one of the few to have a demonic presence contained behind the walls of the Terrible Place; in many examples of the genre, such as *Ju-On: The Grudge* and *Carved*, the grudge associated with the vengeful ghost is able to travel outside the original place of her (his) death and cannot be contained by mere walls.

Carved is one of the most recent Japanese haunted house films, and its portrayal of the demonic mother is much more negative than that in *Sweet Home*. Based upon an urban legend, which took form in Japan in the 1970s (Foster 2007), *Carved* tells the tale of a small community terrorised by the 'Slit-Mouthed Woman' – 'literally mouth (*kuchi*) slit / split (*sake*) woman (*onna*)' (Foster 2007: 699) – who steals and tortures young children. This is the mother at her most demonic and most frightening. Like most female ghosts, the Slit-Mouthed Woman (Maki Mizuno) as immaterial ghost does not have the power to attack the living; instead, she possesses other mothers in order to carry out her bloody deeds. Most obviously, she embodies patriarchal fears around female power, her mouth interchangeable with her vagina, both in imagistic and symbolic terms. It is interesting to note the shift from Shintō myth here in which, as we have already seen, the female genitalia are an object of carnivalesque laughter rather than abject fear. According to Western interpretative frameworks, Foster argues that the Slit-Mouthed Woman can be considered a representation of the Freudian oral sadistic mother, or the pre-Oedipal dyadic mother as theorised by Kristeva, and as such is a paradigmatic example of Creed's monstrous feminine (Foster 2007: 703). At the same time, for young girls the rumour of the Slit-Mouthed Woman encompassed existing anxieties about forthcoming sexual maturity. Akiyama stresses the link between the erotic and the mother in Japanese cultural mythology:

The slit located in the lower part of the mother's body, the big mouth
that gives birth to the child – probably it can also suddenly open up and
swallow the child … A place that is usually covered up and cannot be
seen, it twitches like an entirely independent living thing, and can at
certain times become wide enough to give birth to a baby. (cited in Foster
2007: 703)

Junichiro also makes the connection between the erotic and the demon mother:
'Her beautiful body houses a dark, cruel and evil element. If we examine this
more closely, it is clear that this is not a particular evil inherent in women.
Rather it is an evil desired by men; a reflection of masculine lust' (cited in
Buruma 1984: 49). In *Carved*, this takes the form of the slippage from beautiful
to horrific, the Slit-Mouthed Woman continually asking 'Am I Pretty?' even
as the disfigured face beneath the mask of beauty is revealed. This is 'a representation of the desired in its most sexualised, extreme – unbeautiful – form'
(Foster 2007: 703). Here, female disfigurement, once again, metonymically
articulates the persistence of historical trauma mapped on to contemporary
economic trauma.

In *Carved*, as in the legend, the Slit-Mouthed Woman can be heard
constantly asking whether she is pretty – words that only her son can hear –
only to reveal the abject horror beneath the mask. The first time we see her,
she is a decaying corpse, foregrounding the interplay between monstrosity
and beauty on which the legend plays. The iconography utilised in the film in
terms of the Slit-Mouthed Woman is also very close to the urban legend: long
black hair, a white gauze mask (*masuku*) covering the lower half of her face,
and a long pair of scissors in her hand as she seeks victims. The scissors can be
interpreted as an embodiment of patriarchal castration anxieties; the scissors
that cut, like the mouth, can be understood as a signifier of the vagina dentata
(or the toothed vagina) – that which Freud argued was the uncanniest thing
of all in his essay on the uncanny. The white mask is a symbol of fears about
disease, pollution (environmental and personal) and contagion, together with
evident anxieties about female sexuality, as already discussed. Foster traces the
use of masks in Japan back to 1918 when they were employed against Spanish
influenza and perhaps most notably during the SARS (severe acute respiratory
syndrome) outbreak in 2002 (2007: 707). And, as we have already seen, the
masks central to traditional dramatic forms, including Nō and Kabuki, feature
in many Japanese horror films. A contemporary example of the use of masks
is in *Persona* (Komatsu: 2000), a psychological horror film in which the mask
is used literally to cover up the identity and gender of the murderer; as more
and more students adopt the mask, it becomes increasingly difficult to identify
the murderer. In addition, the image of the slit mouth also has precedents in
contemporary Japanese film and can be found in Miike's *Ichi The Killer* (2000)

in the figure of Kakihara (Tadanobu Asano), the masochist seeking the perfect sadist, the Ichi (Nao Omori) of the title. Kakihara's slit mouth can be seen not only as a form of self-mutilation but also as a type of cosmetic surgery in which the body is reconfigured outside of traditional bodily norms.

Indeed, Foster demonstrates that the figure of the Slit-Mouthed Woman haunted many women's magazines in Japan in the 1970s, frequently appearing in '*Josei jishin* (Woman Herself), *Josei sebum* (Woman Seven) and *Shukan josei* (Weekly Woman)' (Foster 2007: 710) and functioning as a metaphor for the ability of cosmetic surgery to subvert traditional iconic conceptualisations of femininity in Japan. In these terms, she can be read as a symbol of protest in which the female subject 'confront[s] the objectifying male gaze and register[s] a powerful protest against the status quo' (Foster 2007: 718).

Carved opens with an establishing long shot of an almost deserted park. The colour palate of the opening sequences is predominantly a washed-out sepia, which, as we have seen in Japanese horror film, evokes the past. A short montage of scenes showing children talking about the rumour of the Slit-Mouthed Woman are interspersed with three short vignettes showing ordinary family life and continuing with the theme of the urban legend. In the first, we see a father sitting down and talking to his daughter about it, relating its origins back to the time he was at high school. To his wife, he comments that this reminds him of the old days. This observation repeats the inseparability of the past from the present in the formation of social, cultural and national identity. The second short scene shows two young sisters discussing the legend, refusing to go shopping for fear of the monstrous woman, who is rumoured to appear in the park at 5 p.m. when children are on their way back from school. The third scene, the most crucial to the plot, is that of a mother, Mrs Sasaki, hitting her daughter Mika while saying that she wished the Slit-Mouthed Woman would come and take her away, something that soon comes true. These scenes introduce us to a common trope in contemporary Japanese horror: the displacement of the traditional extended family by the fragmented nuclear family in which gender roles have become confused. Finally, we are introduced to the two main characters in the film, a young female teacher, Kyoko Yamashita (Eriko Sato), and a male teacher at the same school, Noboru Matsuzaki (Haruhiko Kato).

It is crucial to the plot that we are introduced to Kyoko just before we see the Slit-Mouthed Woman for the first time, suggesting commonalities between the two women, although at this time Kyoko appears to be the monstrous mother's opposite, the good wife. In the next scene, we see Noboru discovering a crude drawing of the Slit-Mouthed Woman on the blackboard in one of the empty classrooms and we simultaneously hear the voice from the past asking 'Am I pretty?' just before the film cuts to the image of her decaying corpse. Long shots, tracking shots of empty corridors and high-angled vistas of the town from the roof where Kyoko is standing, together with the sepia palate, create an uncanny and uneasy atmosphere. Spatially and emotionally, the community is situated as fractured and individuals alienated. This is a community where mothers beat their children for not talking, as in the case of Mika, or for not loving them, as in the case of Kyoko (as we discover in a flashback towards the climactic sequence of the film). In another flashback sequence, we see Noboru's mother becoming the archetypical Slit-Mouthed Woman, as she beats and kills his brother and sister, who do not so much die as fade out from the frame in the flashback. At the same time, we glimpse the positive side of the Great Mother in a battle with the negative side, as she hands Noboru a knife to kill her with and pleads with him to cut off her head. Instead, Noboru cuts his mother's face, a simulation of the surgical act, which, instead of creating beauty, creates difference configured as female monstrosity.

In *Carved*, the Terrible Place is Noboru's family home, an old house situated in the middle of nowhere on Childbeck hill, its red roof indicating that something terrible lurks inside. In the basement, the Slit-Mouthed Woman tortures and kills children, and it is here that she is finally vanquished as Noboru, crippled at the hands of his demonic and deadly mother, manages at last to decapitate her and put an end to her reign of terror. At the same time, both Mrs Sasaki and Kyoko are restored to appropriate maternity, as Mrs Sasaki becomes the self-sacrificing mother and the encounter with the monstrous mother leads Kyoko to be reconciled with her own daughter.

The mothers portrayed in both *Sweet Home* and *Carved* are the very opposite of the wise mother, each one a modern-day Slit-Mouthed Woman in their aggression and violence towards their daughters. Napier argues that in post-war fantastic narratives women no longer offer a refuge from modernisation but instead 'seem to have become increasingly Other, unreachable, even demonic' (1996: 57). In another film on the same theme, *Apartment 1303* (Oikawa: 2007), young women who rent out the apartment of the title end up dead, supposedly suicides. A young woman, Mariko (Noriko Nakagoshi), investigating the death of her sister, discovers the vengeful ghost of the monstrous mother is behind the deaths of the young women, wanting them as daughter substitutes. Unlike the typical archetypal suffering and wronged women, these monstrous mothers are constructed as threatening to patriarchy, although they are eventually defeated by their surrogate daughters.

These monstrous females are the latest in a long line of dangerous women found in Japanese myths and folktales, as well as in real life: for example, the poison women (*dokufu*), sexually voracious and criminal women of the 1870s. Both Foster and Gössmann agree that the emergence of the demonic mother in film and television can be understood in part as a response to the 'education mother', the growth of the Japanese feminist movement in the 1970s and also in relation to the rapid shifts in Japanese society during and after the economic boom. In his analysis of femininity in Japanese television drama, Mamoru stresses the importance of socio-historical context:

> the period spanning the 1980s and the 1990s was a time of rapid growth in terms of the society's consumption of consumer goods and its access to information; Japan's society became more complex and the self-evident nature of the norms that defined everyday Japanese life were beginning to lose their solid foundations. (2004: 26)

Further, both Foster and Gössmann suggest that the portrait of the demonic mother is not necessarily reactionary, in that she marks a point of resistance to traditional Japanese constructions of femininity and motherhood. While the disfigured and monstrous woman embeds the discourse of *hibakusha*, signalling the persistence of historical trauma, she also represents more contemporary anxieties specific to her cultural and historical location. As Foster writes, 'the Slit-Mouthed Woman legend becomes a symbolically overdetermined allegory of the suffering incurrent in Japan's post-war drive towards economic success' (2007: 708).

THE VENGEFUL FOETUS

Hideo Nakata's *Dark Water* (2002) is based, like his earlier *Ring*, upon a story by Koji Suzuki (known as the Japanese Stephen King). In *Dark Water*, the central character is a young woman, Yoshimi (Hitomi Kuroki), recently separated from her domineering husband, Kunio Hamada (Fumiyo Kohinata), who is struggling to support and maintain custody of her five-year-old daughter, Ikuko (Rio Kanno). Kunio can be interpreted as representative of the 'salaryman', who places duty to the company over and above that to his family.

This is signalled at the beginning of the film, through the dialogue between Yoshimi and the court officials, and through the mise-en-scène of isolation and emptiness that conveys the emotional and physical distance between the couple. Kunio is sitting in the corridor, as Yoshimi walks towards the interview room. As she passes him by, there is no indication of familiarity between the couple. When she is finished, she takes a seat as far away from Kunio as she can manage. In the interview itself, she refers to Kunio as an absent father, who never remembers his daughter's birthday and had no time for her when they were together. At the same time, this opening sequence allows doubts around Yoshimi's state of mind and stability to be introduced. We discover that, in the past, Yoshimi had a nervous breakdown, which required hospitalisation. Yoshimi accounts for this by stating that her job as a proofreader for a large publishing house meant that she had to read violent and sadistic books, over and over again, which resulted in her breakdown. This can be seen as a critique of the prevalence of sadomasochistic pornography in Japanese society, in which women are repeatedly violated, raped and objectified. As such, it could be argued that she is situated as an unreliable narrator, the sort of character that is commonly found in the gothic, who is unable to distinguish between fiction and reality. It also implies that her version of events in terms of her marriage is not one on which we can rely. Just as Yoshimi is portrayed as someone who confuses fiction and reality, Kunio is obsessed with facts and details, rather than their interpretation. In *Dark Water*, femininity is associated with super-stition, the supernatural and the subjective, whilst masculinity is linked with the rational, the observable and the objective.

Suzuki writes of Yoshimi in *Dark Water* that 'The world as she perceived it was largely at odds with the world as others saw it' (2006: 22). In the story, Yoshimi sees herself as destined to be a single parent, just as both her grand-mother and mother were, as she has an irrational fear of sex:

> She had never once found anything enjoyable about the physical union of man and woman. Her only word for it was 'agonizing'. Yet there is never any shortage of talk about sex in the world. She simply couldn't under-stand it. Perhaps some insurmountable barrier separated her from other people. (Suzuki 2006: 22)

In the film, Nakata constructs a back story for Yoshimi, replacing her fear of intimacy with abandonment by her mother in the past, to explain her unstable and neurotic personality. This functions to draw a parallel between the collective past and personal present, in that Yoshimi ultimately abandons her child, mirroring the actions of not only her mother, but also Mitsuko's mother (who abandons Mitsuko, the vengeful ghost who haunts the building in which Yoshimi and Ikuko live). It is key therefore that the film's very first image is that of children being picked up by their mothers, as school ends for the day. Rain is pouring down, and canopies of bright-coloured umbrellas are used to prevent the children and their mothers from getting wet. The camera pulls back and the figure of a young girl, with long brown hair, sitting on the ground by the shut doors of the school and looking outside, is seen from the back. As the children and their parents depart, one of the teachers notices the child. She goes into the school and says to the child, 'Yoshimi, no one's come for you.' This emphasises Yoshimi's isolation; as the camera switches to the outside, the rain cascading down the glass can be seen as an externalisation of her inner psyche. As the camera pans in, capturing the child in close-up, we can no longer see the rain but it can still be heard. The theme of abandonment, central to the main narrative, is emphasised through the economy of this scene. At the same time, the driving rain mirrors the physical and psychical isolation of the child separated from the group. The film cuts to the present – the rain creating continuity between distinct temporal spaces – and we see Yoshimi, now an adult, looking out of a window as rain falls.

The opening sequences also introduce us to the colour imagery that is used to represent the past. The opening credits are placed against a background of brownish-yellow water, and throughout the film yellow and brown are used as the background to flashbacks from the past. In the present, a drab bluish-grey predominates, with the exception of flashes of colour in scenes in the kindergarten, and between the mother and child in the apartment. In *Dark Water*, bright colours are used to represent childhood and freedom; the bluish-grey signifies adulthood, and a sense of nostalgia for an idealised past, associated with childhood and innocence. Writing about Koreeda's *Maboroshi* (1995), McDonald argues that Koreeda 'symbolically links light imagery to color corollary in order to dramatize Yumiko's vacillating state' (2006: 204). The same could be said of the use of colour in *Dark Water*: that is, colour provides an external expression of Yoshimi's inner turmoil. In this manner, Mitsuko's red bag with its white rabbit, which Ikuko finds on the roof of the apartment complex, can be interpreted as signifying death as well as the uncanny. Try as she might, Yoshimi is unable to get rid of the bag and keep the outside at bay; it constantly reappears in the spot beside the water tank on the roof. Its repetition and re-emergence cause Yoshimi to become ever more hysterical, until eventually she discovers Ikuko has brought the satchel into the apartment.

This is a pivotal turning point in the narrative, marking the instant in which death has invaded the domestic space, from which for Yoshimi there can be no turning back. As she grabs the red bag from Ikuko, she has a vision of it falling into deep, dark water. This is also the moment which ultimately will lead to Yoshimi abandoning her daughter for the dead Mitsuko. In fact, she leaves her daughter alone whilst she goes back up to the roof, where the water tank is continuing to overflow with brackish, contaminated water.

On the roof, she has another vision of Mitsuko climbing up the water tank, her bag slipping out of her hands into the water and her body following. In this sequence, the water tank can be interpreted as symbolic of the archaic mother's womb. A sound of banging can be heard, accompanied by bulges in the wall of the tank as if something inside is trying to get out. The metaphor of pregnancy and birth is further solidified by the gushing water coming through the ceiling and out of the taps in the apartment where Ikuko is alone. The water in the bath is dark and muddy, and as Ikuko leans over to try and turn the taps off, a pair of green, decaying arms reach up and grab her, pulling her down under the water. We have already seen that water imagery is not just associated with isolation and alienation, but is often a metaphor for pollution and corruption in Japanese horror cinema. At the same time, water is clearly associated with death in *Dark*

Water, in that it represents the transitory nature of life. McDonald, tracing the etymology of the phrase 'floating weeds', situates it within 'the traditional Buddhist view of the world as fleeting and impermanent' (2006: 96).

Juro Kara, a renowned theatre director associated with the *Angura* movement, emphasises the importance of the 'lower place' in his plays as the site of Japanese collective memory that had become lost in the drive towards modernisation. Kara termed this place *kawara*, or the riverbed. The riverbed was the place where social outcasts congregated, with the aim of committing suicide by throwing themselves into the muddy waters, but instead joined together and became performers instead. Matsui writes:

> In short, *kawara* was a place of rebirth; as its topological deviation from the civilized place made *kawara* the 'outside' of socio-economic rules, people could shake off their learned restraint to live with physical immediacy. (2002: 160)

In Kara's mythological schema *kawara* is also the place of both the violated maternal body (the soil) and the goddess, and he argues that the construction of modern Japan, with its tall skyscrapers, conceals the water that lies underneath these phallic symbols of patriarchal power. Matsui comments: 'Water is a regressive image symbolizing suicide and amniotic fluid, related to the memory of pre-modern Japanese existence' (2002: 160). And in addition, it could be argued that polluted water in *Dark Water* represents the manner in which society has been 'contaminated by modernity' (Napier 1996: 35). The water imagery functions to add a sense of the impermanence of life; hence the importance of the credit sequences. When the dead Mitsuko appears, she leaves a trail of water behind her and water is continuously flowing into her apartment from a damp patch in the ceiling.

In these final sequences, Mitsuko takes on a corporeal materiality and a demonic reality. There is an obvious similarity with *Don't Look Now* (Roeg: 1973) and the moment of revelation when the red-hooded figure (Adelina Poerio) that John Baxter (Donald Sutherland) has been chasing all over Venice, thinking that it was his dead child returned to life, turns around to reveal a monstrous and murderous dwarf. At the same time, the influence of Kubrick's *The Shining* can also be felt, with the tank functioning in a similar manner to the boiler as an externalisation of the central character's madness.

In these terms the overflowing water tank and the gushing waters that come out of the empty lift in *Dark Water* can be interpreted as an external projection of Yoshimi's increasingly disturbed mind. Once again, this suggests that Mitsuko's ghost may well be just a hallucination, a signifier of Yoshimi's increasing inability to cope with work and her duties as a mother in the absence of a father figure. Certainly, one of the key narrative themes of *Dark Water* is the relationship between mothers and their daughters, in both the past and the present. There are two absent mothers, Yoshimi's and Mitsuko's; in the end, Yoshimi chooses to sacrifices herself, and abandons her living child for the dead Mitsuko. It is a poignant moment when Yoshimi in the lift, drenched through by the continuously gushing water, takes hold of the decaying body of Mitsuko and holds her to her breast, as Ikuko stands helplessly watching in the corridor.

Mitsuko can be considered as an archetype of the vengeful foetus from Japanese mythology and folktales. In Japanese folklore, a child is considered a foetus, as not having an identity separate from the mother, until it reaches the age of seven. As Iwasaka and Toelken point out, 'death brings into focus a number of very important elements in the Japanese worldview: obligation, duty, debt, honor, and personal responsibility' (1994: 6). This is clearly demonstrated in traditional *Ubume* stories, such as 'Kosodate-Yūrei', in which a pregnant woman dies suddenly and is buried. However, on the forty-ninth day after her burial, the villagers discover that there are forty-nine funeral cakes (*mochi*) missing from in front of the Buddha, where the cakes had been placed. The coffin is opened and a baby is found in its dead mother's arms, with one of the funeral cakes in its hands. The villagers try to take the child away from its dead mother, but the mother's arms remain clasped tight around her still-living child. The mother only gives up her baby when a nursing mother is brought to her and shows the dead mother her lactating breast. She promises that she will feed and look after the child, and with that the corpse lets go.

Fig. 7.1 Mother and child, *Dark Water* (Hideo Nakata, 2002, Kadokawa Shoten / The Kobal Collection)

Iwasaka and Toelken point to the operation of 'two contrasting, but mutually interactive, modes of obligation and guilt' within the folktale (1994: 64). Firstly, it is the child, rather than the mother, who is a potentially dangerous ghost, as the child, unlike its mother, is unritualised, having not yet been born. And it is consequently the duty of the living to provide the proper rituals which will allow the foetus to rest, and therefore 'the living may prosper, and the community (for the time being) will be safe'. Iwasaka and Toelken argue that the tale 'not only dramatize[s] the obligatory interactions of mother and child but also the living and the dead – which are both concerns which engage the Japanese legend audience' (1994: 64).

The dominant theme of *Dark Water* is the tension between the obligations of mother and child to each other, and those that define the relations of the living and the dead. As we have seen, Yoshimi is forced to choose between her living daughter, Ikuko, and the dead Mitsuko. She decides to become Mitsuko's mother in order to appease the vengeful foetus and to protect Ikuko, thereby putting her obligations to the wider community over her familial duty in the present. As such, *Dark Water* draws on traditional folklore in order to comment and perhaps critique contemporary Japanese society.

Another example can be found in the low-budget *The Locker* (Horie: 2003), loosely based upon the trend in Japan in the 1970s for leaving unwanted babies in coin lockers. A haunted locker at Shibuya station contains the vengeful spirit of an abandoned child, Sachiko. The theme of abandoned and unwanted children is paralleled in the main narrative through the character of Aya (Horikita Maki), whose mother died in childbirth. Aya has a difficult relationship with her mainly absent father, who blames her for his wife's death. Although her friend and tutor, Reika (Mizukawa Asami), tries to reassure her that there is no such thing as an unwanted child, the narrative suggests otherwise. Sachiko, it turns out in the sequel, *The Locker 2* (Horie: 2003), is an unwanted foetus, whose mother abandoned her in the locker, thus giving rise to Sachiko's re-appearance as a vengeful demonic ghost, who literally sucks the lifeblood out of her victims, growing older with each death. Reika, the protagonist in the first film, is clearly placed in the maternal position by her relationship with the unloved Aya.

In *The Locker 2*, the creepy, long-haired Sachiko returns to take Reika, the substitute maternal figure, back to the world of the dead with her, leaving Aya once again abandoned and without a protective 'mother'. As in *Dark Water*, *The Locker* and *The Locker 2* utilise traditional Japanese mythology in order to comment on the contemporary crisis in the family, as demonstrated by the practice of abandoning newly born babies in lockers.

In *Dark Water*, Yoshimi can be interpreted as the archetypical self-sacrificing woman, as commonly found in Japanese horror films of the 1950s and 1960s. As in *Tales of Ugetsu*, the death of mother is necessary in order to reunite the father with his child, and to enable the father to fulfil his familial duty. At the same time, *Dark Water* works within traditional Japanese mythology, which valorises the centrality of the maternal bond.

DOMESTIC VIOLENCE AND THE MONSTROUS FATHER

Similarly, Shimizu's *Ju-On: The Grudge* (2003) utilises traditional Japanese mythology around the wronged woman and the vengeful foetus in order to comment on changes in the shape of the Japanese family in the wake of the economic depression in the late 1990s. Told in episodic fashion, the film brings together the stories of six characters, all of whom come into contact with an accursed house and subsequently die as a reult of the curse: Rika (a social worker), Kazumi (a woman currently living in the house), Hitomi (the sister of Kazumi's husband, Katsuya), Toyama (the brother of the ghostly female *yūrei*, Kayako), Idzumi (the daughter of Toyama) and Mariko (Rika's friend and colleague). The figure of Rika provides a nominal thread that brings together the disparate strands of the narrative. Although in its American remake and in its sequel, *Ju-On: The Grudge 2*, it is the figures of Kayako (Takako Fuji) and her abandoned child, Toshio (Yuya Ozeki), who have become iconic, in the original film it is the jealous husband, Takeo Saeki (Takashi Matsuyama), responsible for the murder of his wife and the abandonment of his child, who is constitutive of the house's curse. The film thus bears similarities to *The Amityville Horror* and *The Shining*, in which male violence and aggression provide the foundations for the horrific events that take place within the narrative.

In *Ju-On: The Grudge*, the opening sequence maps out visually, within the mise-en-scène, the dominant motifs of emptiness and alienation which lead to the eruption of male violence within the home. Establishing shots of deserted streets, caught in grainy black and white footage, present us with an apocalyptic vision of the present, or perhaps the future; they are connected visually with the scene of masculine aggression, as the camera, within the domestic space, pans in on a pair of nervously tapping feet, surrounded by the debris of torn family photographs on the floor. The subsequent montage of shots, which cuts between Takeo's barely concealed aggression – signified by his blood-splattered shirt, face and hands, and captured through close-ups and part shots – and the lifeless face of his female victim, Kayako, creates a visual imagistic system at the heart of which is the destruction of the family unit through male violence. McRoy contends that the underlying masculine violence in the film can be interpreted as a cultural response to the crisis in masculinity that is a result of socio-economic factors. Writing about the opening sequences, McRoy argues:

One can read the fragmented, impressionistic opening montage as illus-
trative of a profound social disorientation, but one can also comprehend
the sequence's implied violence as emblematic of a larger compulsion to
re-establish and/or maintain a regime of masculine dominance. (2005:
179)

McRoy suggests that references to the American slasher film of the late 1970s
and early 1980s can be seen in Shimizu's 'occasional appropriation of visual
tropes' (2005: 179). However, as in *Dark Water*, it is Kubrick's *The Shining*,
with its implied domestic violence and child abuse and portrait of a dysfunctional society, that is most clearly referenced, both thematically and visually
in *Ju-On: The Grudge*. The sepia tones of the opening sequence, the panning
down deserted streets, the high-angled disorientating shot of the outside of
the house, and inside the agitated actions of Takeo, can all be seen as indirect
references to *The Shining*. In his discussion of the supernatural horror film,
Dyson writes, 'Although the Overlook is clearly a "bad" place as Stephen King
puts it, it is Jack Torrance's mental breakdown that allows dark forces to gain
a foothold in the material world' (1997: 252). This is also true of *Ju-On: The
Grudge*, as it is Takeo's violent actions that allow dark forces, in the form of the
curse, to gain a foothold in the material world. The malice and anger of Takeo
are like a virus, in that they infect all those who come into contact with the
house – the family home as a microcosm of Japanese society – and then spread
into the world outside, infecting others. The infectious nature of the curse can
be seen when the security guard dies at the hands of Kayako, a shadowy black
wraith-like figure caught on the security cameras, as Hitomi helplessly watches.
Humphries argues that the eventual outcome of an individualistic society is
'the fragmentation of the social that exposes the subject to aggressive forces
he or she can turn against the other at any moment' (2002: 203). In exploring
social fragmentation or disorientation, as McRoy calls it, *Ju-On: The Grudge*
can be understood as a critique of consumerism, capitalism and commodification as embodied within the individual, as separate to the community. *Ju-On:
The Grudge* also expresses fears around the growing violence within the family.
Buruma writes that 'Random killings are rare in Japan, but families wiped
out by mothers or fathers going berserk are not' (1984: 224). In the opening
sequence, traditional concepts of male activity in its most extreme form are
juxtaposed with the ultimate in female passivity – the dead woman. In her article,
'Japanese Women Confront Domestic Violence', Yukiko Tsunoda emphasises
the commonplace nature of domestic violence in Japanese culture:

In Japan, domestic violence is so pervasive that it is considered a normal
part of marriage, never recognized as a serious social problem, and
lacking even an appropriate term in the Japanese language. Moreover,

battered women have been deprived of any social institution where they can confront domestic violence. (1995)

Tsunoda points out that, until fairly recently, the figure of the battered woman, or indeed the concept of domestic violence itself, was either considered a Western problem, or seen as a consequence of socio-economic inequality and therefore took place only within low-income households. Indeed, the ideology of Japan as a safe country, as compared to the decadent crime-ridden streets of the USA, was at the centre of many discourses of Japanese nationalism. The very concept of domestic violence, therefore, threatened not just the notion of patriarchal privilege within marriage, but also the very construction of Japan as a nation by contrast to its perceived 'Other' – here the West, as implied in the discourse of self-orientalism which was discussed in Chapter 1.

Although there can be little doubt that significant improvements have been made in the area of women's rights in Japan, including landmark rulings with regard to sexual harassment at work and the physical and emotional abuse of woman by their husbands (Tsunoda 1995), cases of domestic violence have escalated in response to the economic recession of the late 1990s. In fact, 30.9 per cent of all divorces in Japan in 1997 were granted on the basis of male violence (Nakamura 2003: 170). Nakamura argues that gender norms in Japan are constitutive of violence towards women:

> While Japanese men learn to express themselves through competition, aggression and violence, for the most part they grow up not verbalizing their inner feelings. Indeed, one important social skill for 'masculine' men is control of their emotions. Expectations of control are higher for men than they are for women.... Painfully pent-up emotions then became directed towards intimate others in the private arena of the home, men's only 'fort' for safety reconfirming their masculine identity and pride (*otoko no koken*). Unfortunately, some men express 'unmanly' emotions in 'manly' fashion, using various (including verbal) forms of violence. (2003: 168)

In *Ju-On: The Grudge*, the murderous Takeo can be best understood as a representation of Japanese masculinity in the aftermath of the so-called economic bubble. The present mirrors the past as the story slowly unfolds. Tokunaga Kazumi (Kanji Tsuda) and her husband, Katsuya Tokunaga (Shuri Matsuda), live with Katsuya's aged mother, Sachie (Chikako Isomura). Once again, the theme of abandonment is central to the main narrative, as it is in *Dark Water*. Both Sachie, who Rika finds alone in the house, and Toshio, who Rika finds hiding in a cupboard in the opening, framing episode, comment on the breakdown of the family, drawing a line of similarity between the abandonment of the very old and the very young in contemporary Japan. Rika's discovery of Sachie, lying on a soiled futon, and the scenes of Kazumi ignoring her mother-in-law in the second episode of the film emphasise the strain that a growing elderly population is putting on the framework of the Japanese family, torn as it is between the traditional *ie* system and the more 'democratic' values epitomised by the triangular formation of the nuclear family.

Katsuya, portrayed as a typical 'salaryman', returns late at night to find his mother alone, and his wife in a catatonic state in the upstairs bedroom. As Katsuya rings for an ambulance, the crouched figure of Toshio appears in the corner of the room and Kazumi breathes her last. The camera pans in on Katsuya's face, as the darkness enfolds him in its violent grasp, both metaphorically and literally. Later in the film, the police discover Katsuya and Kazumi's dead bodies against the wall in the attic, the present mirroring the past.

The parallelism between the two stories, the past and the present, between Takeo and Katsuya, structures a masculine identity defined in and through violence. And yet it is the products of that violence – the seductive and frightening figure of Kayako, the original 'wronged woman', and her child, the vengeful foetus, Toshio – who come to function as figures of dread for most of the narrative, rather than the originator of the curse, Takeo.

In the end sequences, in which Rika goes back to the house to attempt to save her best friend, Mariko (who is already dead), she comes face to face

Fig. 7.2 Takeo corners Rika: domestic violence in *Ju-On: The Grudge* (Takashi Shimizu, 2003, Oz Company Ltd / The Kobal Collection)

with her nemesis, Kayako. As Kayako slowly crawls down the stairs, her limbs broken and bent, Rika stands transfixed in front of a mirror, holding her hands in front of her eyes. A montage of shots reveals that Kayako has been haunting Rika, constructing the two women as doubles of each other. As Rika looks in the mirror, she sees not her own face, but that of the ghostly Kayako. Kayako's hands come out, covering Rika's, as she emerges from her blouse. Taking her hands away from her eyes, Kayako disappears. Here the visual motif of the double situates Kayako as a figure of sympathy rather than fear. However, this separation of woman into beautiful image and abject body could be argued as articulating masculine fears around female subjectivity and empowerment. As she crawls down the stairs, dragging her broken body, Kayako transforms from vengeful *yūrei* into the pitiful 'wronged woman'. This is visually signified through the revelation of the human face behind the mask. At the bottom of the stairs, Kayako holds out her hand towards Rika, as if pleading with her for help. Removing her hands from her eyes, Rika discovers that the room is empty. Another noise can be heard, and this time Takeo appears at the top of the stairs. Repeating the earlier gesture of Kayako, Takeo holds out his bloody hands towards Rika, but this time the gesture signifies menace and male violence. The final shot is of the dead Kayako, lying against the wall of the attic, as the camera pans in; suddenly her eyes open, returning the gaze of the cinematic spectator.

DOMESTIC DISRUPTIONS

The similarity between the contemporary haunted house film in Japanese cinema and earlier films such as *The Amityville Horror* and *The Shining* is not coincidental. Unlike the original Japanese horror story of the 1950s and 1960s, the trope of the vengeful ghost is not a mere embodiment of individual guilt, but rather is a collective projection of societal guilt. All the films discussed, in one way or another, meditate on the prevalence of domestic violence as a result of socio-economic transformations in the very nature of Japanese society. At the centre of these films are the monstrous mother and her equally monstrous progeny. Goldberg argues that New Wave films such as *Blind Beast* marked a shift in the representation of the mother in Japanese cinema: 'It is during this period that the element of blame comes overtly into play, and unnatural mothers who do not fulfil the ideals of Japanese motherhood are depicted as begetting monstrous children' (2004: 374). However, the mother is also a tragic figure, whose disappearance/death functions 'to complete our sense of beauty' (Kawai 1996: 58), working within the Japanese aesthetic of *mono-no-aware*.

It is clear to see how upheavals in Japanese society, brought about by rapid modernisation, have led to a breakdown in the traditional Japanese pre-modern family structure, as embedded within the wider *ie* system that regulated the relationships between people in the broader context of the community and the nation. Societal breakdown, as signified by domestic violence, child neglect and abandonment of the elderly, is negotiated through recourse to traditional Japanese mythology and folktales, within the generic frame of the haunted house narratives.

CHAPTER 8

Serial Killers and Slashers Japanese-Style

Rather than products of dysfunctional families, Japanese psychos are, by and large, products of the contemporary Japanese society where alienation, distance and detachment, lack of affect, indifference towards others and selfishness seem to be rules of the day. (Ognjanovic 2006b)

Unlike America, Japan traditionally has had a low rate of violent crimes against the person. This seems to be changing, in the aftermath of the so-called *Otaku* murders in 1988 and 1989 carried out by Miyazaki Tsutomu, and the notorious flesh-eating media celebrity, Issei Sagawa, in 1981. In June of that year Sagawa shot Renee Hartevelt; he then cut up her body and cooked strips of flesh, which he consumed, before taking pictures of her mutilated corpse. Predating both these cases was the notorious Iwao Enokizu, in 1964, who went on an eighteen-month killing spree before finally being caught. Ognjanovic blames the appearance of the Japanese psychopath on the breakdown of the societal structures through which the subject identifies himself (herself) as embedded within the community, rather than on dysfunctional families. It is the displacing of the situated self by the individual ego associated with Westernisation which, it is implied, is the root cause of the emergence of the Japanese serial killer.

As is true of Ed Gein, whose seemingly normal exterior hid a pathological killer, real-life serial killings have provided the inspiration for Japanese horror film. One of the most notable is Imamura's *Vengeance is Mine* (1979), which focuses on the seventy-eight-day hunt for the charismatic Enokizu, by the Japanese police. More recently came the low-budget *Tokyo Psycho* (Oikawa: 2004), which offers a fictionalised account of the so-called *Otaku* murderer. The notion of the outsider, so essential to both real-life and fictional constructions of the serial killer, has a greater symbolic function, within a society based upon the relational self and underpinned by neo-Confucianism, than in the West where the serial killer can be theorised as the inevitable outcome of a society based upon the sanctity of individualism and underpinned by the imaginary ideology of the American Dream.

In addition to these dramatisations of real-life serial killers is the Japanese version of the slasher film. The key film is *Evil Dead Trap* (1988), which brought together Ikeda (director) and Ishii (writer) for the first time since their collaboration on the *Angel Guts* series of films. *Evil Dead Trap* is generally considered to be a pivotal turning point in Japanese horror, paving the way for the contemporary success of films such as *Ring* and *Ju-On: The Grudge*. However, like the original slasher cycle in America, low-budget exploitation films such as *Entrails of a Virgin* (Komizu: 1986) also proved popular with audiences. Other variations on the fictional serial killer film are *Another Heaven* (Iida: 2000), *Angel Dust* (Ishii: 1994) and *The Guard from the Underground* (Kurosawa: 1992). Fujii's *Living Hell* (2000) is particularly interesting, as it was marketed in the West as *Living Hell: A Japanese Chainsaw Massacre*, thus encouraging audiences to compare it to Hooper's infamous *The Texas Chainsaw Massacre* (1974).

SERIAL KILLERS: BETWEEN FICTION AND FACT

Imamura's *Vengeance is Mine*, about Iwao Enokizu, does not attempt to justify Enokizu's killing spree through recourse to popular psychoanalysis, unlike comparable American films based upon the real-life exploits of Ed Gein, such as Hitchcock's *Psycho* (1960), Hooper's *The Texas Chainsaw Massacre*, the low-budget pseudo-documentary *Deranged* (Gillen and Ormsby: 1974) and Demme's award-winning *Silence of the Lambs* (1991). In all these films, with perhaps the exception of *The Texas Chainsaw Massacre*, the motivation for murder on the part of the fictionalised Gein is clearly linked to a negative Oedipus complex – in other words, the male child's inability to separate from the mother due to the lack of a father as symbol and maintainer of the patriarchal order; this is often connoted through mise-en-scène, costume and props rather than the actual presence of the mother. *Vengeance is Mine* does not offer an explanation of the possible motivations behind the killing spree of Enokizu (played with intensity by Ken Ogata), a charming conman, thief and murderer; nor does it offer a psychological or economic framework which might justify Enokizu's violent acts. Although some factual information, such as Enokizu's Catholic background, his prolific sexual appetite and his desertion of his wife, is offered, none of these facts explains the reasons behind his killing spree.

Vengeance is Mine dispenses with the linear narrative and temporal continuity of the traditional serial killer film. Instead, we have a narrative defined by temporal disunity and incoherence. The use of temporal ellipses – that is, gaps in the temporal framework of the narrative – is signalled early on in the film. In this scene, the first shot is of a dead body in an empty field; the next shot, of a helicopter, provides a transition between the first shot and the following one, in which we return to the field, now swarming with policemen. The manner in which the film is narrated also foregrounds temporal disunity. Beginning with the capture of Enokizu, the subsequent narrative of his crime spree is pieced together non-chronologically through the use of flashbacks and written reports, and is motivated more by the police investigation than the order of the crimes themselves.

In 'Everyday Nightmares: The Rhetoric of Social Horror in the Nightmare on Elm Street Series', Heba distinguishes between coherent and incoherent horror films, arguing that coherent horror films are monoglossic – that is, supportive of the status quo – and that incoherent films are heteroglossic – refusing narrative closure and explanation. He writes: 'incoherent horror movies focus on humanity's capacity to create its own horrors that cannot be contained by the coherent master narrative. In fact, many incoherent horror movies code the dominant culture itself as the source of horror' (1995). This could explain the critical reception of *Vengeance is Mine*, in which the failure of the film to define Enokizu's acts in relation to some societal or psychological ills confounded Japanese critics at the time. In Goldsmith's examination of the film, he quotes the following, taken from a review by a critic from the *Kinema Jumpo* magazine:

> For Japanese film, 1979 was a year in which Imamura Shohei's *Vengeance Is Mine* demonstrated overwhelming strength. While it is the first film in some time for Imamura, if I could venture a personal opinion, I must say that I'm not even sure of the director's viewpoint. (cited in Goldsmith 2005)

It is the middle-class aspirations and status of Enokizu, who is the son of a fisherman-cum-hotel owner, that critics in Japan found so problematic. For them, used to the construction of the outsider as social outcast as a result of his lowly place in the social hierarchy, the representation of Enokizu, whose outsider status cannot be explained by socio-economic constraints, proved difficult to understand. Goldsmith elucidates, 'Enokizu cannot easily be contained in any particular tier of the class system, and this status as a total outsider allows him to mediate between different levels of society at will' (2005). Unlike the traditional left-wing conception of the alienated outsider, the result of class division under the capitalist system of production, Enokizu seems to choose and even revel in his outsider status. He shows no remorse for his crimes, either within the past events or during his present confinement in prison. Further, in *Vengeance is Mine*, spatial dislocation determines the relationships between characters, thus mimicking the isolation of the individual in contemporary Japanese society.

Roberson and Suzuki argue that, as a result of unprecedented economic growth in the early 1960s, 'men's roles became portrayed as those of taxpayers and workers, functioning – as "correct" citizens – as part of a state-sponsored patriarchal industrial-capitalist system ... that place[s] the family in subordinated support of the state' (2003: 7). Gendered assumptions and expectations centred on the idea of *daikokubashira*, which, according to Roberson and Suzuki, means 'literally the large black pillar of traditional Japanese houses' (2003: 8). Gill explains:

> In the image of the *daikokubashira*, man merges with the pillar. It is an image of reliability, of strength, of stasis. The pillar that supports the household has an honour, represented in its/his dominant central position, but also bears a heavy load – supporting the roof/supporting the family. (2003: 144–5)

Enokizu has no fixed identity either within the family or within the corporation as a substitute for the family; instead he assumes the identities of others, including that of a university professor, in order to get close to his victims before robbing and killing them. In this he is a transgressive figure. This is particularly relevant, as mobility of masculine identity in Japanese society was something which, at the time, was associated with the working classes and specifically day labourers. In Gill's terms, day labourers' identities are constructed in terms of 'physicality, immediacy and mobility' (2003: 151), which 'are grounded in a proletarian tradition' (2003: 152). In so far as Enokizu cuts across traditional constructions of masculinity, in both social and cultural terms, he subverts hegemonic constructions of an idealised masculinity that were prevalent at the time.

Enokizu's relationship with women is founded on deceit, but it is a deceit that, even when revealed, as with Haru (Mayumi Ogawa) – one of the women he becomes involved with during his murderous spree – does not seem to matter. Haru chooses to continue her relationship with Enokizu, asking: 'What's the difference?' Goldsmith writes: 'What defines Enokizu is not his position within a social binarism, but his connection to a primal physical energy that Imamura sees as underlying all human life' (2005). As we have already seen, the films of the Japanese New Wave situate the material body (*nikutai*) in opposition to traditional conceptions of the spirit (*seishin*) associated with the 'family-state' and a hyper-militarist position (Standish 2005: 210). As such, Enokizu's search for personal fufilment, irrespective of the societal damage, can be understood as a privileging of the body and materiality against some anomolous concept of the spirit in service of the nation-state, together with a critique of Westernisation. And, as in the Japanese New Wave, the role of the father is questioned. Writing about the *taiyōzoku* genre, Standish comments:

> Within these films the role of the father figure is precarious, as they are emasculated representations of the generation who lost the war and were criminalized through war crimes trials. (2005: 231)

Vengeance is Mine foregrounds this loss of masculine potency through the inadequate father figure. This is demonstrated in the scene where Enokizu's father attempts, but fails, to make love to Enokizu's estranged wife. In addition, in one of the flashback sequences, we see Enokizu's father being humiliated by a Japanese naval officer. In a later scene, Enikozu is shown harassing a young Japanese woman, who is out with a group of American soldiers. While father and son are situated as doubles, the film does not blame the father for the son's actions. In the final sequences, when Enokizu's bones are thrown into Beppu Bay (by his father and his wife), the continued use of the freeze frame to capture the bones frozen in time and space suggests the inability of Japanese paternalism to deal with the shifting nature of class and economic relationships in a rapidly modernising Japan.

THE COLLECTOR

> Closely related to the psychological horror film and to the splatter movie, the stalk-and-slash film was conceived by Hitchcock's *Psycho* (1960), nurtured by Hooper's *The Texas Chainsaw Massacre* (1974) and came of age with Carpenter's *Halloween* (1978). Here the psychopath, supernatural or all-too-natural, figures as a central menace to a string of (usually) women-in-peril, though any vaguely promiscuous teenager is a natural target. (Newman 1996: 300)

Violated Angels (Wakamatsu: 1967), *The Embryo Hunts in Secret* (Wakamatsu: 1966) and *Blind Beast* (Masumura: 1969) can be considered early examples of the stalker film, in which a beautiful young woman is subjected to increasingly brutal attacks and rape by an unsavoury male attacker. Structurally, they are similar in that the actual 'stalking' part of the film is given less time than the graphic scenes of repeated violent attacks on the female victim(s). The endings are also the same: the male attacker's death at the hands of his female victim. In fact, *Violated Angels* was purportedly inspired by the true story of the twenty-five-year-old Richard Speck, who brutally raped and killed a group of young nurses in Chicago on 13 July 1966. Hunter writes:

Legend has it that Wakamatsu, inflamed by this provocative news story from the West, conceived and executed his extraordinary film *Violated Angels* (released in 1967) within a week of hearing about it. Apparently it was not so much the slaughter itself so much as the fact that one nurse survived, which appealed to Wakamatsu's sensibilities. (1998: 40)

Similar to *Violated Angels* is *Tokyo Psycho* (Oikawa: 2004), which was also based upon a true case, but this time one that happened in Japan. Ognjanovic writes: '[The] case is paradigmatic for numerous otaku-like psychos that are later found in the movies like ALL NIGHT LONG, EVIL DEAD TRAP 2 etc.' During the trial, 'The defence argued that the audiovisual culture of videotapes and television, the lack of a sense of reality in the information society and the isolation of youth are behind the crime as sickness of modern society' (2006b).

Between 1988 and 1989, the murders of four young girls, aged between four and seven, took place. The culprit was a seemingly mild-mannered clerk called Tsutomu Miyazaki, who was twenty-seven at the time of his arrest. Due to the fact that he was found with a large collection of pornographic manga, violent horror films and home-made films detailing the molestation and murder of his victims, he was dubbed 'The Collector' by the Japanese press. Ognjanovic details the manner in which Miyazaki's crimes were blamed on his so-called emotional immaturity, articulating contemporary fears around *youjika* (the infantilisation of culture), which is seen to represent an immature or an incomplete identity. Hasegawa argues that the concept of *youjika* is used in terms of 'a hollowness or unisexuality, that is a sexuality that is yet to be distinguished or differentiated' (2002: 157).

Miyazaki's arrest created a moral panic around *Otaku* sub-culture. In 'Amateur Manga Subculture and the Otaku Panic', Kinsella explores the relationship between radical political movements of the 1960s, the development of manga sub-culture, and youth culture. She writes: 'Although the political point of youth radicalism became completely obscure by the early 1970s, younger generations, youth culture, and young women, became the focus of nervous discourse about the apparent decay of a traditional Japanese society' (1998). The Miyazaki case caused a widespread media panic, through which it was perceived that a whole generation of Japanese youngsters were threatening the very foundation of Japanese society. Kinsella comments:

After the Miyazaki murder case, the concept of an otaku changed its meaning at the hands of the media. Otaku came to mean, in the first instance Miyazaki, in the second instance, all amateur manga artists and fans, and in the third instance all Japanese youth in their entirety. (1998)

Like the Ed Gein story in the USA, the '*Otaku*' killer has become firmly embedded within Japanese culture as source of inspiration for post-modern narratives of pathological masculinity. *Tokyo Psycho* substantially changes the 'true-life' story of Miyazaki, transforming him from a paedophile and child murderer into an obsessed transgendered stalker, Komiya Osamu (Taniguchi Masashi), whose object of affection is a beautiful young graphic designer called Yumiko Ōsawa (Kokubu Sachiko).

In *Psycho Paths: Tracking the Serial Killer Through Contemporary American Film and Fiction*, Simpson argues that the serial killer is a post-modern shape-shifter who violates societal taboos through the doubling of normalcy and madness in one composite figure:

The serial killer is a postmodern shapeshifter or changeling child whose spiritual essence was kidnapped by pornography or bad genes or abusive parents and replaced with the soul of Cain. Any given killer has one pleasant or at least non-threatening face with which to conduct public negotiations, and another evil face with which to terrify helpless victims. This doubling strategy allows inhuman evil to lurk behind human 'normalcy', simply because the serial killer's actions by their very nature cannot help but propel him beyond the liminal into what Noel Carroll identifies as the interstitial territory reserved for the most egregious taboo violators. (2000: 3–4)

Loosely working within the conventions of the stalker film, the obsessed stalker, Osamu (who we discover later on is Mikuriya) is typical of the post-modern serial killer, in his ability not only to hide his psychosis behind the mask of normalcy but also to shape-shift between multiple personas, both masculine and feminine. In the opening scene of the film, Yumiko and Moe (Yumiko's work partner and best friend) are in their office, a living/work space in an anonymous grey block. A knock on the door startles Yumiko – Moe is asleep on a couch – but when she peers through the keyhole, the corridor seems empty. However, when she looks a second time, she is horrified to see the visage of a strange woman, with a white eye patch and smeared lipstick, pressed up against the glass – the convex glass distorting the image. The camera follows Mikuriya as he runs away, first through a long shot and ending with an extreme low-angled close-up. Writing about Juraj Herz's *The Cremator* (1968), Scofield argues: 'Magnified body parts on screen are disturbing because they tamper with the continuity of the human form generally beheld during mundane life. When shown mere parts of the body, viewers are denied the unified whole which they desire' (2007). The use of extreme close-ups here distorts the image and imbues a sense of horror linked to the fragmentation of the bodily integrity. Here, as in *The Cremator*, the key to the horror is visual disorientation, as the spectator is positioned within the disturbed consciousness of the serial killer.

In this scene, Mikuriya is holding an open red umbrella, signifying both passion and danger, and creating a caricature of femininity whose overdetermined signs disestablish traditional codings of femininity and masculinity. In his subsequent construction of a macabre sculpture made out of a dead woman's body, piano wire and flashing lights with a photograph of Yumiko in the centre, serial killing is configured as a performance art explicitly linked to the art of cinema itself. Schneider writes: 'a cinematic metaphor is effected whereby the killer gets equated with a kind of artist, and the carnage he leaves behind with works of art' (2001).

In a later scene, like Hannibal Lecter in *The Silence of the Lambs*, Mikuriya disguises himself using the face of the recently butchered Moe and this time gains entry to the work space, allowing him to abduct Yumiko. Halberstam comments in relation to Demme's film that it is 'a horror film that, for once, is not designed to scare women; it scares men instead with the image of a fragmented and fragile masculinity, a male body disowning the penis' (1995: 168). The use of female skin, here as in *The Silence of the Lambs*, can be said to act as a 'fetishized signifier of gender for a heterosexist culture' (Halberstam 1995: 168–9).

However, these similarities apart, *Tokyo Psycho* does not engage with a psychoanalytical framework through which to understand the shifting contours of the serial killer. The little information we have is that he was a loner, an *Otaku*, without friends, who may or may not have strangled his parents with piano wire whilst he was in high school. Instead, the narrative focuses on Yumiko and her attempts to discover the identity of this mysterious visitor and of the writer of a letter she has subsequently received which bears the words 'You were born to marry me'. At a high-school reunion, she remembers a similar letter that she had from Osamu. If we are supposed to identify a traumatic event in the past as an interpretive framework for Osamu's actions in the present, then it would be this rejection by Yumiko of his expressions of love. When Mikuriya eventually manages to kidnap Yumiko, he persists with his declarations of love even when torturing her. As in the *Angel Guts* films and pink cinema, romantic love becomes inseparable from male violence and female violation. Yet Yumiko continues to refuse him. Finally, like many 'final girls' before her, she manages to turn the tables on her attacker, who she drowns in the sea; unlike some, she needs no protector/father figure to help her defeat the monstrous male. It is evident that *Tokyo Psycho* is much more a fictionalisation than *Vengeance is Mine*. This can also be seen in the manner in which *Tokyo Psycho* utilises saturated canvases of primary colours – red, yellow and blue – as an externalisation of the mind of a deranged serial killer, which is in opposition to the more objective semi-documentary style of *Vengeance is Mine*. Mes and Sharp write of the latter: 'Its use of wide long shots with a minimum of edits lends some of the scenes the air of a TV news report, imbuing the depiction of the actual murders with a brutally objective coolness' (2005: 31).

Further, *Tokyo Psycho* is very similar in structure to the American stalker movie in that it focuses on the relationship between a killer and the (usually) female protagonist, with anyone who gets in the way being dispatched to a gruesome and untimely death. In the original cycle of stalker films, the murderous activities of the mainly male monsters, Jason Voorhees (*Friday the 13th*, Cunningham: 1980) and Michael Myers (*Halloween*, Carpenter: 1978), were explained diegetically through an embedded psychoanalytical framework. Jason develops an unhealthy attachment to the dead corpse of his mother when he takes over her mantle in *Friday the 13th Part Two* (Miner: 1981), and it is the sight of his sister having sex whilst their parents are out, interpreted as an incestuous Oedipal impulse, which provokes the development of Michael Myers's pathology – as constructed retroactively through *Halloween 2* (Rosenthal: 1982).

In *Tokyo Psycho*, however, although we learn of rumours that Osamu murdered his parents with piano wire, these are never substantiated, and rather than being motivated by hate, Osamu is dedicated to making the reluctant Yumiko his bride. Whilst the obsessive character of Osamu encompasses attributes of the *Otaku*, it is in the subjective mise-en-scène that isolation and alienation, as causational factors in Osamu's psychosis, are most fully realised. The narrative is mainly located within the grey, minimalist apartment block where Yumiko lives and works. The use of the point-of-view shot of the disembodied killer, an identifiable trope of the original stalker film, tracking down identical corridor after identical uninhabited corridor and swerving round corners, creates an architectural vision of isolation and alienation, and a sensory feeling of deprivation (Balmain 2006). There is a feeling of the uncanny captured by these repeated tracking shots that in places do not seem connected to the obsessed stalker. The serial killer here, as in *Vengeance is Mine*, articulates a crisis in hegemonic constructions of masculinity; multiple identities, as so many masks, can be said to express contemporary Japanese patriarchal anxiety over the shifting of masculinity as a stable sign. Further, in *Tokyo Psycho*, the architecture of the post-modern city mirrors the internal psychosis of the 'Psycho' of the title. Sacchi writes that living in Tokyo has become the art of living in the labyrinth:

> The metropolitan area of Tokyo is today more a non-place, hailing less from architecture and the traditional definition of space than from the ubiquitous, labyrinthine presence of telecommunications networks, intelligent buildings and machines, plant for the accumulation and diffusion of energy and water, waste removal and recycling, and diverse, inter-connect transport systems. (2004: 228–9)

As such, the title of the film suggests perhaps that anyone and everyone in the disorientating urban jungle that is Tokyo must of necessity become a psycho in order to cope with the visual trauma that is the city (Purini 2004: 8).

THE SLASHER FILM: JAPANESE-STYLE

> In these movies, isolated psychotic males, often masked or at least hidden from view, are pitted against one or more young men and women (especially the latter) whose looks, personalities, or promiscuities serve to trigger recollections of some past trauma in the killer's mind, thereby unleashing his seemingly boundless psychosexual fury. (Schneider 2002)

Although stalker and slasher films are often confused as constituting one distinct sub-genre, they are, in fact, not the same. The stalker film, as theorised by Dika (1990), has a distinct two-part temporal structure, the reason behind the killings is usually sexual revenge, and the binary central relationship between the 'final girl' and the 'male killer' can be understood as allowing a female – although not necessarily feminist – rite of passage through the defeat of the male monster. It could be argued that the stalker film is ideologically reactionary in that the end can be seen as affirming rather than challenging the status quo. As Clover points out, the central character may be gendered female, but her androgyny makes her a suitable substitute for the male spectator, who can enjoy the masochistic pleasures of fear from a distance (1992: 42–64). The slasher film, however, does not necessarily stick to the distinct temporal structure of the stalker film and the killer is not necessarily male; neither is the killer necessarily motivated merely by sexual desire. As Heba states, 'the evolution of slasher movies suggests that another, broader set of codes, in addition to the ones Dika identifies, is at work' (1995).

While *Tokyo Psycho*, with its psychopathic killer motivated by sexual desire (rather than rage), falls into the category of the stalker film – although it must be noted that there is no reason given for his psychosexual obsession – the killer in Japanese slasher films, as we will see, often has supernatural origins. Whilst the male antagonists in *Vengeance is Mine* and *Tokyo Psycho* are pathological symptoms of Japanese modernity, the supernatural monsters in *Evil Dead Trap*, *Entrails of a Virgin* and *Living Hell* can be considered revenants of pre-modernity, symptoms of the repressed past whose repetition functions to subvert the aesthetics of shame associated with the sexualised body. In 'An introduction to the American Horror Film', Wood distinguishes between necessary repression (that which is needed for the operation of society) and surplus repression, which functions in the service of the dominant ideology. He writes, 'one can ask what, exactly, in the interests of alienated labor and the patriarchal family, is repressed' (2002: 26). In Japan, it is the materiality of the body linked to the pre-modern, and a time before Westernisation, that has been repressed in order to enable the development of capitalism and ensure economic prosperity.

Entrails of a Virgin (1986) is the first in a trilogy of films by Kazuo 'Gaira' Komizu, which also includes *Entrails of a Beautiful Woman* (1986) and *Rusted Body: Guts of a Virgin III* (1987). *Entrails of a Virgin* is a strange combination of slasher film, Italian exploitation and Japanese pink film, and is an early example of 'gorenography'. Notable for its graphic scenes of sex and violence, its extremely low budget and its not-so-special efforts, *Entrails of a Virgin* features a plot, such as it is, that involves a group of photographers from a pornographic magazine out on a shoot in the woods and their beautiful models, who get lost in the woods and take refuge in an abandoned building, where they find themselves at the mercy of a swamp monster – as some sort of vengeful male deity. *Entrails of a Virgin* is infamous for its sexual violence towards women and its gratuitous sex scenes. One of the more unpleasant scenes features one of the young women, Kazuyo, who is forced to take part in a wrestling match with Tachikawa, assistant to the photographers; while demonstrating his athletic prowess to the male group – all the time berating and insulting Kazuyo, he traumatises her so badly that she wets herself before falling on the ground unconscious. Here, as in the rape-revenge film, the woman as sexualised object is circulated around the male group as some sort of (homoerotic) bonding ritual. In an equally disturbing scene, Kazuyo, having descended into a crazed nymphomania as a result of her treatment by the men in the group, masturbates with a severed arm whilst pleasuring the swamp monster. In response to her cries for more, she is penetrated so deeply that she is disembowelled in the process. One of the other models, Kei, is also ravished by the primal monster and, having been left spent, is decapitated by a shard of a sign which falls off the roof of a building. This is an example of the double binary, in which in order to criticise violence towards women explicitly, along with their objectification, films have first to visualise that violence; as a consequence, they run the risk of being castigated as misogynist. And there is little doubt that the extended scenes of female violation in *Entrails of a Virgin* eroticise the female body, offering up the open and sexualised surfaces of femininity to the penetrating and pornographic gaze of the male spectator. However, unlike its counterpart, the American slasher film, the male group are punished for their treatment of woman by the primal monster. Tachikawa is bludgeoned to death with a hammer; Tachiguichi is penetrated by a spear; and finally, Asaoka, pursued by the enraged Kazuyo, is choked to death as a large hook wielded by the monster lifts him into the air and copious amounts of viscous fluid – the monster's semen – gush into the water nearby. Here, in opposition to the dominant conventions of the slasher film at the time, men are also objects of sexual violation.

Unlike its American predecessors, *Entrails of a Virgin* does not need to substitute the male phallus for an external object, such as knife, chainsaw or axe; instead, it is the monster's enormous phallus (usually depicted in shadow) that is the weapon of choice. The very presence of the phallus as killing machine highlights the sexual inadequacy of the male characters, who can only feel powerful by raping and objectifying women. It is only the swamp monster, it turns out, who can really satisfy the women in the film, thus articulating a male anxiety that, in fact, size does matter. In the end, the 'final girl', Rei (the only virgin amongst the woman at the beginning of the film), ends up impregnated with the monster's progeny. She lives to survive another day but, in the manner of the typical slasher film, 'the heroine is not free' (Dika 1990: 60). Whilst arguably less artistic than the *Angel Guts* series of films, *Entrails of a Virgin* operates within a similar sub-cultural critique of the commodification and exploitation of women in Japan. At the same time, the primal monster's enormous phallus can be interpreted as an external projection of male wish fulfilment and anxieties around masculine power, or indeed the absence of it in a rapidly changing society.

Ikeda's *Evil Dead Trap* also uses the basic format of the slasher film, while adding a specific Japanese flavour to the proceedings. A beautiful young television reporter, Nami (Miyuki Ono), receives a strange videotape, which shows the torture and murder of a woman. In an attempt to confirm the tape's authenticity, Nami and four of her colleagues take a trip to an abandoned army base, the location where the videotape was shot. One by one, her colleagues are killed in a brutal and graphic manner, which calls to mind the *giallo* films of Argento in particular, until Nami is the only one left. Then she meets a strange man, Muraki (Yuji Honma), who seems to know more about what is going on than he lets on; he tries to help her escape.

During the final confrontation between Nami as the archetypical 'final girl' and Muraki, *Evil Dead Trap* takes on a nightmarish, almost Cronenbergian, quality. It turns out that Muraki's twin, Hideki, has been responsible for the killings, but Hideki is part of Muraki, rather than apart from him. Borrowing liberally from Cronenberg's *Videodrome* (1983), Ridley Scott's *Alien* (1979) and earlier films such as *It's Alive* (Cohen: 1974), the film shows the monstrous Hideki bursting out of Muraki's body, determined to reach Nami, who is situated both visually and thematically as a mother substitute for the angry foetus. And, as is typical of the slasher genre, the male monster does not die easily, getting back up after he has been stabbed, burned and shot. In an image reminiscent of the ending of *Halloween*, Nami stabs the angry foetus (still conjoined to Muraki) with a shard of glass, and Muraki falls backwards out of the window. With a nod to *Friday the 13th*, Nami wakes up in a hospital bed to learn that the police did not find any trace of Hideki. The film ends with the grotesque scene of the re-emergence of Hideki from Nami's body in an explosion of blood, plaintively crying, 'Mama'.

Like many contemporary Japanese horror films, *Evil Dead Trap* 'quotes' liberally from a variety of sources, both Western and Japanese, even though Ikeda professes both not to like horror film and not to have watched it (Sharp 2005). The maggots on the ceiling that drop into the hair of one of the victim, before she is brutally eviscerated, pay homage to Argento's supernatural horror film *Suspiria* (1977), as does the sampled soundtrack that accompanies the film. The motif of the penetrated, viscous eyeball recalls similar scenes in both Argento's and Fulci's work. The costume of Muraki when he takes on the persona of Hideki, with its mask and voluminous plastic cape, also combines the conventions of the Italian *giallo* with its remediation in the original American slasher cycle. The names of the central characters, Nami and Muraki, are, of course, the names of the protagonists in the *Angel Guts* series. And the use of blue lighting throughout many of the chase sequences, along with water during the final confrontation – emphasising the distance between Nami and Muraki – is, as we have seen, constitutive of the dominant mise-en-scène in many Japanese horror films.

The addition of a superfluous rape scene, in addition to the obligatory consensual heterosexual sex, seems somewhat out of place, but is, in fact, in keeping with the vast majority of Japanese exploitation and horror films of the time. It is, however, significant that, despite the obvious erotic titillation offered by such a scene, it no longer functions as a mechanism of liberating women's inherent impure nature. In fact, it provides a contrast between forced and consensual sex that signifies shifting changes in attitudes towards women – in the world of cinema, at least. In his review of the film, Galloway points out that it was at the insistence of Japan Home Video, the company that provided the funding for the film and for whom both Hitomi Kobayashi and Eriko Nakagawa (two of the actors involved) worked, that the 'obligatory sex scenes' were inserted. Further, against criticisms by horror film 'purists' of unnecessary explicit sex in the film, he points out that 'sexually active young people are *always* getting murdered in such films – it's a puritanical prerequisite! Here the sex is just more explicit' (2006: 168).

The success of *Evil Dead Trap* led to two sequels: *Evil Dead Trap 2: Hideki* (Hashimoto: 1991) and *Evil Dead Trap 3: Broken Love Killer* (1993), directed by Ikeda. While both are interesting films, they substantially alter the story. In *Evil Dead Trap 2*, the serial killer is a female Jack the Ripper and/or Jekyll and Hyde, called Aki (Shoko Nakajima). An overweight projectionist, Aki has blackouts; when she wakes up she finds herself next to the severely mutilated bodies of prostitutes, and she is eventually revealed as the murderous attacker. In the third film in the series, the heroine, Nami (Kimiko Yo), attempts to track down a serial killer, a high-school teacher called, as is typical in Ikeda's films, Tetsuro Muraki, here played by Shirō Sano.

Although *Evil Dead Trap* is a work of significantly higher quality than *Entrails of a Virgin*, both utilise cultural mythology and supernatural frameworks in their constructions of male monstrosity. Unlike in Western religions, sexuality was an important component of both Buddhism and Shintō – until, of course, Japan started perceiving itself through the Other's eyes. Buisson remarks, 'Unlike the Judaeo-Christian West, which insists on seeing sex as inseparable from evil, Japan does not condemn pleasure in itself' (2003: 63). Indeed, as we have seen in the Shintō creation myth, the earth comes into being because of an act of sexual intercourse between Izanagi and Izanami, who are also brother and sister. The worship of the phallus is also central to Shintō, and can be seen in the story of Susanoo, the brother of the Sun Goddess (Amaterasu), who defeats an eight-headed snake. In Japan, the phallus can be 'a symbol of fertility or primitive purity'. There are shrines dedicated to the phallus, in which the phallus is displayed in 'full anatomical detail' (Buisson 2003: 65). *Shunga* (pornography) prints were popular during the Meiji Era until Japan's gaze came to mimic that of the Western Other. The association between the land, the monster and primal sexuality linked to the pre-modern, in *Entrails of a Virgin*, needs to be considered in light of cultural mythology rather than condemned as out-and-out misogyny. Heba points to a point of identification between the serial killer and the folkloric monster. He writes, 'The supernatural image of the human/monster hybrid is, of course, central to the project of rendering the serial killer into a proper folkloric demon' (1995). The deity/monster in *Entrails of a Virgin* and the vengeful foetus in *Evil Dead Trap* can be seen as eruptions of the pre-modern body, in which the economic and the political converge in a politics of bodily corruption, as in the sub-cultural discourse of *Angura* that we explored in Chapter 5.

A JAPANESE CHAINSAW MASSACRE?

Whilst the Japanese version of the slasher film makes indirect references to the original American cycle of slasher films, as we have seen, Fujii's 2000 film, *Living Hell: A Japanese Chainsaw Massacre*, invites the spectator to make a direct comparison with Hooper's *The Texas Chainsaw Massacre*. As with the earlier film, *Living Hell* critiques the ideology of the family through its representation of a monstrous family of cannibals, but with supernatural overtones. In particular, the demented cannibalistic family reunion towards the end of the narrative clearly demonstrates Hooper's influence. The film has a nightmarish quality, signalled in the opening sequences when an old woman named Chiyo (Yoshiko Shiraishi) and a young girl, Yuki (Naoko Mori), torture and murder a middle-aged couple; and eat the family dog. However, when the police arrive on the scene, they find only the seemingly traumatised Chiyo.

The two women then turn up at the house of Yasu (Hirohito Ho), a wheelchair-bound teenager, who lives at home with his brother, Ken (Kazuo Yashiro), his (adopted) sister Mami (Rumi) and his father, Dr Kuranda (Hitoshi Suwabe). Before this, two scenes, set during the previous day, introduce us to this apparently normal family. The first scene takes place at breakfast and the second later that evening. Crucially, the importance of these scenes is to set up the 'normality' of the nuclear family and to provide a point of contrast to the final grotesque banquet. At the same time, something already off-kilter in the family unit is suggested through switching between the third-person and first-person point of view, as focalised through Yasu. On both occasions, the subjective shot offers a counterpoint to the impersonal third-person point of view. Both times he hears Yuki's name, a piercing sound is heard and the camera cuts to a extreme close-up of Yasu's face; when he looks back towards the family group, the domestic scene is blurred and distorted. The second time, Yasu leaves the table and goes into the next room where a caged bird is hanging. A high-angled camera shot, cutting between Yasu and the trapped bird, creates a line of connection between them; Yasu, who like the bird is helpless, is trapped in his wheelchair. As the director himself points out in the commentary, this is influenced by Robert Aldrich's *Whatever Happened to Baby Jane?* (1962), rather than *The Texas Chainsaw Massacre*.

When the family is out at work, the two women take pleasure in tormenting Yasu, on one occasion offering him his dead bird for lunch, and on another a plate of dead beetles. They take him out in his wheelchair, pushing him into the path of traffic; dump worms on his lap; repeatedly use a stun gun on him; take his teeth out with a pair of pliers; and play darts using him as a sitting target. Yasu is thus situated in a feminine position throughout the narrative. This is made clear in the scene where Chiyo and Yuki tie Yasu to his bed, with his legs spread; they pour water on his shorts and then use the stun gun on his genitals. As with much of the violence in the film, this is implied in a similar manner to Hooper's film, as the camera cuts away at the key moment before the stun gun comes into contact with Yasu.

For much of the film, the spectator is forced into a position of masochism, as structured through the point-of-view shot of Yasu. However, the denouement, which mirrors a similar sequence in *The Texas Chainsaw Massacre* in which the family gather together for a reunion party, subverts the view of Yasu as victim. In this scene, the slim veneer of normality cracks and we view the insanity and craziness beneath. The two women have finished tormenting and torturing Yasu, who is sitting in a corner towards the back of the room. The dead body of Mami is strapped to a chair, whilst Chiyo quietly brushes her hair. Ken returns from work, dragging the unconscious body of his colleague, Mitsuka (played by Shugo Fujii), with him. He sits Mitsuka on a chair at the back of the room, next to Yasu. Just then Dr Kuranda (who we discover is the editor of the paper that both Ken and Mitsuka work on) returns home, and all hopes of rescue for Mitsuka and Yasu disappear. There are minimal reserve shots or eyeline matches in this scene, which forces the spectator into a position of masochistic identification rather than sadistic control.

In relation to *Peeping Tom*, Clover distinguishes between the assaultive (male/sadistic) and reactive gaze (feminine/masochistic). Further, using the beginning of *Halloween* as a case study, she suggests that the use of the subjective point of view of the killer, rather than implying control, actually functions to undermine his (her) omnipotence; she states, 'the "view" of the first-person killer is typically cloudy, unsteady', thereby presuming an 'unstable gaze' (1992: 187). Thus the subjective camera, according to Clover, draws our attention to what cannot be seen and, in doing so, 'gives rise to the sense not of mastery but of vulnerability' (1992: 187). Much of the following scene is shot through the subjective point of view of Yasu, who is sitting at the back of the dining room, and watching in horror as the macabre family reunion takes place. Here the use of the subjective gaze, associated with the wheelchair-bound Yasu, articulates vulnerability rather than mastery, as in Clover's discussions of *Halloween*.

Candles flicker on the table (an obvious reference to *The Texas Chainsaw Massacre*) and 'for dessert' Ken offers the decapitated head of a young woman to Chiyo, who, it transpires, is his mother. Picking up a metal fly swatter, Dr Kurando proceeds to beat his son with it, whilst Chiyo looks on, laughing manically. Then, in a film which foregrounds and operates as self-reflexive commentary on the processes of spectatorship by using Yasu as our diegetic stand-in, Chiyo proceeds loudly and happily to eat Mitsuka's eyeball. The consumption of the eye is thus highly symbolic.

However, there is a final plot twist, which reveals that Yasu is not the innocent victim that he has seemed. Throughout the flashback, shot in negative colour film with added contrast, we learn that Yuki was Yasu's conjoined twin (in other words, they were Siamese twins), and that both children were the product of Dr Kurando's genetic experimentation. A substantial portion of the truth has already been revealed to the viewer through the investigatory strand of the narrative, but it is only during the flashback sequences that we find out that Dr Kurando experimented on Yuki, using Yasu as a control. When the father attempts to separate the twins, Yuki asks him whether he loves her and whether he will marry her when she grows up, thus adding incest to the mix. We see Yasu snatch the knife from his father's hand and kill Yuki instead. This could be seen as either an act of jealousy or the projection of self on to the other in order to eliminate oneself. In the present, Yasu's remembrances cause him to act out violently against his family, killing them all. The film ends in a similar manner to Hitchcock's *Psycho*, with a sequence showing the police and a psychiatrist talking about the causes of Yasu's psychosis; it is suggested that Yuki was a split personality, representing (as the mother does in *Psycho*) the repressed, evil side of Yasu. Then, as in *Psycho*, the film switches to Yasu confined in a mental asylum. The final shot is of Yasu screaming.

In the same manner as *The Texas Chainsaw Massacre*, with its dysfunctional family of cannibals and killers, commenting on the imaginary normalcy of the nuclear family, *Living Hell* also suggests that, behind the veneer of normalcy, perversion and insanity may well hide. Unlike the family in *The Texas Chainsaw Massacre*, Yasu's family appears normal on the surface, as signalled in the scenes where we first meet them. Indeed, their madness seems no obstacle to functioning normally within capitalist society and it could be argued that the madness is a consequence of the conflict in contemporary Japan between traditional ways and the individualism associated with Westernisation.

JAPANESE MONSTERS FROM THE UNDERGROUND

Japanese monsters, whether psychological or supernatural, are substantially different to those that proliferate in mainstream (American) cinema. For example, in Kurosawa's *The Guard from the Underground* (1992), the killer is a former sumo wrestler called Fujimaru (Matsushige Yutaka). Fujimaru has just been employed as a security guard in a large office block, for the Akabone Corporation, where Akiko Narushima (Makiko Kuro) has just started work as an art dealer, in the anonymous 'Department 12'. Her colleagues include Korume (Ren Osugi), her boss, and Hyodo (Hatsunori Hasegawa), Korume's superior. Hyodo is a drunk and Korume a sexual predator. Very much in the tradition of the slasher (or stalk-and-slash) genre, Akiko and her colleagues are trapped in the building, whilst Fujimaru goes on a killing spree. It should come as no surprise that the resourceful Akiko, similar to the 'final girl' in the slasher film, manages to escape from Fujimaru's clutches. However, with its explicit critique of office politics and a sumo-wrestler as a killer, *The Guard from the Underground* is quite unlike the American slasher film.

With its female profiler, the beautiful Setsuko Suma (Kaho Minami), who is putting together a portrait of the serial killer who is murdering women with a poisoned needle on packed commuter trains, *Angel Dust* (Ishii: 1994) seems on the surface to be a Japanese version of *The Silence of the Lambs*. Setsuko begins to suspect that her former lover and colleague, Rei Aku (Takeshi Wakamatsu), who works as a cult deprogrammer, might be behind the murders. Unable to stop the killings, Setsuko becomes increasingly deranged, to a point where she becomes convinced that she is the murderer. Unlike the traditional serial killer and/or slasher narrative, *Angel Dust* offers no clear resolution as to the identity of the killer(s).

Another example of a permutation on the generic features of the serial killer genre is *Another Heaven* (Iida: 2000). In this horror/science fiction hybrid, the serial killer is not only from the future, but also from the land of the dead. In the present of the narrative, like a ghost in the shell, the killer is able to switch bodies at will. Whilst this might sound similar to *Fallen* (Hoblit: 1998), the reason for the killer's appearance in the present time of the narrative is, perhaps, typically Japanese, as is the way in which his ghost can, for short periods of time, live in water. Galloway writes:

> As Manabu pursues the entity, he tries to understand its nature and exactly what it is. This line of inquiry leads him ultimately back to himself, and to something that is in all humans; 'something' repeatedly asserts, 'I am human', leaving Manabu (and us) to contemplate the malevolent aspect of humanity and what the human condition is really about. (2006: 158)

Manabu Hayase (Yosuke Eguchi), a policeman, is led to the conclusion that the beautiful Chizuru Kashiwagi (Yukiko Okamoto) is, in fact, the brain-eating serial killer. However, Chizura dies before Manabu manages to track her down, and the killer escapes from her body into that of Kimura (Takashi Kashiwabara), one of the three men that Chizura had enticed back to her flat for supper (although seduced by her beauty, none of them realises that they are in fact on the menu). Manabu eventually tracks Kimura down, at which time the ghostly spirit inside reveals that he returned to Earth because he was bored in Nirvana. Hence the reason behind the supernatural serial killer murders is explained through recourse to Buddhism. Once more, this suggests that religious frameworks and cultural mythology are important factors in the construction, and our understanding, of Japanese horror cinema as genre.

> Ultimately, the function of incoherent horror movies like the Nightmare series is to continually challenge the codes and authority of the monoglossic master narrative. (Heba: 1995)

While Japanese serial killer and slasher films focus in on unmotivated, or sexually motivated, crimes, it is difficult, if not impossible, to explain their pathologies by recourse to the type of pop-psychoanalysis that is often used in relation to American horror. Neither do socio-economic reasons or class divisions provide the answer. Here the serial killer is identified as a pathological symptom of modernity and the supernatural ghost/monster articulates the return of the repressed pre-modern body. It is clear that, while the Japanese serial killer and slasher films might seem at first glance to be similar to those of the West, they are in fact very different. From a monstrous deity to a murderous foetus and a body-hopping killer, the monsters of Japanese horror exceed taxonomies and pathologies of the psychologically motivated serial killer. What unites these films is their refusal of coherence through reference in a master-narrative – for example, psychoanalysis or Marxism – which would make the actions of their killers make sense. As such, these films challenge dominant ideologies around gender, sexuality and identity. The horror of such films perhaps lies in their refusal to construct an identifiable subject, rather than the actions of that subject.

CHAPTER 9

Techno-Horror and Urban Alienation

There has been no lack of causative factors proposed to account for this crisis, including materialism, consumerism, the collapse of the economic bubble, economic restructuring ('risutora'), the influence of Western 'individualism,' a stressful and rigidly competitive education system, nuclear families, the decline of extended families, smothering mothers, absentee working parents, decline of parental and other authority, non-transmission of normative values, lack of socialization, lack of outdoor activity, urbanization, spatial isolation, media prurience, or solitary absorption in electronic media, particularly electronic games or the Internet. (Taylor 2006)

In contemporary Japanese cinema, the motifs of alienation, emptiness and isolation contained within an apocalyptic mise-en-scène of techno-horror, articulate urban alienation in a society dominated by the image, commodity fetishisation and economic instability. Taylor points to the multiple factors that have resulted in the social crisis in contemporary Japanese society. In 'The Problem of Identity in Contemporary Japanese Horror Films', Iles documents how outbreaks of public violence, as encapsulated in the cases of Aum Shinrikyo and Shōnen A, have amounted to 'an assault on the sanctity, the sense of a close-knit family, of the Japanese and Japan's "island mentality" which saw it as a safe country in some way immune to the social ills of the outside world' (2005).

In addition to this, the rise in domestic violence, outbreaks of *kireru* (unmotivated fits of rage) in primary and secondary schools, economic decline and the erosion of the family unit have provoked what Iles terms 'an assault on its self-image, its sense of security and social stability' (2005) in a manner not experienced since the end of the Allied Occupation in 1952. Napier terms this 'the central Japanese myth', which is that 'Japan is a purely hierarchical, stable society in which all know their place and authority figures know what is best' (1996: 224). Iles asks: 'How could horror not emerge in cinema as a reflection of this social condition?' (2005)

Given the omniscience of the media-spectacle nature of contemporary Japanese society, in which serial killers become media stars and virtual communication is replacing face-to-face encounters, it is no surprise that the dominant form of horror is that in which the source of the horror is technological, whether as cursed video in Nataka's *Ring*, a DVD that demonstrates the best way to commit suicide (*The Manual*, Fukutani: 2003), mobile phone calls that predict the time and date of death (*One Missed Call*, Miike: 2003), a seemingly innocent pop song which leads people to suicide (*Suicide Circle*, Sono: 2000), a video game which becomes all too 'real' (*St John's Wort*, Shimoyama: 2001), the scientific invention of a machine which allows the dead to materialise and whose presence then threatens the world with complete annihilation (*Ghost System*, Nagae: 2002), and a version of the Internet which allows the dead to return to the world of the living (*Pulse*, Kurosawa: 2001).

REPRESSION

In 'The Japanese Horror Film Series: *Ring* and *Eko Eko Azarak*', Tateishi delimits two contradictory responses to the relation between modernity and the past in Japan. The first take the form of a 'cultural nostalgia', which involves an attempt to retrieve the lost past and posit a continuity with the present; the second is 'a repressing of the past in the name of progress and the so-called "modern"' (2003: 296). In the second response, the past becomes defined as monstrous, chaotic and a threat to all things rational and modern. Tateishi refers to the reformation of the education system during the Meiji Restoration, in which all references to folklore and the supernatural were eliminated (2003: 296). She writes: 'Coded as illogical and chaotic, and thus antithetical to the project of modernisation, such elements were targeted as the embodiments of those qualities that needed to be eliminated in the name of progress' (2003: 296). As we have seen, the Japanese horror film is steeped in traditional folkloric mythology in which the 'encounter with the past is shown to have dire consequences' (Takeishi 2003: 297). Writing about *Ring*, Tateishi argues that it 'is a film with modern sensibilities that also displays its ties with the lineage of Japanese horror cinema to which it belongs' (2003: 296).

ERUPTIONS

Nakata's *Ring* (1998) is an adaptation of Koji Suzuki's novel, *Ring* (1992), the first in a trilogy of books. *Ring* was originally premiered on a double bill with *The Spiral* (1998). *The Spiral* was not successful, and Nakata was commissioned to make an alternative sequel, *Ring 2* (1999), which proved much more popular with audiences. In 2000, Tsuruta's prequel, *Ring 0: Birthday*, completed the trilogy.

In *Ring*, the central character, Reiko Asakawa (Nanako Matsushima), is a modern Japanese career woman, who works as a television reporter and is investigating the urban myth of a cursed videotape that, once watched, leads to the death of the viewer exactly seven days later. Significantly, she is also divorced and is struggling to combine her career with her duties as a mother to Yoichi (Rikiya Otaka). Her niece, Tomoko Oishi (Yuko Takeuchi), dies in mysterious circumstances at almost the same time as three of her friends. Reiko discovers that Tomoko and her friends have apparently fallen victim to the videotape of urban legend that she has been investigating. She subsequently locates the tape in a cabin at the Izu Pacific resort and, like the typical woman in the horror film who runs into the arms of the killer rather than away from him, decides to watch it. She receives a phone call as soon as she has viewed the tape, but all she can hear is a sound of buzzing static. The resulting narrative is motivated by Reiko's desperate attempt, together with Ryujii – her ex-husband and father of Yoichi, to decipher the meaning of the videotape before the seven days lapse.

As Tateishi points out, the videotape in *Ring* is a similar mechanism of dread to the parchment in Tourneur's *Curse of the Demon*, also known as *Night of the Demon* (1957), adapted from M. R. James's short story, *The Casting of the Runes* (1931). The videotape, however, embodies contemporary anxieties, in that it is technology through which the repressed past reasserts itself. As such, technology both metaphorically and literally signifies death – the loss of tradition in the face of encroaching modernity is projected on to the female body, making a series of implicit connections between technology, femininity and death. Napier comments:

> Women have gone from being clearly agents of wish-fulfilment in fantasies of escape and cultural retrenchment to becoming aligned with the dark side of modernity, representatives of a world which entraps and destroys the male. These changes seem to parallel both the increased alienation that modernity has brought and the multiplicity of identities now offered to Japanese women. (1996: 224)

The first few scenes of *Ring* map out a series of associations between women, femininity and death, and it is clear to see the relationship between women and the dark side of modernity. The opening credits are superimposed on a background of almost black, crashing waves. The film then cuts to Tomoko and her friend, Masami, discussing an urban legend about a cursed videotape, which leads to the death of the viewer seven days after watching it. Tomoko admits to Masami that she has seen it, but neither girl takes it seriously. When Masami goes to the bathroom, leaving Tomoko alone in the kitchen/lounge, the television suddenly turns on. Tomoko switches it off, but it comes back on again. She turns around and gasps in horror, the moment of her death captured in a still image which freezes the narrative. Water, as we have already seen, is associated in Japanese horror cinema with pollution, impurity and the archaic maternal body. Its juxtaposition with the urban legend of the videotape and Tomoko's subsequent death immediately constructs a relationship between femininity, technology and death.

These associations are also implied by the montage of fragmentary, grainy black and white images contained on the cursed videotape: a circular image of the sky at night; a woman standing in front of a mirror brushing her hair; a short temporal ellipse and a child's figure can be seen standing behind the woman and to the right; another ellipse and we move back to the woman, who is now looking across the room; floating kanji pictograms which spell the word 'eruption'; people crawling across the ground; a figure of a man with a white towel draped over his head, pointing to the left, whilst crashing waves can be seen in the background; a close-up of an eye in which the word Sada, written in kanji (chastity – the first part of Sadako's name which, when translated, means 'chaste child') is reflected; and finally a long shot of a well. Once again, the water symbolism signals impurity and chaos, and the word 'eruption' and the images of people struggling on the ground seem to suggest some sort of dreadful catastrophe. The man pointing symbolises death, and the figures of the woman and her child seem to imply a relation between the images of disaster, chaos and femininity. The fact that the images are some sort of psychic projection of rage on the part of a young girl, Sadako (Rie Inou), whose still-living body we discover was put down a well by her 'father', formalises the connection between monstrous femininity and the threat of technological annihilation. In addition, the film seems to imply that Sadako is the product of an unnatural birth, conceived by her mother and a water deity, which again suggests an association of the maternal with the irrational and chaotic.

The word 'eruption' in the videotape, Reiko and Ryuji discover, is a reference to Mount Mihara on Oshima Island, which erupted in 1950: Shizuko (Masako), Sadako's mother, predicted this before her suicide. Whilst this is important in terms of the narrative plot, in so far as it leads Reiko and Ryuji to the island and eventually to Sadako's body, it also articulates specific cultural anxieties around the perceived vulnerability of Japan to natural disasters. In fact, during the twentieth century, Japan has seen thirteen earthquakes, including the Great

Kanto earthquake in 1923, which killed nearly 100,000 people; the Fukui earthquake of 1948, which left approximately 600,000 injured and nearly 6,000 people dead; and more recently, the Hanshin/Awaji earthquake on 17 January 1995, accounting for 5,500 fatalities. Japan has 108 active volcanoes and an estimated 15 eruptions per year. It is no surprise therefore that the term *tsunami* ('harbour wave') originated from Japan, which helps to explain the fear of the destructive powers of the sea that is central to *Ring*. In a similar manner to *Godzilla*, not only does the natural become mapped on to the technological, in order to articulate fears around the vulnerability of Japan as a nation; it also suggests that the loss of belief in traditional values, as implied through cultural referencing through folklore and mythology, is responsible for the emergence of the past from its watery grave. While critics have discussed the obvious references to the folktales of Oiwa and Okiku, I would argue that the story of the formation of Mount Fuji, which is implied by the reference to volcanoes and natural disaster in the images on the cursed videotape, is an important point of cultural reference in *Ring*; as such, it seems worth while discussing the folktale and its moral message, in some detail.

Although there has not been an eruption since 1707, Mount Fuji, the highest mountain in Japan, functions as a sacred symbol in Japanese folklore and mythology, and has been a place of pilgrimage for centuries. In his discussion of the legends of Mount Fuji (1992: 130–9) F. Hadland Davis describes how Mount Fuji, which is said to have appeared overnight, came to be. In the story, a woodcutter called Visu one day hears a loud sound coming from underneath the earth. Rushing outside, he sees Mount Fuji for the first time. Hadland Davis writes, 'Instead of a desolate plain he perceived a great mountain from whose head sprang tongues of flames and dense clouds of smoke!' Visu names the mountain Fuji-yama, or the Never-dying Mountain. Hadland Davis continues, 'Such perfect beauty suggested to the woodman the eternal, an idea which no doubt gave rise to the Elixir of Life so frequently associated with the mountain' (1992: 136).

A priest comes to visit Visu and accuses him of not praying, threatening him with all sorts of dire consequences as a result. Although the priest leaves, telling Visu to 'work and pray', Visu spends all day praying and not working, thereby neglecting his wife and children. As a consequence of this neglect, his crops wither and die, and his wife and children become thin and emaciated. When his wife confronts him, Visu becomes offended; seizing his axe, he leaves the house and climbs to the top of Mount Fuji, where he discovers three women playing a game of Go.

Transfixed, Visu watches the game, until eventually one of the women makes a mistake, at which point he addresses the women, who turn into foxes and run away. He stands up, his limbs stiff and painful, and makes his way back to his home, only to discover that not only is his home no longer there, but also that he has been away for 300 years. In place of the house, Visu finds an old woman and he asks her about the fate of his family, to which she replies:

> 'Buried!' hissed the old woman, 'and, if what you say is true, your children's children too. The Gods have prolonged your miserable life in punishment for having neglected your wife and little children.' (Hadland Davis 1992: 139)

The horrified Visu is reported to have spent the rest of his life repenting for abandoning his family, and it is said that his white spirit can still be seen on Mount Fuji when the moon is bright. This myth is important in that the story of the neglect of one's familial duties finds specific cultural resonance in contemporary Japan, and is expressed in the horror film through the implicit, or explicit, neglect of one's family obligations.

In *Ring*, the moral message of family values is articulated through the doubling of Shizuko/Reiko and Sadako/Yoichi, and the discourse of child abuse/neglect, both in the past and in the present. Reiko, a typical modern Japanese career woman, struggles to juggle work and family, and as a consequence of these competing demands, ends up neglecting her son, Yoichi. This is made clear in the sequence of scenes leading up the point at which Yoichi watches the cursed video. In the first scene, Reiko and Ryuji are in the newspaper's library, trying to interpret the images from the cursed video. Looking at his watch, Ryuji asks Reiko, 'Is Yoichi OK?', to which she responds, 'He is used to being on his own.' In the next scene, the camera tracks Yoichi as he makes his way out of the apartment building, on his way to school. In a poignant moment, Yoichi turns, looking back up towards the building, before despondently walking away. With no diegetic sound or other people within the frame, the mise-en-scène provides a powerful visualisation of Yoichi's loneliness.

In the following scene, Reiko is shown watching television in her apartment, when she receives a phone call from Ryuji who has deciphered the dialect on the tape. In the next, Ryuji and Reiko are back in the library, looking for more information on the images. Reiko gets up and telephones Yoichi to tell him that she will be late again. It is obvious that he wants her to help him with something because, although we do not hear his part of the conversation, Reiko's response is 'You can do it on your own, can't you?' Her obvious excitement at coming close to solving the mystery evaporates when Ryuji reminds her that she only has four days left to live, and a moment later tells her to stay with Yoichi.

The final short sequence begins with Reiko and Yoichi visiting her father. The scene of the boy and his grandfather fishing provides visual evidence of the gap between Reiko and Yoichi. Yoichi and his grandfather are standing close together in the water, whilst Reiko stands at the edge of the water, away from both of them. The distance between Yoichi and Reiko is both literal and metaphorical. Later that day, Reiko is shown putting Yoichi to bed. The room is lit in blue, which we have seen is a common convention of Japanese horror cinema, connoting isolation and loneliness, as well as suggesting the presence of the supernatural. In the next sequence, a series of visual juxtapositions situates Reiko as the double of Shizuko. During a phone conversation with Ryuji in which he relates Shizuko's suicide, and by association the abandonment of Sadako, the film cuts to a paused image of Shizuko on Ryuji's television before cutting back to Reiko, creating a visual parallel between the two women. In the final scene to be considered, Reiko wakes up suddenly and sees that Yoichi is not in bed. Pulling back the doors that lead to the lounge, she is horrified to discover that Yoichi is watching the tape. These parallels also by implication function to situate Sadako as the double of Yoichi, in that she too is neglected, abandoned and eventually condemned to death as a result of neglect.

In the figure of Sadako, *Ring* is utilising the wronged woman and/or vengeful *yūrei* archetype of conventional Japanese horror. The brief glimpses of the past situate Sadako firmly as an innocent victim of male oppression and maternal neglect. These events are focalised through Ryuji, who possesses psychic powers. In grainy black and white, these images show Shizuko demonstrating her powers at a press conference. One of the journalists gets up and cries 'Freak', and a minute later he falls to the ground dead with a look of horror on his face. Shizuko turns to her daughter, who is standing at the very edge of the stage, and says, 'Sadako – you did that.' As a result, Shizuko and Sadako are ostracised, which leads to Shizuko committing suicide and abandoning her daughter. It is Sadako's 'female' powers that directly lead to her slow and painful death down the well (Balmain: 2004). This can also be seen as a reference to the oppression of the socially disadvantaged in Japanese society. In addition, the ostracisation of Shizuko and Sadako can be seen as criticism of the importance of Groupism (simply being a part of a group) in contemporary Japanese society, in which to be outside the group is considered as a metaphorical death. In 'Culture and Social Structures', Bada highlights the continued importance of the collective in Japanese society:

> To function alone, and thus be part of no group in particular, is almost undesirable and incomprehensible …. Conformity to a group is so integral to Japanese society that a popular saying is 'the nail that sticks up gets hammered down'. (2003)

The emergence of the monstrous past is therefore implicitly connected to the demise of the family and to the *On* system of obligations that dictate wider relationships with the community. As such, rather than challenging an oppressive reality, as *Ring* seems to in its sympathetic representation of Sadako as the archetypical wronged woman, consciously or unconsciously, it also reaffirms that reality by constructing Reiko as a neglectful mother, who does not look after her son properly. The fact that the only way to escape the curse is to copy the video and give it to someone else suggests that there is no way to escape the technological alienation of a post-modern, media-saturated society. At the same time, the fact that Reiko gives the copy of the tape to her father, who, as we find out in the sequel, *Ring 2*, watched the video but did not pass it on, seems to suggest a conflict between the different value systems of the modern nuclear family and of the pre-modern extended family as embedded within the community. The final sequences provide an example of the apocalyptic mise-en-scène of techno-horror. A high-angled, long-distance shot of a car disappearing into the distance on a deserted road and containing Reiko and Yoichi signals the eventual outcome of the video virus, as a threat to the whole community. The seemingly endless road and the foreboding dark skies seem to suggest the presence of some dreadful catastrophe, just out of sight.

ISOLATION

In Miike's *One Missed Call*, technology also provides a conduit between past and present, its very existence paradoxically enabling the return of the monstrous repressed past. Instead of the videotape, it is the mobile phone that functions as a transmitter of death, utilising the same sort of viral metaphor as found in *Ring*. In addition, also similar to *Ring*, the dysfunctional family is the causational factor in the production and reproduction of terror. In the credit sequences, a fluorescent orange sweet tracks the credits across the screen, from right to left; a montage of clips of mobile phones divides the space horizontally, and the only sound is the ringing of mobile phones. This is followed by a long-distance, high-angled shot of a busy Tokyo, as commuters make their way home. Childhood, isolation, abandonment, disconnection: are all signified in the film's establishing sequences.

In the following scene, a group of college students in a restaurant exchange mobile numbers. One by one, members of the group die in mysterious circumstances. Each death is prefigured by the 'one missed call' of the title, in which the future self can be heard screaming in terror. These phone calls give the time and date, but not the manner, of their owners' deaths. As such, *One Missed Call* utilises the same sort of premonition of death as *Ring*.

In 'Social, Cultural and Economic Issues in the Digital Divide – Literature Review and Case Study of Japan', Otani comments that 'Japan has one of the most developed telecommunication infrastructures in the world. Japan has wired phone lines everywhere, and high levels of Internet availability.' In addition to this, 79.2 per cent of Japanese have access to the Internet from their mobile phones (Otani 2003). In Japan, advances in mobile phone technology have created a sub-culture, known as *keitai* culture. In *keitai* culture, the user can not only access the Internet and send text messages and emails; but can also watch television, produce home movies and transmit them to others, pay bills, utilise GPS technology, subscribe to dating services, scan and pay for goods, and play computer games (Nguyen 2005). As such, the mobile phone has become an extension of the self, an inseparable part of one's personal identity. In 'Japan, a Wireless Vision of Future for US: Mobile Internet is Mainstream as Phones take Place of Computers', Faiola writes:

> 'Cell phones have created extensions of personal space in Japan,' said Yuichi Kogure, who teaches a class on keitai culture at Tokyo's Toita Women's College. 'You take your world with you when you have your keitai in your hand. In the keitai world, people forget where they are, and women [with cell phones], for instance, can be seen putting on makeup or brushing their hair in the subway, something considered highly rude in Japan in the past. But now, people are walled inside their own little world with their keitai and aren't even aware of what they're doing in public.' (2008)

In *One Missed Call*, a number of outside crowd scenes depict Tokyo as a city of strangers; every member of the crowd is holding a mobile phone and either texting or speaking on the phone to someone; immersed in their self-constructed *keitai* world, they are indifferent to the world outside.

At Bukkyo University in Japan, fifty-two courses are taught utilising the mobile phone as a mechanism of communication between lecturers and staff. Instead of asking direct questions, students send their queries and comments to the lecturers through their mobile phones (Faiola: 2008). Around seventy per cent of all Japanese own one *keitai* or more, and there are eighty-nine million *keitai* subscriptions. Although the use of mobile phone technologies has been critiqued as causing the breakdown of the family in an 'age of the absent family', Kohiyama suggests that it may well lead to the formation of a new, improved 'age of the family', in that it can be seen as allowing better, rather than worse, communication (2005). In *One Missed Call*, *keitai* culture is viewed from the negative position, as constitutive of a lack of communication, with characters isolated in their own walled worlds.

The protagonist in *One Missed Call* is Yumi Nakamura (Kou Shibasaki), who is studying social sciences at university. The theme of child abuse, abandonment and neglect is introduced early in the film with a scene set during a lecture on child abuse. In this scene, Yumi is sitting in front of her friends, Yoko Okazaki (Anna Nagata) and Natsumi Konishi (Kazue Fukiishi). Distracted, Yoko and Natsumi chat and send messages on their mobile phones. However, when asked about the content of the lecture, Yoko stands up and says 'abuse spawns more abuse'. As in *Ring*, the breakdown in relations between children and their mothers, as displayed in *One Missed Call* through the rhetoric of child abuse, is situated as a causational factor in the ensuing production of the vengeful ghost, who kills indiscriminately.

Immediately following the scene in the lecture theatre is a brief montage of shots which relate visually to the main theme: a close-up of a pair of adult hands as they brutally cut the toenail of an unidentified subject; a disorientating shot past screen doors; a close-up of a closed eye, which then looks through a peephole; and finally, a close-up of a mobile phone. The camera cuts to Yumi, sitting in darkness in her apartment, creating an explicit association between the fragmentary images from the past and Yumi in the present. Further, Yumi's abuse at the hands of her mother is a significant narrative thread, in that not only does it parallel the past, but also, importantly, leaves Yumi susceptible to possession by evil forces: a factor which becomes key towards the conclusion of the film.

Later that night, whilst Yumi is on the phone to Yoko, Yoko is pushed off a platform by a mysterious force into the path of a speeding train. The next day, another of her friends, Kenji Kawai (Atsushi Ida) is killed when he falls into an empty lift shaft. When Yumi's close friend, Natsumi, also receives a video clip of her forthcoming death, Yumi and Hiroshi Yamashita (Shin'ichi Tsutsumi), whose sister died after receiving a similar message on her mobile phone, decide to try to find out who or what is behind the deaths. However, Yumi and Hiroshi do not uncover the identity of the vengeful ghost until it is too late to save Natsumi.

The presence of the media, who are quick to latch on to the story of these phone messages, which predict the time and date when the recipient will die, functions as a mechanism through which to critique the media-saturated spaces of contemporary Japanese society, in which the real has been replaced by the hyper-real. Natsumi is persuaded to participate in a live transmission of an exorcism by an unpleasant male reporter. The scene of the attempted exorcism functions not only as an explicit critique of the invasion of the media into everyday life, but also to highlight the increasing disconnection between people in contemporary Japanese society; neither the film crew nor the people in the Tokyo square outside the studio where the events are being projected demonstrate any interest in Natsumi's plight.

The stage set for the exorcism utilises conventional colour codings associated with the supernatural in Japanese horror cinema. Bathed in red light, the screen door behind Natsumi can be seen as an intertextual reference to the original cycle of ghost stories in the 1950s and 1960s, as can the green light with which part of the studio is lit. The long black hair that comes out of the ground and down from the ceiling, by this time a common convention in Japanese horror film, indicates the presence of a vengeful *yūrei* or deity. However, the psychic researcher, Masakazu Hiroyama, is unable to stop the demonic vengeful ghost and the exorcism is halted mid-way through. Here *One Missed Call* departs from the traditions and superstitions of pre-modern Japan, as captured in the original cycle of ghost stories in the 1960s, in which the appropriate rituals would lay the unquiet spirit to rest. As such, there is an implied nostalgia for the pre-modern, before the commodification of the self and the dispersion of tradition into pure signifiers without origin.

The interweaving of present and past is shown in the next scene. This is significant, as it operates to throw the diegetic and extra-diegetic spectator on to the wrong path, as well as foregrounding Yumi's vulnerability. In this extension of the previous short montage of clips, the camera pans up to the face of Yumi, as her mother tears out her toenails with the clipper. Her mother grabs her and drags her to her grandmother's room, forcing her to look through a peephole in the door where she is confronted with the sight of her grandmother's hanging body. This traumatic past event explains Yumi's seemingly irrational fear of peepholes, introduced at the beginning of the film.

As in *Ring*, the source of the horror seems to be tied up with the death of a young girl. In *One Missed Call*, it is the death of a ten-year-old, Mimiko Mizunuma, from an asthma attack, that appears to be the precipitating factor for the strange murders by mobile. It transpires that the girl's sister, Nanako, had been in and out of hospital with unexplained injuries, leading to what turns out to be a mistaken belief that the mother, Marie (Mariko Tsutsui), suffers from Munchausen's syndrome by proxy. As a consequence, Nanako is placed in a children's home, where Yamashita manages to track her down. It appears, at least on the surface, that the girl has been abandoned by her mother, who has not been to visit her in six months. Yumi tracks Marie down to an old abandoned hospital. In typical horror film fashion, Yumi is chased down the corridors, as she desperately tries to get away from a monstrous force from the past. Green and red lighting, as in traditional Japanese horror cinema, is used to connote the presence of the supernatural. Hiroshi turns up just in time to rescue her, but it is Yumi who has to confront the monstrous maternal on her own.

The rotting body of Marie is found in a wooden box in one of the rooms. It seems that she has been dead since she disappeared. However, as is common in Japanese horror cinema, being dead is not sufficient to keep the body from continuing to live; the proper funeral rites and remembrances need to be said in order to lay the unquiet spirit to rest. As Yumi is confronted by the abject mother figure, past and present coalesce, and the dead body switches between the decaying corpse of Marie and the form of Yumi's mother. In an acceptance of responsibility for the sins of the other, Yumi is an evocative remnant of the past. When the rotting corpse puts her hands around Yumi's neck, Yumi forgives the mother (both present and past), and reassures the monstrous maternal corpse. She tells the 'mother', 'I'll be a good girl,' and promises not to leave her alone. At this stage, Yumi appears to be the typical self-sacrificing woman. Hiroshi breaks into the room and finds that Yumi has taken on the role of the mother, sitting with the corpse of the dead Marie cradled in her arms. This image of child and mother (with the child holding the mother) is a subversion of the iconic image of mother and child that was a prominent feature in Japanese horror cinema in the 1950s and 1960s. With the corpse of the monstrous mother laid to rest, it would appear that the primal chaotic past has been defeated.

However, an old film found at the children's home sheds a different light on past events, and shows that it was in fact Mimiko, desperate for attention, who caused her sister's injuries. The significance of the orange sweet is explained; it was the treat that Mimiko would give her sister in order to keep her from telling anyone about what was happening. The film within the film shows Marie catching Mimiko in the act of hurting her sister. As Marie grabs her daughter and draws back, Mimiko has an asthma attack but, instead of looking after her, Marie walks out of the apartment, leaving Mimiko to die. In a further subversion of conventions, Mimiko is not the typical innocent victim of either maternal or paternal oppression; instead, *One Missed Call* seems to imply that Mimiko is the result of the sort of extreme narcissistic individualism that has replaced the communal system of obligations of the pre-modern. The film replaces the wounded figure of the wronged woman killed before her time, which can be understood, with pure evil, which cannot.

In addition, in the final sequences, Mimiko takes possession of Yumi's body. This transformation could be interpreted as the abused child becoming the abuser. Indeed, in *One Missed Call 2*, it is suggested that the evil child, whether Mimiko or Li-Li, is not a separate individual but rather an external projection of an internal evil. In *One Missed Call* Hiroshi fails to recognise Yumi's transformation and, as a consequence, becomes another victim of the vengeful female spirit when Yumi stabs him. The final scene takes place in the hospital where Hiroshi is recovering from his injuries. Dressed all in white, with her long dark hair flowing, Yumi is clearly positioned as an unquiet *yūrei*. The final shot is of Yumi leaning over Hiroshi, placing an orange sweet in his mouth – mirroring the actions of Mimiko when torturing Nanako; as she steps back, a knife can be seen in the hand behind her back. Creed's comments on the final shots of the *femme castratrice* in Brian de Palma's *Sisters* (1973) seem applicable here: 'The threatening power of woman lingers in the final shot, pointing to the insecurity of the male imagination. Man must be ever on the alert, poised in phallic anticipation wherever signs of the deadly femme castratrice are present' (1993: 138). It seems that the wronged woman archetype, central to traditional mythology, has been replaced by the monstrous feminine more commonly associated with the American horror film.

DISCONNECTION

Yukio Saito, a Japanese Methodist minister and the instigator of Lifeline, Japan's first suicide hotline, suggests that high suicide rates in Japan amongst the young stem from the disconnection between people as a result of mobile, Internet and other technologies:

> a particular form of modern loneliness washing over Japan, where nuclear families occupy the same home but scarcely communicate, where dating and friendships are negotiated on the tiny screens of mobile phones, and where the phenomenon of shut-ins is total, housebound seclusion has become endemic. 'What we have seen is the collapse of the family throughout Japan, even in small towns,' said Mr. Saito, who is married and has a grown son. 'Loneliness has become universal.' (cited in French 2003)

Sono's 2002 film, *Suicide Circle* (also known as *Suicide Club*), takes a negative view of Japan's media-saturated culture as epitomised by the banal surfaces of J-pop and *keitai* culture. Loneliness is the dominant theme in this film, which deals with the growing trend in Japanese society for suicide amongst the young, as well as the unexplained outbreaks of violence at the home and in the classroom. Suicide is inscribed as a type of post-modern virus, travelling through the Internet, mobile phones and video technologies, and mainly affecting the younger, disillusioned generation. Crawford writes:

> Although the suicide surge seems to have affected many age groups in Japan, there has also been an unnerving escalation in youth crime and violence, a cultural development that is also explored in *Suicide Club*. (2003: 306)

Suicide Circle's shocking opening sequences, with fifty-four schoolgirls holding hands and jumping off a platform in front of a train, sets the tone for the resulting surreal, spiralling violence. Hundreds of young people, mainly but not exclusively female, acting in groups and on their own, commit suicide in ever more innovative and disturbing fashion: a group of schoolgirls and boys jump off a roof; a mother nonchalantly cuts through her hand as she prepares the family dinner; and two actors stab themselves in the stomach during a live performance. In an interview, Sono talks about the replacement of real communication between people with virtual conversations though cyberspace, as articulating some type of suicidal impulse on behalf of the Internet generation:

> The Internet is a way of communication which I think is suicidal. Anonymous words or opinions travel around the world. It has a freedom,

but at the same time it is very dangerous. It weakens the responsibility and originality of the words. It doesn't have a face at all. (cited in Crawford 2003: 311)

Crawford argues that the urban techno-alienation in *Suicide Circle* is most fully encapsulated in the figure of the 'Bat', a teenage girl who spends her time watching an Internet website which logs suicides as flashing circles by gender before they happen (2003: 311). A group of nihilistic young men, led by the charismatic and sadistic Genesis, are also signifiers of techno-alienation. With his blond hair and *gunguro* outfit (*gunguro* being a street fashion identifiable through bleached hair and goth-like clothes), Genesis (played by real-life musician Rolly) is a sociopath, brutally kicking animals to death and instigating the rape of young women, including the 'Bat' whom he has kidnapped. The police eventually capture Genesis, who is all too keen to take credit for the wave of suicides, as he poses for the flashing cameras of the media. For Genesis, image and celebrity are everything; his nihilistic obsession with surfaces can be interpreted as an implied criticism of contemporary Japanese culture. In 'Japan's Gross National Cool', McGray writes:

the Japanese art magazine BT ... equate[s] contemporary Japanese culture with 'Super Flat' art, 'devoid of perspective and devoid of hierarchy, all existing equally and simultaneously.' 'We don't have any religion,' painter Takashi Murakami told the magazine, a bit more cynically. 'We just need the big power of entertainment.' (2002)

The film stresses that it is ultimately the lack of connection between individuals that causes the suicides, irrespective of who is instigating them. In fact, as Iles points out, the scenes of the suicides seem to suggest that their whole point is the desire of the individual to be part of a group, rather than an isolated individual. Iles writes: 'Visually, this is apparent in the camera's treatment of the victims of the mass suicides, presenting their corpses as a jumbled assortment of body parts, the identity of one indistinguishable from that of any other in the pile' (2005).

The reluctance of the police to take the suicides seriously, as a social rather than an individual issue, is explicitly condemned. The officer in charge of the investigation, Detective Kuroda (Ryo Ishibashi), receives strange phone calls that seem to be from someone who has knowledge of who or what is causing the suicides. However, Kuroda takes little notice of the calls and seems reluctant to designate the suicides as '*hanzai*' (a crime rather than *jiken*, or accident, as suicides are understood by the police), which would imply social responsibility. Instead, it is easier to deem them accidents, or the acts of one individual, even after a white bag containing a circle of flesh sewn together from the next wave of potential suicides is found at the site of each death. This circle of flesh can be interpreted as a reference to *giri*, or the social cloth that binds individuals together. As such, *Suicide Circle* articulates a nostalgia for the loss of pre-modern traditions, which embedded the individual within the community.

At the same time, Kuroda is a representation of the absent father, who spends all his time at work and therefore neglects his family. Therefore, it comes as little surprise when he returns home from work one day to find his family have also become victims. In a moment of epiphany, Kuroda realises that his neglect is responsible for his family's deaths; his failure to consider the suicides as murder – because they did not directly affect him – has directly caused his family's actions. Kuroda is left with little alternative but to reproduce the acts that caused the loss of his family and commit suicide. In this manner, suicide can be seen as a viral metaphor for social crisis.

The banal J-pop songs played by a group made up of young children, called 'Dessert', appear to be related to the suicides in some way or form, thus expressing cultural anxieties over childhood. This is also the case in *One Missed Call*, when the ring tone is identified as being from a children's television programme. Their music seems omnipresent. The first song, 'Mail Me', opens the film, and can be seen playing on the television in a number of houses where the suicides take place; their second song provides a backdrop to the scenes of multiple suicides; and the film concludes with the band's final performance.

One young teenager, Mitsuko (Saya Hagiwara), who resists the temptation to commit suicide even after her boyfriend kills himself, attempts to track down the code transmitted by mobile phone. She discovers that the answer lies in a poster showing Dessert. Mitsuko attends Dessert's final performance as a group (and final performance in the film), at which she seems to be the only viewer. She is asked by Dessert if she has connections with her family, with her boyfriend and with the Group itself. She insists, however, that she is herself and the group applaud her answer. The denouement, though, is still to come. Mitsuko joins a group of young people behind the stage who are having strips of their skin shaved off. Does this mean that Mitsuko too is going to commit suicide? This ending is, as Iles (2005) points out, ambiguous. The final scene is set in the underground station where the first mass suicide took place. Having been forced to take the matter seriously, the police are now patrolling the platform. As a train pulls in, Mitsuko joins hands with a line of others, thus repeating the opening sequence. Just before the train arrives in the station, a policeman puts his hand on Mitsuko's shoulder, signifying perhaps his desire to reconnect, but she shrugs it off. Iles comments:

> *Jisatsu sakura* thus presents no resolution to the urban problem, only a critique of its sources and analysis of its form. Its rejection of interpersonal

communication and care is pessimistic, suggesting the impossibility of urban, consumerist society as something substantiable – and yet its suggestion that children hold the answer to overcome the alienation of the age is a welcome hint of hope. (2005)

Ueno's *Ambiguous* (2003), supposedly based on a real incident in Japan, also concentrates on a group of individuals brought together by loneliness and isolation, who plan to commit suicide together. They communicate with each other through text messages. However, whilst waiting for a fifth person to turn up, the other members of the group connect with each other. This connection is through acts of material physicality, such as eating, having sex and working together. When the fifth member arrives and commits suicide in front of the others, they suddenly decide that, in fact, they no longer wish to die. *Ambiguous* seems to offer a more redemptive vision of the ability of technology to connect people, in a world of disconnection, than *Suicide Circle*.

ANNIHILATION

It is in Kurosawa's films that a critique of the postmodern, or 'post-individual,' form of identity finds its most consistent expression, and where characters struggle most desperately against the overwhelming commodification of their selves. (Iles 2005)

The premise for Kurosawa's *Pulse* is that the world of the dead is overcrowded and that they are trying to escape into the world of the living, using the Internet as a conduit between the two planes of existence. These shadowy figures begin to seep into the real world and people start to disappear, uttering 'Help me' before their body disintegrates into black ashes, leaving a transient mark of their being in the process. Rather than being able to move on to the world of the dead, individuals who die like this are condemned to spend eternity in isolation. An Internet site directs the isolated and alienated to a forbidden room, whose door is closed with red tape. These forbidden rooms can be seen as an explicit reference to Internet chat rooms. Once the victims unseal the door, they fall prey to the hungry wraith-like ghosts of the dead. In its delimitation of the isolated subject who makes contact only through the computer keyboard, *Pulse* is commenting on the generation of Internet users, or *Otaku*, who prefer the company afforded by technology and virtual relationships rather than real connections. The ghosts within the machine, sucking the life out of its victims, are clearly a metaphor for the centrality of disconnection amongst the younger generation in Japan.

The narrative is presented from the perspective of Michi (Aso Kumiko) and Ryosuke Kawashima (Katou Haruhiko), both of whom come into contact with dangerous ghosts and barely escape with their lives. By the end of the film, only Michi survives; Ryosuke simply fades away, turning into a pile of ashes. Like the disfigured face of the vengeful female *yūrei*, the ashes of those who disappear signify the persistence of historical trauma (Iles 2008).

Visually and thematically, the opening sequences introduce isolation, emptiness and apocalypse, which form the dominant themes of the subsequent narrative. The first shot is of an ocean liner. A conversation takes place between unnamed men about their position at sea and about their course. The next shot shows one of the men walking towards the edge of the boat. A female figure can be seen against the ship's railing. She is standing with her back to the camera. A female voice-over says, 'It began one day without warning.' The next scene is of a dark, deserted room; for a few seconds, the image flickers like a light going on and off. Here the idea of the embodied gaze is dispensed with; instead, perspective, as in Japanese *ukiyo-e* images and paintings, focuses on empty spaces and unusual angles. In the following scene, the location changes to what appears to be a rooftop garden. Green plants and the bright costumes of the female characters offer a pastoral mise-en-scène, which is the opposite of the dark and dingy room in the preceding scene. These opening sequences produce a series of oppositions: emptiness/fullness, death/life, technology/nature and dark/light. Again, water imagery is omnipresent in the opening shots of the ship at sea, connoting the presence of the chaotic and threatening.

Fig. 9.1 Sole survivors: Ryosuke and Michi, *Pulse* (Kiyoshi Kurosawa, 2001, Tōhō / Magnolia / The Kobal Collection)

The mainly static camera in the scenes in the garden and the placement of the camera behind a glass partition create a distance between the screen and the extra-diegetic spectator. In *Pulse*, the pastoral is situated in opposition to the technological and the apocalyptic. Scenes of Michi working, towards the beginning of the film, utilise a saturated palate of colours reflecting the natural world. As the world becomes ever more empty, the colour palate shifts into greyish-green, as if technology were somehow responsible for sucking the life out of nature.

The use of predominantly medium and long shots, and deep focus, throughout the narrative effectively mirrors the feeling of quiet despair that exists between the main characters. The following scene, in which Michi goes to see what is happening with a co-worker, Taguichi (Kenji Mizuhashi), whom no one has heard from for a week, foregrounds the increasing disconnection between people. Michi takes the bus to Taguichi's apartment. She seems to be the only passenger, which prefigures the gradual disappearance of people from the real world. Long shots cross-cut with medium shots are used to track Michi as she walks across a deserted street and up the stairs to Taguichi's apartment.

Fig. 9.2 Spaces within spaces, *Pulse* (Kiyoshi Kurosawa, 2001, Tōhō / Magnolia / The Kobal Collection)

Inside, the apartment seems deserted and unlived-in. The camera remains mainly static and there is only silence. The use of deep focus and the plastic curtains that divide the room into two separate spaces function to create a visual distance between Michi and Taguichi, who suddenly appears in the background against the wall. In a later shot in the sequence, Michi is shown with her back towards the camera, giving the impression that she is being watched. However, a reverse shot shows that the space occupied by Taguichi is now empty. This disruption of the shot–reverse shot structure generates an overwhelming feeling of quiet dread, as well as isolating characters within a generalised emptiness. When Michi looks for Taguichi, she finds his body hanging from the ceiling. This suicide anticipates many of the later deaths in *Pulse*. By doing so, the motif of suicide, omnipresent in many contemporary Japanese horror films, is used to imply that the subsequent deaths can be seen as a consequence of suicidal impulses which allow the ghosts in the machine to seep into the world of the diegesis. This is foregrounded in a conversation between Michi and her friends at a café later that day, in which they attempt to understand why Taguichi committed suicide. One of them responds: 'Maybe he just suddenly wanted to die, I get that way sometimes.'

In many ways, *Pulse* is similar to Cronenberg's *Videodrome* (1983), with Internet technologies replacing the televisual screen in the latter. The dead, who appear within cyberspace, are shown with black plastic bags over their heads, providing a direct visual link to *Videodrome*. The relationship between Ryosuke and the beautiful computer lab worker, Harue Karasawa (Koyuki), is analogous to that between Max Renn (James Wood) and Nicki Brand (Deborah Harry) in *Videodrome*. At the start of *Pulse*, Ryosuke is shown as being almost computer-illiterate, having to use a guide to the Internet in order to operate his computer. Harue is the opposite, proficient in Internet technologies. As in *Videodrome*, femininity is aligned with technology, as Harue becomes Ryosuke's guide (as does Nicki Brand in *Videodrome*) to the Internet, which eventually leads to his death. Unlike Ryosuke, Harue embraces the deathly technology that she discovers as a result of the pair's investigation into the mysterious disappearances of friends and colleagues. Ryosuke actively resists the seductive technologies of death but, because he is already isolated, and Harue provides the only contact for him with the world outside his self-contained isolation, her eventual death must lead to his. This again draws a line of connection between *Videodrome* and *Pulse*, as in *Videodrome* Nicki Brand's death prefigures that of Max Renn. As Bukatman comments in relation to *Videodrome*, 'Image is virus; virus virulently replicates itself; the subject is finished' (2004: 234).

Only Michi and a few others survive the viral plague of the ghosts within the machine. Michi survives because she retains her ability to connect with others, unlike Ryosuke, who, when he first meets Michi, cannot remember his name or indeed who he is. While Iles (2008) suggests that the purpose of the voice-over at the end, in which Michi states that she had gained happiness through her relationship with Ryosuke, articulates the continuance of a desire for connection between individuals, the ending is typical of Japanese fairy tales and the sense of *mono-no-aware* that we have seen is an integral component of them.

DYSTOPIAS

Techno-horror constructs a dystopian view of society, whether in the present or in the future. Death, both symbolic and literal, is omnipresent, as the eventual outcome of technological progress. Monstrous mothers are superseded by their demonic daughters and adolescent angst leads to mass suicides, while ghosts from the Internet take over the world and no one seems to notice or care. In the wake of the bursting of the Japanese economic bubble in the 1990s, it is not surprising that dystopian visions of the future would dominate Japanese culture. Napier writes, 'In the 1980s this image of Japan as a technological and social Utopia came increasingly under attack from both inside and outside' (1996: 182). And yet one has to wonder whether, walled into their own worlds, the consumers of *keitai* culture will even notice.

Conclusion

Since the success of the remake of Nakata's *Ring*, as *The Ring*, a growing number of Japanese films have been remade for Western audiences. These include *Ju-On: The Grudge*, *Dark Water* and *Pulse*, which have been remade respectively as *The Grudge* (Shimizu: 2004), *Dark Water* (Salles: 2005) and *Pulse* (Sonzero: 2003), with varying degrees of success. *Pulse* is, perhaps, one of the least successful, as the horror in Kurosawa's version is not so much thematic as cinematic, as we have seen. As in *Ring*, the adaptation reworks *Pulse* to fit in with the structure of the slasher film, but not as effectively as in the former. Nakata's own adaptation of *Ring Two* (2005) clearly points out the problems with East–West adaptations; the complexity of *Ring* 2 is reduced to a simple supernatural possession film, which bears little relation to its source. In terms of Iwabuchi's concept of cultural odour, it would seem that racial and national borders have been erased through the process of adaptation. In order to clarify this, I have chosen to conclude this study of Japanese horror by comparing the denouement in *Ju-On: The Grudge* with that in *The Grudge*. This begins when the central female character, Rika (Megumi Okina) in the former film and Karen (Sarah Michelle Geller) in the latter, comes face to face with her nemesis, the monstrous Kayako.

In my analysis of this scene in Chapter 7, I suggested that Kayako (Takako Fuji) transforms from vengeful *yūrei* to the more sympathetic archetype of the wronged woman. In *The Grudge*, there is no Takeo, and rather than going to rescue a friend, as is the case with Rika, Karen goes to save her boyfriend, Doug (Jason Behr). Here it is possible to interpret Kayako as working with stereotypes of the dangerous Orient, in her role as iconic *fatal femme* who is a threat to white masculinity and therefore the very foundations of American society. Indeed, the manner in which she bends over Doug visually suggests the rape of the Self (Doug/America) by the threatening Other (Kayako/Japan) (Balmain: 2007a).

In addition, unlike the passive respectable femininity of Rika in *Ju-On: The Grudge*, Karen is the typical 'final girl' of American horror film in that she defeats, if only for a short time, the monstrous Other. The casting of Sarah Michelle Geller, known to Western audiences for her role as Buffy in the long-running television series, *Buffy the Vampire Slayer*, meant that not only was the character of Karen associated with strength, determination and power, but also that it would not be good publicity for her character to die, unlike her counterpart Rika in the original. However, Karen is killed off in Shimizu's sequel and her role in the narrative is taken over by her sister, Audrey (Amber Tamblyn), who succeeds where Karen fails and defeats the murderous Kayako.

In *Ju-On: The Grudge*, Rika is situated, at both a visual and thematic level, as the double of Kayako, two women in an oppressive patriarchal world. Just before Kayako crawls down the stairs, Rika looks in the mirror and sees, not her own reflection, but that of Kayako staring back at her. And Rika, like Kayako before her, becomes a victim of male violence; Takeo reaches his bloody hand towards Rika's face and the screen fades to black. In *The Grudge*, however, Karen remains separate to the monstrous Kayako; when Karen looks in the mirror she sees, not Kayako as Rika does, but her own reflection. As such, this maintains rather than subverts binary distinctions between Self (America/good) and Other (Japan/evil), reproducing Western fears around the oriental Other which can be traced back to the discourse of 'Yellow Peril' which emerged in the 1920s and 1930s. China (and other East Asian nations) were constructed as a place of mystery and danger that threatened the stability of the democratic order in the West. The archetypical figure of Fu Manchu is the literary and cinematic embodiment of the Yellow Peril. First appearing in the novels of British writer Sax Rohmer, Fu Manchu was a popular figure both in silent and sound films, including Don Sharp's films of the 1960s and 1970s in which the character was played by Christopher Lee.

In the final scene of *The Grudge* Karen is in hospital, where her dead boyfriend's body is awaiting identification. As she stands by the body, which is obscured from view by a white sheet, long black hair falls over the rail of the trolley. Then we hear a loud noise, as a white arm comes out from under the sheet and the murderous Kayako appears behind Karen. The final shot of the film is a close-up of Kayako's eye, her hair obscuring her features, as seen from the point of view of Karen. This image is very similar to that of Sadako in *Ring*, constructing perhaps a deliberate relationship between the two films and, as such, conforming to Western expectations about the vengeful ghost in the Japanese horror film.

In *Ju-On: The Grudge*, the final image is that of Kayako as wronged woman, her broken body leaning against a wall in the attic. As the camera pans in, Kayako's eyes suddenly open, staring straight towards the extra-diegetic spectator. While this look can be considered a signifier of the threat she continues to pose, it can also be seen as requiring an empathic response from the audience – Kayako is situated as the wronged woman of traditional Japanese mythology. In *The Grudge*, however, the final look is both horrific and threatening, and the corresponding fragmentation of the female body can be seen to act as a fetish, or disavowal, of the power of the gaze of the 'Other'.

In these terms, *Ju-On: The Grudge* can be seen as working within the conventions of Japanese horror, with its message of female oppression and violent men, articulated through reference to the archetype of the wronged woman that has dominated Japanese horror from its earliest days. It is also slower, more episodic and less structured than the remake. As such, it could be argued that the difference between the films is structural and stylistic rather than thematic.

Just as the West has rewritten the script of Japanese horror, so has Japan adapted Western horror, bringing its own cultural mythology to bear on the iconic figure of Dracula in *Legacy of Dracula* (1970), *Lake of Dracula* (1971) and *Evil of Dracula* (1974), all of which were directed by Michio Yamamoto. Further, Hirai Tarō (1894–1965), a famous Japanese writer of mystery and detective fiction and one of the country's most noted authors, was better known as Edogawa Rampo, a pseudonym which paid homage to Edgar Allan Poe. It was the opening up of Japan to the West at the start of the Meiji Era that inaugurated a new age of Japanese crime fiction, which, up until then, had been based around old court trials (Sharp 2006: 26). There have been many film versions of Rampo's work, including *Blind Beast*, *The Mystery of Rampo* (Mayuzumi and Okuyama: 1994) and, most recently, *Rampo Noir* (Jissoji et al.: 2005) – films which themselves have arguably influenced Western horror cinema.

It is clear, therefore, that global flows and cultural exchange between the West and Japan have led to the cross-fertilisation of contemporary horror cinema, both in Japan and the West. The concept of fusion, based on equality rather than dominance, can provide a way of interpreting this cultural exchange. As Said writes:

> Rather than a manufactured clash of civilizations, we need to concentrate on the slow working together of cultures that overlap, borrow from each other, and live together in far more interesting ways that any abridged or inauthentic mode of understanding can allow. ([1973] 2003: xxii)

Select Filmography

Many of the films are available in the UK, although some are still to be released in either the UK or the USA. These titles are available from reputable on-line companies, including Amazon (www.amazon.co.uk). The main on-line company that I used for difficult-to-find DVDs was YesAsia (www.yesasia.com).

A Certain Night's Kiss (*Aru yo no seppun*, Yasuki Chiba: 1946).
Ambiguous (Toshiya Ueno: 2003).
Angel Dust (*Enjeru dasuto*, Sogo Ishii: 1994).
Angel Guts: High School Co-Ed (*Jokōsei: tenshi no harawata*, Chusei Sone: 1978).
Angels Guts: Nami (*Tenshi no harawata: Nami*, Noboru Tanaka: 1979).
Angel Guts: Red Classroom (*Tenshi no harawata: Akai kyōshitsu*, Chusei Sone: 1979).
Angel Guts: Red Dizziness (*Tenshi no harawata: Akai memai*, Takashi Ishii: 1988).
Angel Guts: Red Lightning (*Tenshi no harawata: Akai senkō*, Takashi Ishii: 1994).
Angel Guts: Red Porno (*Tenshi no harawata: Akai inga*, Toshiharu Ikeda: 1981).
Another Heaven (*Anazahevun*, Jōji Iida: 2000).
Audition (*Ōdishon*, Takashi Miike: 1999).
Band of Ninja (*Ninja bugei-cho*, Nagisa Ōshima: 1967).
Battle Royale (*Batoru rowaiaru*, Kinji Fukasaku: 2000).
Bedroom, The (*Shisenjiyou no Aria*, Hīsayasu Sato: 1992).
Black Snow (*Kurio Yuki*, Tetsuji Takechi: 1965).
Blind Beast (*Mōjuu*, Yasuzo Masumura: 1969).
Bride from Hell (*Botan-dōrō*, Satsuo Yamamoto: 1968).
Carved: A Slit-Mouthed Woman (*Kuchisake-onna*, Kōji Shiraishi: 2007).
Ceiling at Utsunomiya, The (*Kaii Utsunomiya tsuritenjo*, Nobuo Nakagawa: 1956).
Children of Hiroshima (*Genbaku no ko*, Kaneto Shindō: 1952).
Crazed Fruit (*Kurutta ka*, Kō Nakahira: 1956).
Crazy Lips (*Hakkyousuru kuchibiru*, Hirohisa Sasaki: 2000).
Cursed (*Chō' kowai hanashi A: yami no karasu*, Yoshihiro Hoshino: 2004).
Dark Tales of Japan (*Kumo Onna*, Takashi Shimizu et al.: 2004).
Dark Water (*Honogurai mizu no soko kara*, Hideo Nakata: 2002).
Daydream (*Hakujit sumu*, Tetsuji Takechi: 1964).
Discarnates, The (*Ijintachi tono natsu*, Obayashi Nohuhiko: 1988).
Dolls (Takeshi Kitano: 2002).

Double Suicide (*Shinjū: Ten no Amijima*, Masahiro Shinodam: 1969).

Eko Eko Azarak: The Birth of the Wizard (*Eko Eko Azaraku II*, Shimako Sato: 1996).

Eko Eko Azarak: Misa the Dark Angel (*Eko Eko Azaraku III*, Katsuhito Ueno: 1998).

Eko Eko Azarak: Wizard of Darkness (*Eko Eko Azaraku*, Shimako Sato: 1995).

Embryo Hunts in Secret, The (*Taiji ga mitsuryosuru toki*, Koji Wakamatsu: 1966).

Empire of Passion (*Ai no borei*, Nagisa Ōshima: 1978).

Empire of the Senses (*Ai no Corrida*, Nagisa Ōshima: 1976).

Entrails of a Beautiful Woman (*Bijo no harawata*, Kazuo 'Gaira' Komizu: 1986).

Entrails of a Virgin (*Shōjo no harawata*, Kazuo 'Gaira' Komizu: 1986).

Evil Dead Trap (*Shiryo no wana*, Toshiharu Ikeda: 1988).

Evil Dead Trap 2: Hideki (*Shiryo no wana 2: Hideki*, Izō Hashimoto: 1991).

Evil Dead Trap 3: Broken Love Killer (*Chigireta ai no satsujin*, Toshiharu Ikeda: 1993).

Evil of Dracula (*Chi o suu bara*, Michio Yamamoto: 1974).

Face of Another (*Tanin no kao*, Hiroshi Teshigahara: 1966).

Face to Face (Casey Chan: 2002).

Floating Weeds (*Ukigusa*, Yasujiro Ozu: 1959).

Freeze Me (Takashi Ishii: 2000).

Frightful School Horror, A (*Kyoufu Gakuen*, Yamaguchi Makoto: 2001).

Ghost Cat of Otama Pond, The (*Kaibyo Otamagaike*, Yoshiro Ishikawa: 1960).

Ghost Story of Yotsuya (*Tokaido-Yotsuyakaidan*, Shozu Makino: 1912).

Ghost Story of Yotsuya (*Tokaido-Yotsuyakaidan*, Nobuo Nakagawa: 1959).

Ghost System (*Gosuto shisutemu*, Ikazu Nagae: 2002).

Ghosts of Kagama-Ga-Fuchi (*Kaidan kagamigafuchi*, Masaki Mori: 1959).

Ghosts of Kasane Swamp, The (*Kaidan Kasanegafuchi*, Nobuo Nakagawa: 1957).

Godzilla (*Gojira*, Ishirō Honda: 1954).

Go Go Second Time Virgin (*Yuke yuke nidome no shōjo*, Koji Wakamatsu: 1969).

Grudge, The (Takashi Shimizu: 2004).

Guard from the Underground, The (*Jigoku no keibīn*, Kiyoshi Kurosawa: 1992).

Haunted Lantern (*Otsuyu: Kaidan botan-dōrō*, Masaru Tsushima, 1998).

Haunted School 1 (*Gakkou no Kaidan 1*, Hirayama Hideyuki: 1995).

Hell (*Jigoku*, Nobuo Nakagawa: 1960).

Hellish Love (*Seidan botan-dōrō*, Chusei Sone: 1972).

Howl's Moving Castle (*Hauru no ugoku shiro*, Hayao Miyazaki: 2004).

Ichi the Killer (*Koroshiya 1*, Takashi Miike: 2000).

Illusion of Blood (*Yotsuya Kaidan*, Shirō Toyoda: 1966).

Infection (*Kansen*, Masayuki Ochiai: 2004).

Inugami (Masato Harada: 2001).

Isola (*Isola: Tajuu jinkaku shōjo*, Toshiyuki Mizutani: 2000).

Japanese Horror Anthology II: Horror of Legend (Kiyomi Yada et al.: 2002).

Junk: Evil Dead Hunting (*Junk: Shiryō-gari*, Atsushi Muroga: 2000).

Ju-On: The Curse (*Ju-On*, Takashi Shimizu: 2000).

Ju-On: The Grudge (Takashi Shimizu: 2003).

Ju-On: The Grudge 2 (Takashi Shimizu: 2003).

Ju-Rei The Uncanny (Koji Shiraishi: 2004).

Kuroneko (*Yabu no naka no Kuroneko*, Kaneto Shindō: 1968).

Kwaidan (*Kaidan*, Masaki Kobayashi: 1964).

Lake of Dracula (*Noroi no yakata: Chi o sū me*, Michio Yamamoto: 1971).

Legacy of Dracula (*Yūreiyashiki no kyōfu: Chi o suu ningyō*, Michio Yamamoto: 1970).

Living Hell: A Japanese Chainsaw Massacre (*Iki-jigoku*, Shugo Fujii: 2000).

Locker, The (*Shibuya Kaidan*, Kei Horie: 2003).

Locker 2, The (*Shibuya Kaidan 2*, Kei Horie: 2003).
Lucky Dragon No. 5 (*Daigo Fukuryu-Maru*, Kaneto Shindō: 1959).
Lunch Box (*Tamamono*, Shinji Imaoka: 2004).
Mail (Iwao Takahashi: 2004).
Mansion of the Ghost Cat, The (*Borei kaibyo yashiki*, Nobuo Nakagawa: 1958).
Manual, The (*Jisatsu manyuaru*, Osamu Fukutani: 2003).
Marebito (Takeshi Shimizu: 2004).
Mystery of Rampo, The (*Rampo*, Rintaro Mayuzumi and Kazuyoshi Okuyama: 1994).
Naked Blood (*Nekeddo burāddo: Megyaku*, Hisayasu Satō: 1995).
One Missed Call (*Chakushin ari*, Takashi Miike: 2003).
One Missed Call 2 (*Chakushin ari 2*, Renpei Tsukamoto: 2005).
Onibaba (Kaneto Shindō: 1964).
Only Son, The (*Hitori musuko*, Yasujiro Ozo: 1936).
Organ (Kei Fujiwara: 1996).
Original Sin (*Shinde mo ii*, Takashi Ishii: 1992).
Parasite Eve (*Parasaito Ivu*, Masayuki Ochiai: 1997).
Persona (*Kamen gakuen*, Takashi Komatsu: 2000).
Pitfall (*Otoshiana*, Hiroshi Teshigahara: 1962).
Please Rape me Again (*Mo Ichido Yatte*, Giichi Nishihara: 1976).
Premonition (*Yogen*, Norio Tsuruta: 2004).
Pulse (*Kairo*, Kiyoshi Kurosawa: 2001).
Punishment Room (*Shokei no heya*, Kon Ichikawa: 1956).
Rampo Noir (*Rampo jigoku*, Akio Jissoji, Atsushi Kaneko et al.: 2005).
Rape! (*Okasu!*, Yasuharu Hasebe: 1976).
Reincarnation (*Rinne*, Takashi Shimizu: 2005).
Resident Evil (Paul W. S. Anderson: 2002).
Resident Evil: Apocalypse (Alexander Witt: 2004).
Resident Evil: Extinction (Russell Mulcahy: 2007).
Ring 0: Birthday (*Ringu 0: Bāsudei*, Norio Tsuruta: 2000).
Ring (*Ringu*, Hideo Nakata: 1998).
Ring 2 (*Ringu 2*, Hideo Nakata: 1999).
Rusted Body: Guts of a Virgin III (*Gōmon kifujin*, Kazuo 'Gaira' Komizu: 1987).
School Day of the Dead (*Shisha No Gakuensai*, Shinohara Tetsuo: 2000).
School Mystery (*Hanako-san*, Joji Matsuoka: 1995).
Shadow of the Wraith (*Ikisudama*, Toshiharu Ikeda: 2001).
Shikoku (Shunichi Nagasaki: 1999).
Sky High (Ryuhei Kitamura: 2003).
Souls on the Road (*Rojo no Reikon*, Minoru Murata: 1921).
Spiral (*Rasen*, Jōji Iida: 1998).
Spirited Away (*Sen to Chihiro no kamikakushi*, Hayao Miyazaki: 2001).
St John's Wort (*Otogiriso*, Ten Shimoyama: 2001).
Stacy (Naoyuki Tomomatsu: 2001).
Suicide Circle (*Jisatsu saakuru*, Sion Sono: 2002).
Sweet Home (*Suito Homu*, Kiyoshi Kurosawa: 1989).
Tales of Terror From Tokyo and All Over Japan: The Movie (Akio Yoshida et al.: 2004).
Tales of Ugetsu (*Ugetsu monogatari*, Kenji Mizoguchi: 1953).
Tandem (*Chikan densha hitozuma-hen: Okusama wa chijo*, Toshiki Sato: 1994).
Three Hundred and Sixty Nights (*Sambyaku-rokujugo Ya*, Kon Ichikawa: 1948).
Toilet Hanako-San: New Student (*Shinsei Toire no Hanako-san*, Tsutsumi Yukihito: 1998).
Tokyo Psycho (*Tōkyō densetsu: ugomeku machi no kyôki*, Ataru Oikawa: 2004).

Tokyo Story (*Tokyo monogatari*, Yasujiro Ozu: 1953).
Tokyo Zombie (*Tōkyō Zonbi*, Sakichi Satō: 2005).
Tomie (Ataru Oikawa: 1999).
Twenty-Year-Old Youth (*Hatachi no sei sieshun*, Yasushi Sasaki: 1946).
Vengeance is Mine (*Fukushū suruwa wareniari*, Shohei Imamura: 1979).
Versus (Ryuhei Kitamura: 2000).
Village of Eight Gravestones, The (*Yatsu haka-mura*, Nomura Yoshitaro: 1977).
Violated Angels (*Okasareta hakui*, Koji Wakamatsu: 1967).
Vital (Shinya Tsukamoto: 2004).
Watcher in the Attic, The (*Edogawa Rampo Ryoukikan: Yaneura No Sanposha*, Noboru Tanaka: 1976).
Woman in Black Underwear, The (*Raigyo*, Takahisa Zeze: 1997).

Bibliography

Addis, Stephen (1985), 'Conclusion: The Supernatural in Japanese Art', in S. Addis, *Japanese Ghosts & Demons: Art of the Supernatural*, New York: George Braziller, in association with the Spencer Museum of Art, University of Kansas, pp. 177–9.

Alexander, James R. (2003), 'Obscenity, Pornography and the Law in Japan: Reconsidering Oshima's *In the Realm of the Senses*', *Asian-Pacific Law & Policy Journal*, Vol. 4.1, Winter, pp. 148–68.

Allison, Anne (1998), 'Cutting the Fringes: Pubic Hair at the Margins of Japanese Censorship Laws', in A. Hiltebeital and B. D. Miller (eds), *Hair: Its Power and Meaning in Asian Cultures*, New York: New York University Press, pp. 195–218.

Allison, Anne (2004), 'Sailor Moon: Japanese Superheroes for Global Girls', in T. J. Craig (ed.), *Japan Pop! Inside the World of Japanese Popular Culture*, New York: M. E. Sharpe, pp. 259–78.

Allsop, Samara Lee (2004a), '*Gojira / Godzilla*', in J. Bowyer (ed.), *The Cinema of Japan and Korea*, London: Wallflower, pp. 63–72.

Allsop, Samara Lee (2004b), '*Ai No Corrida / In the Realm of the Senses*', in J. Bowyer (ed.), *The Cinema of Japan and Korea*, London: Wallflower, pp. 103–10.

Altman, Rick (1998), 'Reusable Packaging: Generic Products and the Recycling Process', in N. Browne, *Refiguring American Film Genres: History and Theory*, Berkeley, CA: University of California Press, pp. 1–41.

Anderson, Joseph L. and Donald Richie (1982), *The Japanese Film: Art and Industry* (expanded edition), Princeton, NJ: Princeton University Press.

Anderson, Mark (2006), 'Mobilizing Gojira', in W. M. Tsutsui and M. Ito (eds), *In Godzilla's Footsteps: Japanese Pop Culture on the Global Stage*, New York: Palgrave Macmillan, pp. 21–40.

Australian Journal of Media and Culture, The (1994), Vol. 7, No. 2; http://anarchy.translocal.jp/non-japanese/popular.html; accessed 12 November 2007.

Avella, Natalie (2004), *Graphic Japan: From Woodblock and Zen to Manga and Kawaii*, Hove: RotoVision.

Bachnik, Jane M. (1994), 'Uchi/Soto: Authority and Intimacy, Hierarchy and Solidarity', in J. M. Bachnik and C. J. Quinn Jr (eds), *Situated Meaning: Inside and Outside in Japanese Self, Society and Language*, Princeton, NJ: Princeton University Press, pp. 223–46.

Bada, Myonnie (2003), 'Culture and Social Structures', 44th Annual International Studies Association Convention'; http://www.isanet.org/portlandarchive/bada.html; accessed 27 October 2006.

Bakhtin, Michel [1941] (1993), *Rabelais and his World*, H. Iswolsky (trans.), Bloomington, IN: Indiana University Press.

Balmain, Colette (2004), 'Lost in Translation: Otherness and Orientalism in *The Ring*', in G. Wisker (ed.), *Diagesis: Journal of the Association for Research into Popular Fictions* (Special Horror Edition), No. 7 (Summer), pp. 69–77.

Balmain, Colette (2006), 'Inside the Well of Loneliness: Towards a Definition of the Japanese Horror Film', *Electronic Journal of Contemporary Japanese Studies*, 2 May; http://www.japanesestudies.org.uk/discussionpapers/2006/Balmain.html; accessed 8 February 2008.

Balmain, Colette (2007a), 'The Enemy Within: The Child as Terrorist in the Contemporary American Horror Film', in N. Scott (ed.), *Myths and Metaphors of Ending Evil*, Amsterdam: Rodopi.

Balmain, Colette (2007b), 'Evil, Responsibility and Shintoism: *Illusion of Blood* (*Yotsuya kaidan*, Toyoda, Japan: 1966)', conference paper, *Perspectives on Evil and Human Wickedness*, 8th Global Conference, 19–23 March, Salzburg, Austria.

Balmain, Colette (2007c), 'Myths of Monstrous Maternity in Japanese Horror Film: Kurosawa's *Sweet Home*', conference paper, *Monsters and the Monstrous: Myths and Metaphors of Enduring Evil*, 17–20 September, Mansfield College, Oxford.

Balmain, Colette (2008), 'The "Demonic" Other in Contemporary American Adaptations of Japanese Horror Film', in C. Balmain and L. Drawmer (eds), *Something Wicked This Way Comes*, New York: Rodopi.

Barber, Stephen (2002), 'Tokyo's Urban and Sexual Transformations: Performance Art and Digital Cultures', in F. Lloyd (ed.), *Consuming Bodies: Sex and Contemporary Japanese Art*, London: Reaktion, pp. 166–85.

Barrett, Gregory (1989), *Archetypes in Japanese Film: The Sociopolitical and Religious Significance of the Principal Heroes and Heroines*, London: Associated Presses.

BBC News (2003), 'Fury over Japan Rape Gaffe', 27 June; electronic version http://news.bbc.co.uk/1/hi/world/asia-pacific/3025240.stm; accessed 18 August 2006.

Benedict, Ruth (1946), *The Chrysanthemum and the Sword: Patterns of Japanese Culture*, New York: Meridian.

Bernardi, Joanne (2006), 'Teaching Godzilla: Classroom Encounters with a Cultural Icon', in W. A. Tsutsui and M. Ito (eds), *In Godzilla's Footsteps: Japanese Pop Culture Icons on the Global Stage*, New York: Palgrave Macmillan, pp. 111–27.

Bornoff, Nicholas (2002), 'Sex and Consumerism: The Japanese State of the Arts', in F. Lloyd (ed.), *Consuming Bodies: Sex and Contemporary Japanese Art*, London: Reaktion, pp. 41–68.

Botting, Fred (1996), *Gothic*, London: Routledge.

Boyle, Karen (2005), *Media and Violence*, London: Sage.

Brophy, Philip (1986), 'Horrality: The Textuality of Contemporary Horror Films', *Screen* 27 (1), pp. 2–13.

Buisson, Dominique (2003), *Japan Unveiled: Understanding Japanese Body Culture*, London: Hachette.

Bukatman, Scott (2004), 'Who Programs You? The Science Fiction of the Spectacle', in S. Redmond (ed.), *Liquid Metal: The Science Fiction Film Reader*. London: Wallflower, pp. 228–38.

Burch, Noel (1979), *To the Distant Observer: Form and Meaning in the Japanese Cinema*, Berkeley, CA: University of California Press.

Burgess, Chris (2004), 'Maintaining Identities: Discourses of Homogeneity in a Rapidly Globalizing Japan', *Electronic Journal of Contemporary Japanese Studies*, 19 April; http://www.japanesestudies.org.uk/articles/Burgess.html; accessed 8 November 2007.

Buruma, Ian (1984), *A Japanese Mirror: Heroes and Villains in Japanese Culture*, London: Phoenix.

Buruma, Ian (2006), *Film Notes to Godzilla*, London: British Film Institute.

Carroll, Noël (1981), 'Nightmare and the Horror Film: The Symbolic Biology of Fantastic Beings', *Film Quarterly* 34:3, pp. 16–25.

Carroll, Noël (1990), *The Philosophy of Horror or, Paradoxes of the Heart*, New York: Routledge.

Carroll, Noël (2002), 'Why Horror', in M. Jancovich (ed.), *Horror: The File Reader*, London: Routledge, pp. 33–46.

Cazdyn, Eric (2003), *The Flash of Capital: Film and Geopolitics in Japan*, Durham, NC: Duke University Press.

Chaudhuri, Shohini (2005), *Contemporary World Cinema: Europe / Middle East / East Asia / South Asia*, Edinburgh: Edinburgh University Press.

Clover, Carol J. (1992), *Men, Women and Chainsaws: Gender in the Modern Horror Film*, London: British Film Institute.

Crawford, Travis (2003), 'The Urban Techno-alienation of Sion Sono's *Suicide Club*', in S. J. Schneider (ed.), *Fear without Frontiers: Horror Cinema Across the Globe*, Godalming: FAB, pp. 305–11.

Creed, Barbara (1993), *The Monstrous-Feminine: Film, Feminism, Psychoanalysis*, London: Routledge.

Cummings, Doug (2005), Film Notes, *Kurenoko*, Eureka Entertainment Ltd.

Davies, Roger J. and O. Ikeno (eds) (2002), *The Japanese Mind: Understanding Contemporary Japanese Culture*, Tokyo: Tuttle.

Davis, Darrell Williams (2006), 'Japan: Cause for (Cautious) Optimism', in A. T. Ciecko (ed.), *Contemporary Asian Cinema*, Oxford: Berg, pp. 193–206.

Dennison, Stephanie and Song Hwee Lim (2006), 'Situating World Cinema as a Theoretical Problem', in S. Dennison and S. H. Lee (eds), *Remapping World Cinema: Identity, Culture, and Politics in Film*, London: Wallflower, pp. 1–18.

Desser, David (1992), *Reframing Japanese Cinema*, Indiana: Indiana University Press.

Desser, David (2008), 'New Kids on the Street: The Pan-Asian Youth Film', in J. Burton (ed.), *21st Century Film Studies: A Scope Reader*, Scope: An Online Journal of Film and TV Studies, issue 10, February; http://www.scope.nottingham.ac.uk/reader/chapter.php?id=4; accessed 30 March 2008.

Diamond, Milton (1999), 'Pornography, Rape and Sex Crimes in Japan', *International Journal of Law and Psychiatry* 22(1): 1–22; http://www.hawaii.edu/PCSS/online_artcls/pornography/prngrphy_rape_jp.html; accessed 8 November 2007.

Dika, Vera (1990), *Games of Terror: Halloween, Friday the 13th, and the Films of the Stalker Cycle*, New York: Fairleigh Dickson University Press.

Domenig, Roland (2004), 'The Anticipation of Freedom: Art Theatre Guild and Japanese Independent Cinema', *Midnight Eye*; http://www.midnighteye.com/features/art-theatre-guild.shtml; accessed 22 August 2007.

Douglas, Mary (1966), *Purity and Danger: An Analysis of the Concepts of Pollution and Taboo*, London: Routledge.

Dubro, Alec and David Kaplan (1986), *Yakuza: The Explosive Account of the Japanese Criminal Underworld*, Reading, MA: Addison-Wesley.

Dworkin, Andrea (1989), 'Introduction', in *Pornography: Men Possessing Women*, 2nd edn; http://www.nostatusquo.com/ACLU/dworkin/PornIntro4.html.

Dyson, Jeremy (1997), *Bright Darkness: Lost Art of the Supernatural Horror Film*, London: Continuum.

Ebersole, Gary (1998), '"Long Black Hair like a Seat Cushion": Hair Symbolism in Japanese Popular Religion', in A. Hiltebeital and B. D. Miller (eds), *Hair: Its Power and Meaning in Asian Cultures*, New York: New York University Press, pp. 75–104.

Edmundson, Mark (1997), *Nightmare on Main Street: Angels, Sadomasochism, and the Culture of Gothic*, Cambridge, MA: Harvard University Press.

Faiola, Anthony (2008), 'In Japan, a Wireless Vision of Future for U.S.: Mobile Internet is Mainstream as Phones Take Place of Computers', *MSNBC*; http://www.msnbc.msn.com/id/4306834; accessed 18 October 2006.

Foster, Michael Dylan (2007), 'The Question of the Slit-Mouthed Woman: Contemporary Legend, The Beauty Industry, and Women's Weekly Magazines in Japan', *Signs: Journal of Women in Culture and Society*, 32:3, pp. 699–726.

Frank, Alan (1977), *Horror Films*, London: Hamlyn.

Freiberg, Freda (2000), 'Comprehensive Connections: The Film Industry, the Theatre and the State in the Early Japanese Cinema', *Screening the Past*, 1 November, issue 11; http://www.latrobe.edu.au/screeningthepast/firstrelease/fr1100/fffr11c.htm; accessed 10 October 2006.

French, Howard W. (2003), 'The Saturday Profile; Japanese Pastor Reaches Out With Suicide Line', *New York Times*, electronic version http://query.nytimes.com/gst/fullpage.html?res=9F02E1DF1430F932A05756C0A9659C8B63&sec=health&pagewanted=print; accessed 10 October 2006.

Freud, Sigmund [1919] (1990), 'The Uncanny', in J. Strachey (trans. and ed.), *The Penguin Freud Library Volume 14: Art and Literature*, London: Penguin, pp. 335–74.

Freud, Sigmund [1920] (1995), 'Beyond the Pleasure Principle', in P. Gay (ed.), *The Freud Reader*, London: Vintage, pp. 594–626.

Freud, Sigmund [1924] (1995), 'The Dissolution of the Oedipus Complex', in P. Gay (ed.), *The Freud Reader*, London: Vintage, pp. 661–5.

Galloway, Patrick (2006), *Asia Shock: Horror and Dark Cinema from Japan, Korea, Hong Kong, and Thailand*, Berkeley, CA: Stone Bridge.

Gauntlett, David (2006), 'Ten Things Wrong with Media Effects', in C. K. Weaver and Cynthia Carter (eds), *Critical Readings: Violence and the Media*, Maidenhead: Open University Press, pp. 54–66.

Gerow, Aaron (2006a), 'Fantasies of War and Nation in Recent Japanese Cinema', *Japan Focus: An Asia-Pacific e-journal*; http://www.japanfocus.org/products/details/1707; accessed 8 November 2007.

Gerow, Aaron (2006b), 'Wrestling with Godzilla: Intertextuality, Childish Spectatorship, and the National Body', in W. A. Tsutsui and M. Ito (eds), *In Godzilla's Footsteps: Japanese Pop Culture Icons on the Global Stage*, New York: Palgrave Macmillan, pp. 63–82.

Gill, Tom (2003), 'When Pillars Evaporate: Structuring Masculinity on the Japanese Margins', in J. E. Roberson and N. Suzuki (eds), *Men and Masculinities in Contemporary Japan: Dislocating the Salaryman Doxa*, London: Routledge, pp. 144–61.

Goldberg, Ruth (2004), 'Demons in the Family: Tracking the Japanese "Uncanny Mother Film" from *A Page of Madness* to *Ringu*', in K. Grant and C. Sharratt (eds), *Planks of Reason: Essays on the Horror Film*, revised edn, Lanham, MD: Scarecrow, pp. 370–86.

Goldsmith, Leo (2005), 'Review of *Vengeance is Mine*, Not Coming to a Theatre Near You'; http://www.notcoming.com/reviews/vengeanceismine/; accessed 12 January 2008.

Gössmann, H. M. (2000), 'New Role Models for Men and Women?', in T. J. Craig (ed.), *Japan Pop! Inside the World of Japanese Popular Culture*, New York: M. E. Sharpe, pp. 207–21.

Grant, Barry K. (1999), 'American Psycho/sis: The Pure Products of American Go Crazy', in C. Sharratt (ed.), *Mythologies of Violence in Postmodern Media*, Detroit, MI: Wayne State University Press, pp. 23–40.

Grant, Barry K. (2004), 'Sensuous Elaboration: Reason and the Visible in the Science Fiction Film', in S. Redmond (ed.), *Liquid Metal: The Science Fiction Film Reader*, London: Wallflower, pp. 17–23.

Green, Shane (2002), 'Once were Corporate Warriors, Japan's Salarymen Walk Desolation Row',

The Age, 5 October; http://www.theage.com.au/articles/2002/10/04/1033538769771. html; accessed 19 October 2006.

Grossman, Andrew (2002), 'The Japanese Pink Film: *Tandem, The Bedroom* and *The Dream of Garuda* on DVD', *Bright Lights Film Journal*, Vol. 36, April; http://www.brightlightsfilm. com/36/pinkfilms1.html; accessed 12 February 2007.

Gunde, Richard (2005), '*Godzilla* and Postwar Japan: William M. Tsutsui (Univ. of Kansas) Explores the Role of the *Godzilla* Film Series in Popular Culture', UCLA International Institute; http://www.international.ucla.edu/article.asp?parentid=24850; accessed 10 February 2007.

Hadland Davis, F. (1992), *Myths and Legends of Japan*, New York: Dover.

Halberstam, Judith (1995), *Skin Shows: Gothic Horror and the Technology of Monsters*, Durham, NC: Duke University Press.

Hamabata, Matthews M. (1994), 'The Battle to Belong: Self-Sacrifice and Self-Fulfilment in the Japanese Family Enterprise', in J. M. Bachnik and C. J. Quinn Jr (eds), *Situated Meaning: Inside and Outside in Japanese Self, Society and Language*, Princeton, NJ: Princeton University Press, pp. 192–208.

Hamamoto, Ben (2006), 'Entertainment Re-oriented - Atomic Pop Part I: It Created a Monster', *Nichi Bei Times*, 3 August, electronic version http://www.nichibeitimes.com/articles/ artsent.php?subaction=showfull&id=1154637480&archive=&start_from=&ucat=3&; accessed 8 November 2007.

Hand, Richard J. (2005), 'Aesthetics of Cruelty: Traditional Japanese Theatre and the Horror Film', in J. McRoy (ed.), *Japanese Horror Cinema*, Edinburgh: Edinburgh University Press, pp. 18–28.

Hantke, Steffen (2005), 'Japanese Horror Under Western Eyes: Social Class and Global Culture in Miike Takashi's *Audition*', in J. McRoy (ed.), *Japanese Horror Cinema*, Edinburgh: Edinburgh University Press, pp. 54–65.

Harper, Stephen (2002) 'Zombies, Malls, and the Consumerism Debate: George Romero's *Dawn of the Dead*', *Americana: The Journal of American Popular Culture (1900-present)*, 1.2; http://www.americanpopularculture.com/journal/articles/fall_2002/harper.htm, accessed 4 January 2008.

Hasegawa, Yuko (2002), 'Post-identity *Kawaii*: Commerce, Gender and Contemporary Art', in F. Lloyd (ed.), *Consuming Bodies: Sex and Contemporary Japanese Art*, London: Reaktion, pp. 127–41.

Hearn, Lafcadio [1904] (1924), *Japan: An Attempt at Interpretation*, New York: Macmillan.

Hearn, Lafcadio [1932] (2006), *Glimpses of an Unfamiliar Japan*, second series, Middlesex: Echo Library.

Heba, Gary (1995), 'Everyday Nightmares: the Rhetoric of Social Horror in the *Nightmare on Elm Street* Series', *Journal of Popular Film and Television*, 22 September; http://www. encyclopedia.com/doc/1G1-17923437.html; accessed 5 November 2007.

Hibi, Sadao (2000), *The Colors of Japan*, Tokyo: Kodansha International.

Higson, Andrew (2002), 'The Concept of National Cinema', in C. Fowler (ed.), *The European Cinema Reader*, London: Routledge, pp. 132–42.

Hirano, Kyoko (1992), *Mr. Smith Goes to Tokyo: Japanese Cinema under the American Occupation, 1945-1952*, Washington, DC: Smithsonian.

Hochberg, Deborah (2000), 'Realm of Shades: Japanese Ghost Films Bring the Chills Back into Horror', *Metro Times Online*, 25/10; http://www.metrotimes.com/editorial/story. asp?id=779; accessed 12 January 2008.

Horeck, Tanya (2004), *Public Rape: Representation Violation in Fiction and Film*, London: Routledge.

Hughes, Henry (2000), 'Familiarity of the Strange: Japan's Gothic Tradition', *Criticism*,

Winter; http://www.findarticles.com/p/articles/mi_m2220/is_1_42/ai_63819091; accessed 8 November 2007.

Humphries, Reynold (2002), *The American Horror Film: An Introduction*, Edinburgh: Edinburgh University Press.

Hunter, Jack (1998), *Eros in Hell: Sex, Blood and Madness in Japanese Cinema*, London: Creation.

Hunziker, Steven and Ikuro Kamimura (1994), *Kakuei Tanaka: A Political Biography of Modern Japan*; http://www.rcrinc.com/tanaka/index.html; accessed 8 November 2007.

Hutchinson, Rachel (2006), 'Orientalism or Occidentalism? Dynamics of Appropriation in Akira Kurosawa', in S. Dennison and S. H. Lim (eds), *Remapping World Cinema: Identity, Culture and Politics in Film*, London: Wallflower, pp. 173–87.

Igarashi, Yoshikuni (2005), 'Edogawa Rampo and the Excess of Vision: An Ocular Critique of Modernity in 1920s Japan', *positions: East Asia Cultures Critique*, Vol. 13.2, Fall, Durham, NC: Duke University Press, pp. 299–327.

Iles, Timothy (2005), 'The Problem of Identity in Contemporary Japanese Horror Films', *Electronic Journal of Contemporary Japanese Studies*; http://www.japanesestudies.org.uk/discussionpapers/2005/Iles2.html; accessed 12 January 2007.

Iles, Timothy (2007), *The Crisis of Identity in Contemporary Japanese Film*, Leiden: Brill.

Irigaray, Luce (1996), *I Love to You: Sketch of a Possible Felicity in History*, London: Routledge.

Ishii, Takeshi (2005), 'Interview with Jasper Sharp', *Angel Guts*, Five Disc Collector's Edition, Artsmagic.

Ishii-Kuntz, M. (2003), 'Balancing Fatherhood and Work: Emergence of Diverse Masculinities in Contemporary Japan', in J. E. Roberson and N. Suzuki (eds), *Men and Masculinities in Contemporary Japan: Dislocating the Salaryman Doxa*, London: Routledge, pp. 198–216.

Itakura, Fumiaki (2004), 'Japaneseness in Japanese Cinema from the War Period to the Current', conference paper, *Through the Surface: Collaborating Textile Artists from Britain and Japan*; http://www.throughthesurface.com/symposium/Fumiaki_Itakura.html; accessed 8 November 2007.

Iwabuchi, Koichi (1994), 'Complicit Exoticism: Japan and its Other', *Continuum: The Australian Journal of Media & Culture*, Vol. 8.2; http://wwwmcc.murdoch.edu.au/ReadingRoom/8.2/Iwabuchi.html; accessed 8 November 2007.

Iwabuchi, Koichi (2002), *Recentering Globalization: Popular Culture and Japanese Trans-nationalism*, Durham, NC: Duke University Press.

Iwabuchi, Koichi (2004), 'Time and the Neighbor: Japanese Media Consumption of Asia', in K. Iwabuchi, S. Muecke and M. Thomas (eds), *Rogue Flows: Trans-Asian Cultural Traffic*, Aberdeen: Hong Kong University Press, pp. 151–74.

Iwamura, Rosemary (1994), 'Letter from Japan: From Girls Who Dress Up Like Boys To Trussed-up Porn Stars – Some of the Contemporary Heroines on the Japanese Screen', in T. O'Regan and T. Miller (eds), *Screening Cultural Studies, Continuum: The Australian Journal of Media & Culture*, Vol. 7, No. 2 (1994); http://wwwmcc.murdoch.edu.au/Reading Room/7.2/Iwamura.html; accessed 12 November 2007.

Iwasaka, Michiko and Barre Toelken (1994), *Ghosts and the Japanese: Cultural Experience in Japanese Death Legends*, Logan, UT: Utah State University Press.

Jackson, Rosemary [1981] (2000), *Fantasy: The Literature of Subversion*, London: Routledge.

Jacoby, Alexander (2005), 'Horizons East: or, A Dialogue on the Japanese Silent Cinema, its Themes, Forms and Influences', *Film Intelligence*; http://filmintelligence.org/horizons.htm; accessed 8 November 2007.

Jameson, Frederic (1991), *Postmodernism, or, The Cultural Logic of Late Capitalism*, Durham, NC: Duke University Press.

Jancovich, Mark (2002), 'General Introduction', in M. Jancovich (ed.), *Horror: The Film Reader*, London: Routledge, pp. 1–20.

JETRO (Japanese External Trade Organisation) (2004), 'Japan's Soft Power Moves into the Limelight', 2 September; http://www.jetro.go.jp/en/market/report/pdf/2004_48_r.pdf; accessed 8 November 2007.

Jordan, Brenda (1985), 'Yūrei: Tales of Female Ghosts', in S. Addis (ed.), *Japanese Ghosts and Demons: Art of the Supernatural*, New York: George Braziller, in association with the Spencer Museum of Art, University of Kansas, pp. 25–48.

Kamir, Orit [2000] (2004), 'Judgment by Film: Socio-Legal Functions of *Rashomon*', *Yale Journal of Law and the Humanities*, Vol. 12, No. 101, pp. 102–63.

Kawai, Hayao (1996), *The Japanese Psyche: Major Motifs in the Fairy Tales of Japan*, Woodstock: Spring.

King, Stephen [1981] (1994), *Danse Macabre*, London: Warner.

Kinsella, Sharon (1998), 'Amateur Manga Subculture and the Otaku Panic', *Journal of Japanese Studies*, 24 (2), pp. 289–316; http://basic1.easily.co.uk/04F022/036051/nerd.html; accessed 12 February 2007.

Kipnis, Laura (2006), 'How to Look at Pornography', in P. Lehman (ed.), *Pornography Film and Culture*, New Brunswick, NJ: Rutgers University Press, pp. 118–32.

Knowles, Joe (2002), 'Popcorn and Sake', *In These Times*, 7 June; http://www.inthesetimes.com/article/1494; accessed 12 January 2008.

Kohiyama, Kenji (2005), 'The Meaning of Keitai', *Japan Media Review*, University of Southern California, 28 July; http://www.japanmediareview.com/japan/stories/050728kohiyama/; accessed 8 November 2007.

Kristeva, Julia (1982), *Powers of Horror: An Essay on Abjection*, Leon S. Roudiez (trans.), New York: Columbia University Press.

Kushmer, Barak (2006), '*Gojira* as Japan's First Postwar Media Event', in W. A. Tsutsui and M. Ito (eds), *In Godzilla's Footsteps: Japanese Pop Culture Icons on the Global Stage*, New York: Palgrave Macmillan, pp. 41–50.

Lafond, Frank (2005), 'Case Study: Ishii Takashi's *Freeze Me* and the Rape-Revenge Film', in J. McRoy (ed.), *Japanese Horror Cinema*, Edinburgh: Edinburgh University Press, pp. 77–88.

LaMarre, Thomas (2005), *Shadows on the Screen: Tanizaki Jun'inchirō and 'Oriental' Aesthetics*, Ann Arbor, MI: Michigan University Press.

Lehman, Peter (1993), 'Don't Blame this on a Girl', in S. Cohen and I. R. Hark (eds), *Screening the Male: Exploring Masculinities in Hollywood Cinema*, London: Routledge, pp. 103–17.

Lillywhite, Jamie and Akira Y. Yamamoto (1985), 'Snakes, Serpents, and Humans', in S. Addis (ed.), *Japanese Ghosts and Demons: Art of the Supernatural*, New York: George Braziller, in association with the Spencer Museum of Art, University of Kansas, pp. 139–68.

Littleton, C. Scott (2002), *Understanding Shinto*, London: Duncan Baird.

Lloyd, Fran (2002), 'Introduction: Critical Reflections', in F. Lloyd (ed.), *Consuming bodies: Sex and Contemporary Japanese Art*, London: Reaktion, pp. 9–22.

Lowenstein, Adam (2005), *Shocking Representation: Historical Trauma, National Cinema and the Modern Horror Film*. New York: Columbia University Press.

Lunsing, Win (2003), 'Transgender practices among Japanese "men"', in J. E. Roberson and N. Suzuki (eds), *Men and Masculinities in Contemporary Japan: Dislocating the Salaryman Doxa*, London: Routledge, pp. 49–77.

McDonald, Keiko I. (2006), *Reading a Japanese Film: Cinema in Context*, Honolulu: University of Hawai'i Press.

McGray, Doug (2002), 'Japan's Gross National Cool', *Foreign Policy: The Magazine of Global Politics, Economics and Ideas*; electronic version http://www.japansociety.org/web_docs/grossnationalcool.pdf; accessed 8 November 2007.

Macias, Patrick (2001), *TokyoScope: The Japanese Cult Cinema Companion*, San Francisco: Cadence.

Macias, Patrick and Tomohiro Machiyama (2004), *Cruising the Anime City: An Otaku Guide to Neo Tokyo*, Berkeley, CA: Stone Bridge.

McKinlay, Megan (2002), 'Unstable Mothers: Redefining Motherhood in Contemporary Japan', in *Intersections: Gender, History and Culture in the Asian Context*; http://wwwsshe.murdoch.edu.au/intersections/issue7/mckinlay.html; accessed 8 November 2007.

McLelland, Mark (2003), 'Review of *Men and Masculinities in Contemporary Japan: Dislocating the Salaryman Doxa*', in *Intersections: Gender, History and Culture in the Asian Context*; http://wwwsshe.murdoch.edu.au/intersections/issue9/mclelland_review.html; accessed 8 November 2007.

McRoy, Jay (2005), 'Case Study: Cinematic Hybridity in Shimizu Takashi's *Ju-On The Grudge*', in J. McRoy (ed.), *Japanese Horror Cinema*, Edinburgh: Edinburgh University Press, pp. 175–84.

McRoy, Jay (2008), *Nightmare Japan: Contemporary Japanese Horror Cinema*, Amsterdam: Rodopi.

MacWilliams, Mark W. (2000), 'Japanese Comics and Religion: Osamu Tezuku's Story of the Buddha', in T. J. Craig (ed.), *Japan Pop! Inside the World of Japanese Popular Culture*, New York: M. E. Sharpe, pp. 109–37.

Mamoru, Ito (2004), 'The Representation of Femininity in Japanese Television Dramas', in K. Iwabuchi (ed.), *Feeling Asian Modernities: Transnational Consumption of Japanese TV Dramas*, Aberdeen: Hong Kong University Press, pp. 25–42.

Mathews, Gordon (2003), 'Can a "Real Man" Live for his Family?: Ikigai and Masculinity in Today's Japan', in J. E. Roberson and N. Suzuki (eds), *Men and Masculinities in Contemporary Japan: Dislocating the Salaryman Doxa*, London: Routledge-Curzon, pp. 109–25.

Matsui, Midori (2002), 'The Place of Marginal Positionality: Legacies of Japanese Anti-Modernity', in F. Lloyd (ed.), *Consuming Bodies: Sex and Contemporary Japanese Art*, London: Reaktion, pp. 142–65.

Meikle, Denis (2005), *The Ring Companion*, London: Titan.

Mes, Tom (2001), 'Truth, Hope and Violence Kinji Fukasaku', *Midnight Eye*, 3 March; http://www.midnighteye.com/features/focus_fukasaku.shtml, accessed 8 March 2008.

Mes, Tom (2004), '*Ōdishon/Audition*', in J. Bowyer (ed.), *The Cinema of Japan and Korea*, London: Wallflower, pp. 199–206.

Mes, Tom and Jasper Sharp (eds) (2005), *The Midnight Guide to New Japanese Film*, Berkeley, CA: Stone Bridge.

Miller, Laura (2004), 'Those Naughty Teenage Girls: Japanese Kogals, Slang, and Media Assessments', *Journal of Linguistic Anthropology*, 17:2, pp. 184–203.

Miller, Roy Andrew (1982), *Japan's Modern Myth: The Language and Beyond*, New York: Weatherhill.

Mishima, Yukio [1961] (1995), *Patriotism*, G. W. Sargent (trans.), New York: New Directions.

Mulvey, Laura [1975] (1989), 'Visual Pleasure and Narrative Cinema', in L. Mulvey, *Visual and Other Pleasures: Language, Discourse, Society*, Basingstoke: Macmillan, pp. 14–28.

Mulvey, Laura [1981] (1989), 'Afterthoughts on "Visual Pleasure and Narrative Cinema". Inspired by King Vidor's *Dual in the Sun* (1946)', in L. Mulvey, *Visual and Other Pleasures: Language, Discourse, Society*, Basingstoke: Macmillan, pp. 29–38.

Nadeau, Randall (1996), 'Dimensions of Sacred Space in Japanese Popular Culture', *Intercultural Communication Studies*, VI: 2, pp. 109–14.

Nagib, Lúcia (2006), 'Towards a Positive Definition of World Cinema', in S. Dennison and S. H. Lee (eds), *Remapping World Cinema: Identity, Culture and Politics in Film*, London: Wallflower, pp. 30–7.

Nakamura, Karen and Hisako Matsuo (2003), 'Female Masculinity and Fantasy Spaces: Transcending Genders in the Takarazuka Theatre and Japanese Popular Culture', in J. E.

Robertson and N. Suzuki (eds), *Men and Masculinities in Contemporary Japan: Dislocating the Salaryman Doxa*, London: Routledge, pp. 59–76.

Nakamura, Tadashi (2003), 'Regendering Batterers: Domestic Violence and Men's Movements', in J. E. Roberson and N. Suzuki (eds), *Men and Masculinities in Contemporary Japan: Dislocating the Salaryman Doxa*, London: Routledge, pp. 162–79.

Napier, Susan (1996), *The Fantastic in Modern Japanese Literature: The Subversion of Modernity*, London: Routledge.

Napier, Susan (1998), 'Vampires, Psychic Girls, Flying Woman and Sailor Scouts: Four Faces of the Young Female in Japanese Popular Culture', in D. P. Martinez (ed.), *The Worlds of Japanese Popular Culture: Gender, Shifting Boundaries and Global Cultures*, Cambridge: Cambridge University Press, pp. 91–109.

Napier, Susan (2006), 'When Godzilla Speaks', in W. A. Tsutsui and M. Ito (eds), *In Godzilla's Footsteps: Japanese Pop Culture Icons on the Global Stage*, New York: Palgrave Macmillan.

Neale, Stephen (1980), *Genre*, London: British Film Institute.

Newman, Kim (1996), 'Introduction', in K. Newman (ed.), *The BFI Companion to Horror*, London: BFI, pp. 11–16.

Nguyen, Keaton (2005), 'The Agency of Keitai', *E-ASPC: An Electronic Journal of Asian Studies*; http://mcel.pacificu.edu/easpac/2005/nguyen.php3; assessed 8 November 2007.

Noreiga, Chon (2006), 'Godzilla and the Japanese Nightmare: When *Them*! Is U.S.', in D. Eleftheriotis and G. Needham (eds), *Asian Cinemas: A Reader and Guide*, Edinburgh: Edinburgh University Press, pp. 41–55.

Ognjanovic, Dejan (2006a), 'The Best Japanese Horror Films of All Time, Part 1', *KFC Cinema. Com*; http://www.kfccinema.com/features/articles/besthorrorjapan1/besthorrorjapan1.html; accessed 8 November 2007.

Ognjanovic, Dejan (2006b), 'The Best Japanese Horror Films of All Time: Part 2', *KFC Cinema. Com*; http://www.kfccinema.com/features/articles/besthorrorjapan2/besthorrorjapan2.html; accessed 8 November 2007.

Otani, Shuho (2003), 'Social, Cultural and Economic Issues in the Digital Divide – Literature Review and Case Study of Japan', *Online Journal of Space Communication*, Fall; http://satjournal.tcom.ohiou.edu/Issue5/social.html; accessed 8 November 2007.

Phoenix, Woodrow (2006), *Plastic Culture: How Japanese Toys Conquered the World*, Tokyo: Kodansha International.

Pidduck, Julianne (1995), 'The 1990s Hollywood Fatal Femme: (Dis)Figuring Feminism', *Cineaction*, pp. 64–72.

Purini, Franco (2004), 'Introducstion', in L. Sacchi, *Tokyo: City and Architecture*, Milan: Skira, pp. 7–11.

Quinn, Charles J. Jr (1994), 'Uchi and Soto as Windows on the World', in J. M. Bachnik and C. J. Quinn Jr (eds), *Situated Meaning: Inside and Outside in Japanese Self, Society and Language*, Princeton, NJ: Princeton University Press, pp. 38–72.

Raine, Michael (2005), 'Imagining a New Japan: The *Taiyozoku* Films', *The Criterion Collection*; http://www.criterionco.com/asp/release.asp?id=295&eid=423&section=essay; accessed 8 November 2007.

Rauer, Julie (2005), 'Persistence of a Genetic Scar: Japanese Anime, Manga, and Otaku Culture Fill an Open National Wound', *Little Boy: The Art of Japan's Exploding Subculture*, 13 June; http://www.asianart.com/exhibitions/littleboy/intro.html; accessed 8 November 2007.

Richie, Donald (1992), *A Lateral View: Essays on Culture and Style in Contemporary Japan*, Berkeley, CA: Stone Bridge.

Richie, Donald (2001), *A Hundred Years of Japanese Films: A Concise History with a Selective Guide to Videos and DVDS*, London: Kodansha Europe.

Roberson, James E. (2003), 'Japanese Working-class Masculinities: Marginalized Complicity', in J. E. Roberson and N. Suzuki (eds), *Men and Masculinities in Contemporary Japan: Dislocating the Salaryman Doxa*, London: Routledge, pp. 126–43.

Roberson, James E. and N. Suzuki (2003), 'Introduction', in J. E. Roberson and N. Suzuki (eds), *Men and Masculinities in Contemporary Japan: Dislocating the Salaryman Doxa*, London: Routledge, pp. 1–19.

Ross, Catrien (1996), *Supernatural and Mysterious Japan*, Tokyo: Tuttle.

Rubin, Norman A. (2000), 'Ghosts, Demons and Spirits in Japanese Lore', *Asian Art*; http://www.asianart.com/articles/rubin/; accessed 12 November 2007.

Sacchi, Livio (2004), *Tokyo: City and Architecture*, Milan: Skira.

Said, Edward W. [1978] (2003), *Orientalism*, London: Penguin.

Schilling, Mark (1999), *Contemporary Japanese Film*, New York: Weatherhill.

Schneider, Steven J. (2001), 'Killing in Style: The Aestheticization of Violence in Donald Cammell's *White of the Eye*', *Scope*; http://www.scope.nottingham.ac.uk/article.php?issue=jun2001&id=273&section=article; accessed 10 October 2007.

Schneider, Steven (2002), 'Slasher Films', *St. James Encyclopedia of Pop Culture*; http://findarticles.com/p/articles/mi_g1epc/is_tov/ai_2419101116; accessed 5 January 2008.

Schneider, Steven (2004), 'Introduction: "Psychoanalysis in / and /of the Horror Film"', in S. Schneider (ed.), *Horror Film and Psychoanalysis: Freud's Worst Nightmare*, Cambridge: Cambridge University Press.

Scofield, Adam (2007), 'A Black Pearl of the Deep: Juraj Herz's *The Cremator*', *Senses of Cinema*, Issue 44; www.sensesofcinema.com/contents/07/43/cremator-juraju-herz.html; accessed 8 November 2007.

Secor, L. James and S. Addis (1985), 'The Male Ghost in Kabuki and Ukiyo-e', in S. Addis (ed.), *Japanese Ghosts and Demons: Art of the Supernatural*, New York: George Braziller, in association with the Spencer Museum of Art, University of Kansas, pp. 49–56.

Sedgwick, Eve (1986), *The Coherence of Gothic Conventions*, New York: Methuen.

Shabecoff, Phillip (1970), 'Mishima: A Man Torn Between Two Worlds', *New York Times*, 26 November; electronic version http://www.nytimes.com/books/98/10/25/specials/mishima-torn.html; accessed 8 November 2007.

Shapiro, Jerome F. (2002), *Atomic Bomb Cinema*, New York: Routledge.

Sharp, Jasper (2005), 'Commentary to the *Angel Guts* Series', *Angel Guts*, Five Disc Collector's Edition, ArtsMagic.

Sharp, Jasper (2006), 'Edogawa Rampo: A Hellish Mirror', *Film International*, issue 19, vol. 4, no. 1, pp. 24–43.

Sharratt, Christopher (2005), 'Preface', in J. McRoy, *Japanese Horror Cinema*, Edinburgh: Edinburgh University Press, pp. xi–xviii.

Shaw, Richard Shaw (2003), 'Through a Glass Darkly: Bergman as Critical and Cultural Bellwether', *Bright Lights Film Journal*, Issue 40, May; http://www.brightlightsfilm.com/40/bergman.htm; accessed 8 November 2007.

Shimada, Yoshiko (2002), 'Afterword: Japanese Pop Culture and the Eradication of History', in F. Lloyd (ed.), *Consuming Bodies: Sex and Contemporary Japanese Art*, London: Reaktion, pp. 186–92.

Simpson, Phil (2000), *Psycho Paths: Tracking the Serial Killer Through Contemporary American Film and Fiction*, Carbondale, IL: Southern Illinois University Press.

Slantchev, Branislav L. (2006), '*The Ghost Cat of Otama Pond (Kaibyo Otamagaike*, 1960), *Gotterdämmerung.Org*; http://www.gotterdammerung.org/film/reviews/g/ghost-cat-of-otama-pond.html; accessed 12 November 2007.

Slater, Jay (2002), 'Introduction', in J. Slater (ed.), *Eaten Alive: Italian Cannibal and Zombie Films*, London: Plexus, pp. 12–21.

Standish, Isolde (1998), '*Akira*, Postmodernism and Resistance', in D. P. Martinez (ed.),

The Worlds of Japanese Popular Culture: Gender, Shifting Boundaries and Global Cultures, Cambridge: Cambridge University Press, pp. 56–74.

Standish, Isolde (2005), *A New History of Japanese Cinema: A Century of Narrative Film*, New York: Continuum.

Steele, Bruce (2005), 'The Horror! The Horror! Pitt Professor Adam Lowenstein Examines how Horror Films Probe, Reflect National Traumas', *Pitt Chronicle*, 10 January; http://www.umc.pitt.edu/media/pcc050110/theHORROR.html; accessed 18 November 2007.

Stephens, Chuck (2005), 'Heat Stroke! Japanese Cinema's Season in the Sun', *The Criterion Collection*; http://www.criterionco.com/asp/release.asp?id=295&eid=422&section=essay&page=3; accessed 8 November 2007.

Stockwin, James Arthur Ainscow (2003), 'Series Editor's Preface', in J. E. Robertson and N. Suzuki (eds), *Men and Masculinities in Contemporary Japan: Dislocating the Salaryman Doxa*, London: Routledge, pp. xiii–xv.

Suzuki, Koji (2005), 'Interview with Koji Suzuki, Novelist of the Dank and Dread', *Kateigaho International Edition*; http://int.kateigaho.com/win05/horror-suzuki.html; accessed 8 November 2007.

Suzuki, Koji (2006), *Dark Water (Honogurai mizu no soko kara)*, London: HarperCollins.

Tanaka, Yuki (2005), 'Godzilla and the Bravo Shot: Who Created and Killed the Monster?', *Japan Focus*; http://www.japanfocus.org/products/todf/1652; accessed 12 January 2008.

Tanizaki, Jun'inchirō [1918] (2005), 'The Tumor with a Human Face' (*Jinmenso*)', in T. LaMarre (trans.), *Shadows on the Screen: Tanizaki Jun'inchirō and "Oriental" Aesthetics*, Ann Arbor: The University of Michigan, pp. 86–102.

Tanizaki, Jun'inchirō [1929] (2005), 'A Women's Face' (Onna no kao, 1929), T. LaMarre (trans.), in *Shadows on the Screen: Tanizaki Jun'inchirō & 'Oriental' Aesthetics*, Ann Arbor, MI: University of Michigan Press, pp. 264–5.

Tateishi, Ramie (2003), 'The Japanese Horror Film Series: *Ring* and *Eko Eko Azarak*', in S. J. Schneider, *Fear without Frontiers: Horror Cinema Across the Globe*, Godalming: FAB, pp. 295–304.

Taylor, Matthew (2006), 'Strategies of Dissociation: A Mimetic Dimension to Social Problems in Japan', *Anthropoetics – The Journal of Generative Anthropology*, vol. XII, no. 1, Spring/Summer; http://www.anthropoetics.ucla.edu/ap1201/taylor.htm; accessed 12 January 2008.

Tetsuo, Kogawa (1985), 'New Trends in Japanese Popular Culture', *Telos*, no. 64, Summer, pp. 147–52.

Toelken, Barre (1994), 'Dancing with the Departed: Japanese Obon in the American West', *The World and I*; http://www.worldandi.com/public/1994/august/cl2.cfm; accessed 6 October 2006.

Totaro, Donata (2002), 'The Final Girl: A Few Thoughts on Feminism and Horror', *Offscreen*; http://www.horschamp.qc.ca/new_offscreen/final_girl.html; accessed 12 November 2007.

Tsunoda, Yukiko (1995), 'Japanese Women Confront Domestic Violence', *The Journal of the International Institute*, Vol. 3.1, Fall; http://www.umich.edu/~iinet/journal/vol3no1/jpndv.html; accessed 12 November 2007.

Tsutsui, William M. (2006), 'Introduction', in W. A. Tsutsui and M. Ito, *In Godzilla's Footsteps: Japanese Pop Culture Icons on the Global Stage*, New York: Palgrave Macmillan, pp. 153–66.

Tucker, Richard N. (1973), *Japan: Film Image*, London: Studio Vista.

Turnball, Stephen (2002), *War in Japan 1467–1615*, Oxford: Osprey.

Weisser, Thomas and Yoko Mihara Weisser (1998), *The Sex Films: Japanese Cinema Encyclopaedia*, Miami: Vital.

Wells, Paul (2000), *The Horror Genre: From Beelzebub to Blair Witch*, London: Wallflower.

White, Carla (2006), 'Japanese Ghosts and Spirits', *The Shadowlands: Ghosts and Hauntings*, http://theshadowlands.net/ghost/japanese.html; accessed 24 November 2007.

White, Eric (2005), 'Case Study: Nakata's *Ringu* and *Ringu 2*', in J. McRoy (ed.), *Japanese Horror Cinema*, Edinburgh: Edinburgh University Press, pp. 38–50.

Williams, Linda (1984), 'When the Woman Looks', in M. Ann Doane, P. Mellencamp and L. Williams (eds), *Re-vision: Essay in Feminist Criticism*, Frederick, MD: University Publications of America, pp. 83–99.

Williams, Linda (1993), 'A Virus is Only Doing its Job', *Sight & Sound*, May.

Williams, Linda (2006), 'Generic Pleasures: Number and Narrative', in P. Lehman (ed.), *Pornography Film and Culture*, New Brunswick, NJ: Rutgers University Press, pp. 60–85.

Williams, Linda Ruth (1995), *Critical Desire: Psychoanalysis and the Literary Subject*, London: Edward Arnold.

Wood, Robin [1979] (2002), 'The American Nightmare: Horror in the 70s', in M. Jancovich (ed.), *Horror: The Film Reader*, London: Routledge, pp. 25–32.

Wyver, John (1989), *The Moving Image: An International History of Film, Television and Video*, London: BFI and Blackwell.

Yamamoto, Fumiko Y. and Akira Yamamoto (1985), 'Two and a Half Worlds: Humans, Animals and Inbetweens', in S. Addis (ed.), *Japanese Ghosts and Demons: Art of the Supernatural*, New York: George Braziller, in association with the Spencer Museum of Art, University of Kansas, pp. 169–76.

Yamamoto, Tsunetomo (2002), *Bushido: The Way of the Samurai*, J. F. Stone (ed.), M. Tanaka (trans.), New York: Square One.

Yano, Christine R. (2006), 'Monstering the Japanese Cute: Pink Globalization and Its Critics Abroad', in W. A. Tsutsui and M. Ito, *In Godzilla's Footsteps: Japanese Pop Culture Icons on the Global Stage*, New York: Palgrave Macmillan.

Yoshimoto, Mitsuhiro [2000] (2005), *Kurosawa: Film Studies and Japanese Cinema*, Durham, NC: Duke University Press.

Yoshimoto, Mitsuhiro (2006), 'The Difficulty of Being Radical: The Discipline of Film Studies and the Postcolonial World Order', in D. Eleftheriotis and G. Needham (eds), *Asian Cinemas: A Reader and Guide*, Edinburgh: Edinburgh University Press, pp. 27–40.

Index